BEFORE BARBED WIRE

Joseph's Last Figh...

BEAR PAW MTS.

ANDY ADAMS' HERD OF ○S IN "LOG OF A COWBOY"

TETON R.

MARIAS R.

× Ft. Benton

Ft. Shaw

SUN R. ×

SQUARE BUTTE

MISSOURI R.

Car...

NORTH JUDITH MTS.

ARROW CR.

HIGHWOOD MTS.

MULLAN ROAD

SMITH R.

JUDITH R.

DS ×
Ft. Maginnis
SOUTH JUDITH MTS.

× Reed's Fort N

MC DONALD CR.

BOX E...

LITTLE BELT MTS.

BIG SNOWY MT.

FLAT WILLOW CR.

Helena

Deer Lodge

JUDITH GAP

CARROLL TRAIL

MUSSELSH...

CRAZY MTS.

Montana Territory

JEFFERSON R.

MONTANA-OREGON TRAIL

SHIELDS R.

PO...
TO...

Bozeman
× Ft. Ellis

BOZEMAN TRAIL

Coulson (Billings)

Nevada

MADISON R.

GALLATIN R.

YELLOWSTONE R.

STILLWATER R.

PRYOR CR.

RUBY R.

Virginia City

CLARK FORK

Bannack

BEAVERHEAD R.

PRYOR MTS.

RAYNOLD'S PASS

RED ROCK CR.

TARGHEE PASS

MONIDA PASS

✗ Camas Meadows

YELLOWSTONE LAKE

ABSAROKA RANGE

STINKING WATER R.

SHOSHONE R.

YELLOWSTONE NATIONAL PARK

GREYBULL R.

Ranches and Cattle Trails
OF EARLY MONTANA

R. D. Palacios

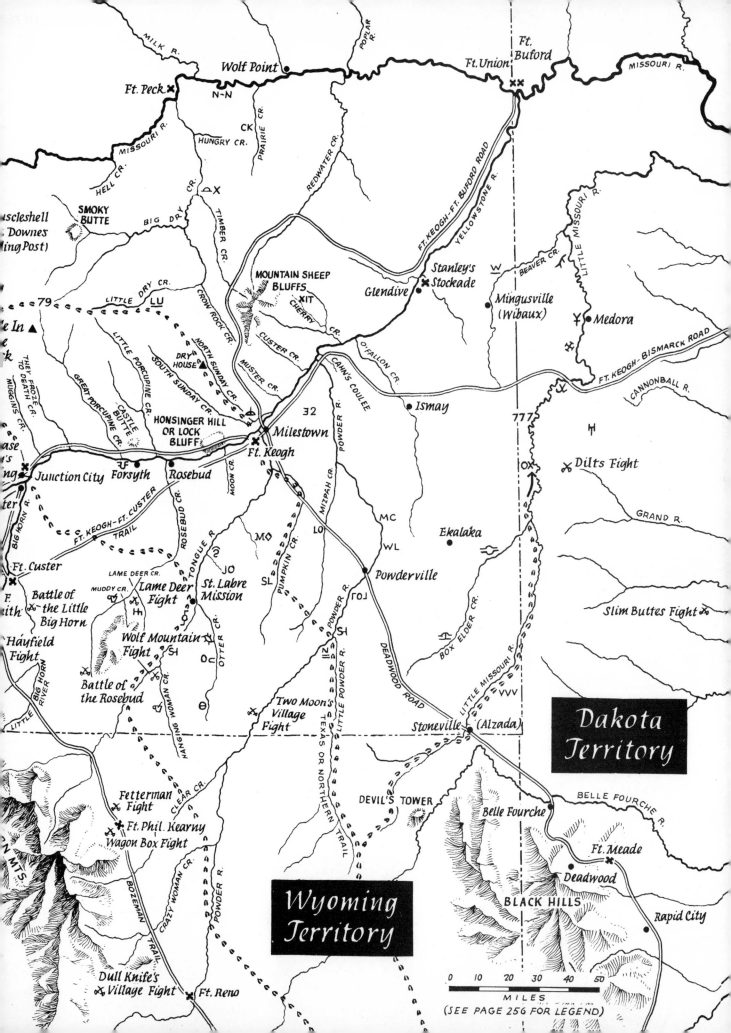

DEDICATED to Bessie Huffman Felton and other
old-timers who helped bring the breath of life to
these pages before they crossed the Big Divide.

by Mark H. Brown
and W. R. Felton

BEFORE BARBED WIRE

L. A. HUFFMAN, Photographer on Horseback

Illustrated with Photographs

BRAMHALL HOUSE · NEW YORK

Contents

1. "The Hat X Roundup Outfit camped on Hungry Creek, North Montana, Aug. 1904."

Prologue

Dream back beyond the cramping lanes
    To glories that have been—
The camp smoke on the sunset plains,
    The riders loping in:
Loose rein and rowelled heel to spare,
    The wind our only guide,
For youth was in the saddle there
    With half a world to ride.[1]

These poignant words recall memories of the open range—the days before barbed wire. For in the Short Grass Country—that broad sweep of prairie and badlands from Mexico's Rio Grande del Norte to the plains of Alberta and Saskatchewan—barbed wire has always been regarded as the thing that stripped the range of that quality so dear to the hearts of old-timers—*freedom*. In story and in song that loss has been told a thousand times, but never with more feeling than in the ode to "The Old Cow Man":

I rode across a valley range
   I hadn't see for years.
The trail was all so spoilt and strange
   It nearly fetched the tears.
I had to let ten fences down
   (The fussy lanes ran wrong)
And each new line would make me frown
   And hum a mournin' song.

  •   •   •   •   •   •   •   •   •

When my old soul hunts range and rest
   Beyond the last divide,
Just plant me in some stretch of West
   That's sunny, lone and wide.
Let cattle rub my tombstone down
   And coyotes mourn their kin,
Let hawses paw and tromp the moun'
   But don't you fence it in! [2]

Much of the color and spirit of these early days has been preserved on the printed page by trail bosses like Andy Adams, by cowboys like Teddy Blue, John Rollinson, Philip Ashton Rollins, and Will James, and by wives of the range country like Hughie Call and Nannie Alderson.

Artists, too, have left their impressions on canvas, on paper, and in bronze. Of these, many have caught a facet of the cowpuncher's life, but Charles M. Russell alone succeeded in being the cowboys' "cowboy artist." Russell, great as he was, however, had one failing: he painted only those of good breeding—man and beast. He never painted scrubs. Of this short-coming he was reminded on occasion and on none more pointedly than at a Montana exhibition when a cowhand asked, "Where'd yuh find all them good-lookin' cowboys yuh put in yer pitchers?"

Only the photographers preserved a truly accurate pictorial record, and to their work one must turn for an exact picture of this life. Of these, four are worthy of note: William Henry Jackson of Omaha who made a few pictures of ranch life[3]; M. C. Ragsdale of Fort Concho, Texas, whose plates burned in 1907; Erwin E. Smith who photographed in the Texas Panhandle after 1900[4]; and L. A. Huffman of Miles City, Montana.

Huffman came to Fort Keogh just outside "Milestown" in 1878 as post photographer. His record of the Indian in the last days of the buffalo-skin tepee, the hide hunter at work on the bleak plains of Montana in the dead of winter, the soldier, the scout, the bull-whacker, the jerkline teamster, and the growth of the frontier towns has been presented by the authors in *The Frontier Years: L. A. Huffman Photographer of the Plains.*[5] When the rancher came, Huffman was already at home on the plains soon to be covered with cattle. With the eye of an artist and the perspective of an historian, this photographer caught and preserved the spirit of life on the unfenced Montana ranges.

Huffman did his work so well that then (and now) he towered head and shoulders above his contemporaries. One Plains historian, who probably knows better than any other the range photographs of these early days, passed judgment in these words: "For sheer versatility of significant and historic subject matter close to the range of grass . . . [Huffman's collection] surpasses them all." [6] On the pages that follow, Huffman's pictures tell the story of the cowboy at work, at rest, and at play. These were the days when, for weeks at a time, the only roof a cowpuncher knew was the sky, when the beans, meat, and coffee were sometimes seasoned with ashes whipped up from the cook's fire by the ceaseless wind, and when the central figure of many an evening campfire story was—*a horse*.

Kind fate had it I should be Post Photographer with the Army during the Indian campaigns close following the annihilation of Custer's command. This Yellowstone-Big Horn country was then unpenned of wire, and unspoiled by railway, dam or ditch. Eastman had not yet made the Kodak, but thanks be, there was the old wet plate, the collodion bottle and bath. I made photographs. With crude home-made cameras, from saddle and in log shack, I saved something.

Round about us the army of buffalo hunters—red men and white—were waging the final war of extermination upon the last great herds of American bison seen upon this continent. Then came the cattleman, the "trail boss" with his army of cowboys, and the great cattle roundups. Then the army of railroad builders. That—the railway—was the fatal coming. One looked about and said, "This is the last West." It was not so. There *was* no more West after that. It was a dream and a forgetting, a chapter forever closed.

L. A. Huffman

ONE

L. A. Huffman, Frontier Photographer

I T WAS a bleak day in December, 1878. The thermometer stood at twenty degrees below zero and the wind, sweeping unobstructed across a hundred miles of Dakota prairie, howled down over the barren hills of the Missouri at Bismarck, Dakota Territory. There was much activity in Bismarck, for the construction engineer of the Northern Pacific Railroad was pushing heavy equipment and supplies across the frozen Missouri to be used in extending the line the following summer. But the famous "ice bridge" and the construction activity held no interest for a slender young man of twenty-four. He was fascinated by a Diamond R bull train with its blue wagons on a hill just across the river; by the knowledge that Comanche, sole survivor of Custer's detachment at the battle of the Little Big Horn, was at nearby Fort Abraham Lincoln; and by the realization that his destination was three hundred miles beyond, beside the trail that led to the westward over the snow-covered hills.

Laton Alton Huffman was on his way to Fort Keogh, Montana Territory, to apply for the position of post photographer. However, the prospect of a business was but part of the attraction, for Huffman's forebears were frontiersmen when Ohio and West Virginia were the *West,* and in his veins ran the blood of that restless breed to whom the country beyond the horizon was always an irresistible attraction. Huffman wanted to see and become a part of this last fragment of the American Frontier. When he died fifty-three years later, he had not only fulfilled this desire but he had made a

2. L. A. Huffman—*circa* 1880.

priceless record of this country and its people from the days of the Indian in his buffalo-skin tepee to those when the plowman turned the buffalo grass "wrong side up."

Huffman never forgot his trip from Bismarck to Fort Keogh in the open buckboards of the mail carriers. Exposed to the wind and subzero temperatures without adequate clothing, he suffered so severely that he was forced to lay over at a little stage station midway along the trail. The first night out an outlaw who was under suspicion in connection with the disappearance of some army mules stopped the stage and climbed in. Curiously, he sized Huffman up as a fellow fugitive and generously offered to attempt a stand-off while Huffman got away should an attempt be made to apprehend them.

Although Colonel (later General) Miles was in the field with some troops, Huffman persuaded the adjutant to stretch his authority and let him move into the log shack occupied by the previous post photographer. This position was a civilian position and, as such, carried no remuneration other than the right to occupy this rough building and to engage in a private business on the post. His income was to be the profits—if any—from his work. As his predecessor had gone broke, put up his equipment

3. "Officers Quarters and Cavalry Barracks, Fort Keogh, June 1880."

for a loan, and then left the country, the financial prospects were not bright. However, these difficulties did provide Huffman with an opportunity to buy the equipment put up as security and thus set up shop.

As soon as he had squared himself away, Huffman acquired a horse and a camping outfit and headed north into the great area of prairie and badlands between the Yellowstone and the Missouri which he later affectionately referred to as "The Big Open." After a few days of wandering about he located the camp of a group of buffalo hunters. Then he returned to the post for his camera and equipment and went back to photograph the buffalo and the hide hunters, thus beginning the collection of frontier pictures that was to make him famous.

The active fighting of the Sioux war was over when Huffman came to Fort Keogh, but the situation had not settled down completely. Miles held some three hundred Northern Cheyennes and Sioux in a prisoner of war camp near the fort; Little Wolf and Dull Knife had just made their famous break from the reservation in Indian Territory and were on their way back to their Montana homeland; and bands of "lariat Indians," many of them from Sitting Bull's Hunkpapa Sioux just across the Canadian border, roamed the countryside. In one letter to his father, dated February 6, 1880, he casually mentioned that he was in the adjutant's office when Miles sent Sergeant Glover out to chase one raiding band. This incident, which Huffman referred to as "nothing of importance," resulted in the capture of this particular band and was an important link in negotiating the surrender of about two thousand of Sitting Bull's followers. This surrender brought to Fort Keogh a number of important chiefs, among them Spotted Eagle, Broad Trail, and Rain-in-the-Face.[1]

Huffman was anxious to collect pictures of these famous Indians and,

4. "Guard Mount in Buffalo Coats, Ft. Keogh, Mont. [*circa* 1880]."

in the case of Rain-in-the-Face, he resorted to a subterfuge which landed him "on the carpet" before Miles. As Indians were not allowed out of camp without a military escort, Huffman and an Irish teamster smuggled Rain-in-the-Face out of camp in a covered wagon used to deliver supplies, and took him to the studio. Here the Indian posed for Huffman for a couple of hours or more. In the meantime the Indians at the camp, thinking the soldiers had spirited Rain-in-the-Face away for no good purpose, became restless. This was noted by an officer who quickly ferreted out the trouble; and, although Huffman successfully smuggled the Indian back into the camp, he was soon summoned to Miles' office. The Colonel, obviously "hot around the collar," issued strict instructions not to take prisoners out of the camp again without permission. But Huffman had his pictures, one of which was to become the most widely used picture of this Indian.

In later years Huffman treasured his memories of these days when he was post photographer. He recalled that Major Ilges and Two Moon would come to his studio to smoke and talk in sign language; that one day Captain Clark and the scout and interpreter, Johnny Bruguier, joked old Spotted Bear and wanted to know if the story was true that the latter sat on the hill and cried the day the Sioux and Cheyennes killed Custer; and that he, Clark, and Little Wolf planned to record the Indian sign language in photographs but the other Indians did not take kindly to the idea. And he also recalled how the famous trapper and scout, "Yellowstone" Kelly, would loaf in his studio between scouting trips, reading books and sleeping on a pile of buffalo robes in one corner.

As the business opportunities were better in nearby Milestown—as Miles City was then called—he opened a studio in town after a couple of

5. "Old trader's store and residence, Ft. Keogh, 1879."

years at the post. Here he occupied several studios, one of which burned and with it some early negatives he prized highly. Another was a curious building built of salvage lumber from the *F. Y. Bachelor,* a steamboat on which some of the staterooms were torn out to make room to load on more buffalo hides in the days when hide-hunting was at its height. As some of the lumber was "cut on the bias" the construction of this studio involved some unique problems.

Business was scanty in those early days, and Huffman turned to other tasks for additional income. He hunted buffalo for hides and meat, although his buffalo hunting was usually limited to a trip or two each winter.[2] On two occasions he guided and photographed for George Shields, a sports writer. Shields used his photographs to illustrate a hunting story in a holiday number of *The American Field* in 1880, thus providing the first known use of Huffman's photographs for illustrations. In the spring of 1880 he helped guide Granville Stuart, noted Montana pioneer and rancher, on an extensive search for a suitable range for the DHS outfit of which he and three others were the owners. It was this trip that probably launched Huffman into the ranching business, for he wrote that the fall of this year found him and a partner, Eugene Lamphere, the nephew of Captain Baldwin, "building a cabin, making hay, and preparing to winter some stock" in the valley of the Rosebud near where the buildings of the Northern Cheyenne Agency were later located. Thus he became the first rancher in the valley of the Rosebud.[3] This venture petered out in a few years, but Huffman was always proud of the days when he was part owner of the H-Lazy L and repped at the roundups.

6. "Old Buffalo Hunters Camp. A relic of the Seventies."

Huffman sometimes wrote to his father, who was also a photographer, about his business. These letters and the notes in the negative collection provide a general picture of his professional problems. The early pictures were taken with a stereographic camera. This camera used a five-by-eight-inch wet plate, which the photographer had to coat and sensitize before using: then he had to develop the exposed plate before the sensitized material dried. These early plates imposed certain limitations, for exposures were measured in fractions of a minute rather than fractions of a second, and the carrying of solutions and a portable darkroom was something of a problem when the means of transportation was a pack horse. Unfortunately, Huffman left no record of the technical problems with which he had to cope when he photographed buffalo hunters on the Montana prairies in the middle of the winter. The task must have been a formidable one.

About 1885 Huffman changed to a camera using a six-and-a-half-by-eight-and-a-half-inch dry plate, thus eliminating the problems created by the solutions and the need for immediate processing of the exposed plate. However, there were other problems. "Eastman's Instantaneous," which he mentioned in one letter, was far from being a "fast" film, and his Perry shutter, one of the first iris shutters, which he worked "as quick as it can be

7. "Taking the Tongues."

worked," probably did not yield an exposure speed of over one-twentieth or one-twenty-fifth of a second. Furthermore, cameras were large and bulky. Huffman once remarked that his was a home-made affair weighing about fifty pounds; and, of course, such cameras were usually used on a tripod with a black cloth and a ground glass back for focusing.

Although it is true that some of these early pictures have technical shortcomings, they have never been excelled. Their popularity is ample proof that the man who took them was a fine technician, had the eye of an artist, and the perspective of a historian.

While Huffman is widely known for his pictures, those who knew him remembered him for other things. Granville Stuart wrote in the journal he kept while on his range hunting trip that "Huffman is one of the most companionable men I ever traveled with." Badger Clark, the range poet, remembered him as a "modest man, rather mild spoken, kindly with gentlemanly manners, and not a trace of swagger." And Louis Grill, editor of the Miles City *Star,* summarized his opinion in the terse fashion of the Old West: "Huffman," said he, "was more than an ordinary character—*he was an institution.*" A casual survey of old correspondence and clippings shows clearly the reason why Huffman might be considered an *institution:* George Bird Grinnell requested the skulls of some of the mountain sheep that once ranged the Montana badlands; Harlan Smith of the American Museum of

8.　"A skin Hunter Taking robes and Tongues, North Montana."

9. "Sioux Chief Spotted Eagle—Wa ma laga lisca, 1880."

Natural History asked for advice on how to make a profitable trip to gather Indian relics; Dr. William T. Hornaday, then taxidermist for the U. S. National Museum, begged some buffalo grass and sagebrush for the buffalo group that stands today in this museum; and the author Hamlin Garland was indebted for introductions to some of the old Cheyenne warriors. For these, and many others, Huffman provided various bits and pieces that were necessary in their work.

As might be expected with anyone who was well liked, sincere, and capable, Huffman served in several public offices. In the mid-1880's he was elected to the school board in Miles City—"school twister" as he put it. Shortly afterward he became one of the county commissioners. At this time Custer County comprised a large part of the southeastern part of Montana, and it fell his lot to be in office when the never-to-be-forgotten winter of 1886-1887 struck. With public funds radically reduced, it was necessary to assess closely all property in 1887. As the major part of this property was cattle that some ranchers moved over the state line into North Dakota

10. "Spotted Eagle's Tepee, 1880."

11. "Rain-in-the-Face at his tepee, 1880."

or Wyoming just before the assessor arrived, and brought back after he had left, there were difficulties. As chairman of the board of commissioners, Huffman was the recipient of some caustic criticism from several prominent cattlemen. As Huffman had tried to act fairly, he felt these criticisms deeply; and later in life he was grateful to one wealthy cattleman who "made what restitution he could."

In 1893 he was elected to the Montana House of Representatives, where he introduced one of the first bills to promote irrigation in the state. However, although Huffman was progressive in his ideas for the development of the state, his heart was always with the wild, free days. After attending the opening of an irrigation project in the Yellowstone Valley near Huntley, he wrote an article for *The Yellowstone Journal* in which he stated: "I

12. "Indian buck and squaw. Two Sans Arc Sioux with antelope skins on ponies in front of my old shack at Ft. Keogh, 1879."

would that there were yet a few waste places left untouched by the settler and his cursed wire fence, good in its way, but not for me." Huffman was a frontiersman at heart as long as he lived.

Perhaps the one characteristic of Huffman that his acquaintances remembered best was his love of humor and practical jokes. Tucked away here and there in his notes, and in his letters to his father, are references to various bits of humor. One of these relates to a "sawed off" range cook named Fritz who once substituted tobasco sauce for catsup; and another pertains to White Bull, the famous Cheyenne medicine man, who wanted to plant raisins in a garden because he considered them the best food the white man had. Of one Fourth of July typical of his bachelor days, he wrote his father that he and sixteen friends celebrated in the very early hours of the morning with a barrel of rosin, six kegs of blasting powder, ten gallons of kerosene, and other incidentals to amplify the noise as iron cans to fire charges in, empty whisky barrels, and couple of anvils. He also noted that the firing of heavy charges in the anvils with his cigar gave him a headache.[4]

13. "Two Moon's Children, Fort Keogh June 1879."

Difficult times in 1890 forced Huffman to close out his business in Miles City. The next few years found him working at various tasks, one of them being in a photographic establishment in Chicago. However, in the end, the wide open spaces called him back. In 1896 he opened a studio in Billings, Montana, but after a few years he closed it and returned to Miles City.

About 1905 he closed his studio to casual business and devoted all of his time to the production and sale of pictures from his negatives of the frontier days. These he sold in various forms from small contact prints from the old gelatin plates to enlargements several feet long. He also carefully tinted some of his enlargements, and these have become collectors' items. This work kept him busy until the end; and visitors to his studio were usually entertained with fascinating stories of the human-interest details pertaining to these pictures.

In December, 1931, Huffman and his wife went to Billings to visit a daughter during the holiday season. On the morning of the twenty-eighth he was stricken by a heart attack and died a few minutes later. Thus passed

14. "Main Street, Miles City. 1882."

15.   Huffman's studio on East Main Street.

16. "My first grizzly bear, Big Horn, 1879."

a pioneer who had watched with pride the development of a prairie frontier, but who had loved best those days when the sod was etched by the trails of the buffalo.[5]

Of all the photographs Huffman took, he prized most of all those dealing with the days of the open range. As he was an early rancher and many of his acquaintances were ranchers, this is to be expected. Not only did Huffman value these pictures above the others, but they comprise the largest and best part of his collection. His record of such subjects as hide-hunting, Indian life, and freighting is fragmentary; and to get a complete picture it is necessary to fill in the gaps with material from other sources. However, this shortcoming does not extend to that part of the collection dealing with range life: this aggregate is both rich and reasonably complete.

Various phases of ranch life are reflected, in one way or another, in the records Huffman left. Beginning with a short account (quoted later) of the arrival of the first trail herd at Fort Keogh, he preserved in fragmentary manuscripts, in notes, and in letters considerable of the intimate color that was a part of the early days of ranching.[6] The following extracts are typical of the comments he set down in letters to his father.

Of the cowboys celebrating a few days in town between the spring and fall roundups—customers for an inexpensive tintype now and then[7]—he noted:

July 1st 1884
. . . The Roundup is nearly finished and the boys are coming in to *rest* up a little before the beef drive commences— Its soothing to see them resting in bands of

17. "Black Canyon, Big Horn Range. Baldwin's Exploring Expedition, 1879."

10 to 25— they cant rest real hard unless they have their shaps [*sic*] and 6 shooters on— ...

Just what was "soothing" about a bunch of cowboys whooping up the town is not clear unless it was that it broke the monotony that prevailed during busy seasons.

The following winter he was concerned about the effects of the cold on the livestock:

Jan 16th 1885

Yours of the 4th at hand and finds us still enjoying intense cold weather— for example yesterday was bright and clear   a real smiling sunny day to look out upon but the mercury only rose from 36° in the morning to 12° below zero at noon   and in the afternoon slid down to 40°   This morning the mercury was in the ball at 9 OC—spirit thermometers in two exposed localities were respectively 58° & 60° —The official sig[nal] station says 51°   The cowmen shake their heads some   no heavy losses are yet reported but are daily expected if this holds on much longer. indications are tonight that it will be about like last night and we hope that the end of the 3rd snap for this winter will be reached— since the 1st Dec I have never seen so much solid cold crammed into 48 days and I guess no one ever did—if stock unfed and unsheltered can stand this and live then we do live in the "green cow land" ...

18. "Tall Bull and Indian Police. Lame Deer, 1892."

A few months later spring had pushed these fears into the background:

April 5 1885

Our summer has fairly begun. today its really too warm for comfort. the past 30 days have been as a whole spotless and faultless and the cowmen are more than gay as they go about the preparation for the largest spring calf gathering picknic . . .

The optimism of the ranchers was apparently infectious, for Huffman packed his gear and headed for the roundups too. Here he tried out his "modern" equipment and two months later, in a jubilant mood, he wrote:

June 7 1885

Yours of the second at hand finds us all well at home. I Just returned a few days ago from a 12 days ride with the Powder River Roundup— I shall soon show you what can be done from the saddle without ground glass and tripod— Please notice when you get the specimens that they were made with the lens wide open and many of the best exposed when my horse was in motion— . . .

Huffman's comments in the last letter quoted is one of the few instances

19. "Young 'Plenty Bird,' Cheyenne, in his sweat lodge."

where he alluded to the difficulties he encountered in taking pictures of frontier life. Here, as in all other such notes, it is necessary to read between the lines to fully understand the problems to which he referred.

The equipment with which Huffman was now working was a definite improvement over that which he used when he photographed hide hunters at work on the bleak plains in midwinter. Gone were the days when he had to coat and sensitize glass plates literally on the spot, expose, and then develop them before the emulsion dried. Gone, too, were the days when exposures had to be measured in fractions of a minute. The new *dry* plates, which were purchased "ready made" and did not require immediate processing, were an immense improvement over the old wet plates. Furthermore, shutter speeds up to one-twenty-fifth of a second could be used, but even this was slow compared to the fast film of the present day which, with a proper lens, permits shutter speeds of one-one-thousandth of a second. Compared to modern cameras and film, Huffman's equipment was still very crude.

His home-made camera was bulky and heavy and, to secure the very best results, it had to be supported on a tripod. Because its focus was very

20. "Crow Warrior named [Sits Down Spotted] ..., Fort Keogh, Montana Territory . . . [*circa* 1881?]."

critical at close distances, it was necessary either to use a small lens opening and a long exposure or to focus very carefully when photographing nearby subjects. These large cameras were focused by slipping a piece of ground glass into the back instead of the plate-holder and then shutting out the distracting light by covering the body of the camera with a black cloth while the critical adjustment was made. Unfortunately, cutting horses "turning on a dime" at full speed as they pursued a wily cow, broncos unloading their riders, and little calves fighting on the end of lariats as they were being dragged to the branding fire were not the sort of subjects well suited for this fussy sort of preparation or for long exposures. And these were the kind of pictures Huffman wanted to balance out his collections.

But Huffman was the sort of genius who refused to be balked by such

21. "Old Swing Ferry at Buffalo Rapids near Miles City."

22. "Main Street, Miles City [*circa* 1882]."

23. "Roping Calves on the Open Range."

difficulties. As he could not work around a roundup herd on foot, he discarded his tripod, black cloth, and ground glass focusing back, and climbed on a horse with his "snappin' machine" and the necessary plate-holders. As the riding horses of that day often possessed an unpredictable temperament, probably even the most gentle animals constituted a hazard with unusual objects on their backs. Perhaps Huffman had a way with horses—some riders did—at any rate, he never told of having any serious spills.

With a four-legged "tripod" that not only provided a desirable perspective but was also capable of self-propulsion, the only serious difficulties remaining were those inherent in the camera. These Huffman recognized and avoided as far as possible. He opened the lens as wide as possible, set the fastest speed into the shutter, and then stayed far enough away from his subject so that depth of focus did not become a critical factor. The lack of definition, sometimes called fuzziness, that resulted from using an imperfect lens wide open will be noted at the extreme edges of some of the pictures. This shortcoming Huffman tolerated in order to capture the action he desired.

Now and then he tried to push his camera beyond the limits of its capabilities. One such instance produced—everything considered—a very remarkable action shot. In this case the securing of a picture of a bronc in

24. Cutting out a steer.

the act of unloading his rider was a noteworthy achievement—particularly when it is considered that the horse on which Huffman was working was undoubtedly in motion following the subject. What the picture lacks in sharpness and detail is supplied by the photographer's vivid description:

> The big red broncho bolted and threw "Dutchy" at the third pitch. The photograph is not over sharp, but shows "Dutchy" high in the air, however it does not show the three deep purple blats that the horse uttered as he bucked to "get his man." There is nothing more terrifying, at first, than the bawl of a maddened broncho, but you soon get used to it, for it goes on every day at the roundup. You soon grow to like it—if some other fellow is doing the riding.

Huffman wrote short descriptive sketches such as this for many of his pictures. These he sent to prospective mail-order customers along with a list of titles. Today these little vignettes are delightful supplements as well as being extremely valuable additions from a historical standpoint, for they inject a unique breath of life and realism into the pictures.

On the following pages is reproduced a part of Huffman's record of the frontier of the rancher's wife, the sheepherder, and the cowpuncher. In the notes for some of the pictures are the highlights as the photographer saw them. Except in two instances these sketches contain no hint of the

25. A bucking bronco.

obstacles that had to be overcome. Of one sheep picture he noted, "This picture . . . , like many others, cost some days of patient waiting." And, of an outstanding picture of a roundup on the move, he recalled, "The choice of the situation cost more than a week of riding, watching and waiting." The difficulties involved in making this superb collection the reader must —for the most part—imagine for himself.

They was dirt-roofed, an' homely, an' ramblin' an'
  squat—

Jest logs with mud-daubin'; but I loved 'em a lot.

Their latch-strings was out, an' their doors wouldn't
  lock:

Get down an' walk in ('twas politer to knock).[1]

Frank Bird Linderman

TWO

Their Latchstrings

Hung Out

IN APRIL, 1883, a young bride from West Virginia, traveling with her husband in a spring wagon from Miles City to their ranch at the mouth of Lame Deer Creek, observed with some apprehension the low, drab, mud-chinked log shacks with dead weed stalks on their dirt roofs that were to be seen occasionally along the hundred miles of trail. When an old lady she still remembered that, as the second day of travel passed, her heart sank lower and lower. Finally she gathered enough courage to ask her husband if their cabin was as unattractive as the others along the trail. He confirmed her fears by stating that theirs was even worse.

What her husband had called an unattractive shack was a little

dirt-roofed cabin, hardly any taller than a man, with one door and only *one window*. In this country where windows had to be hauled many miles they were usually used sparingly, one being made to do the work of two—a half to each room. An immense pair of elk antlers hung over the door, one prong supporting a human skull which . . . had been picked up on the battle ground of Lame Deer . . .[2]

The inside, with a new wagon sheet spread on the dirt floor, a bright fire in the fireplace, and a white bedspread on the bed, provided a pleasant surprise. However, the bride was to regret the white bedspread, for the bedroom doubled for the family living room and she could never keep that bedspread clean.

26. "The Old [Spear] Cow Camp on Bitter Creek."

27. A line camp.

28. Interior of the line camp.

That evening the bride ate supper in a dirt-floored kitchen having for its furnishings a stove, some three-legged stools that had not been designed for stability, and a box such as was used on a chuck wagon—the compartments of which served as a kitchen cabinet and its folding lid for a table. Around the table with her were her husband and his partner, a cowboy, a logger, and another hired man who was an expert with a whipsaw. A wave of homesickness swept over her as she sat down with these grizzled men in their grimy-looking clothes, but she soon forgot it in the enjoyment of an excellent supper of hot biscuits, venison and bacon, potato chips, dried fruit, and coffee.

These experiences of Nannie Alderson, whom Huffman and his family came to know well some years later, were typical of those had by many wives on the Montana frontier. This rough cabin represented the cruder type of ranch home, though certainly it was larger and perhaps better constructed than the little shacks and dugouts that served as line camps on big ranches. However the latter were not *homes* in the true sense of the word but merely a sort of permanent camp.

Alderson was building a new house when his wife arrived. This home represented the opposite extreme. It had four rooms and was constructed of small, carefully hewn logs that fitted closely together. The floors were of boards, laid double for warmth, and the kitchen even had a built-in cupboard with drawers and a flour bin. The walls of the living room, which was also the owner's bedroom, were lined with muslin and papered with a flowered paper. A fireplace that took logs five feet long provided warmth, and the room had the unusual luxury of a carpet, walnut furniture, and pictures on the wall. "There was no house," Mrs. Alderson wrote afterward, "like it anywhere in eastern Montana, outside of Miles City. And we never had one like it again."

In contrast to this small "spread," which followed the unusual practice of having the cowboys live with the owners, was the home ranch of the DHS, constructed in 1880. Of this establishment Granville Stuart wrote:

> I selected a spot on Ford's creek near some nice cold springs, about three miles from the foot of Judith mountains, and began the construction of a log stable that would accommodate ten horses, a cabin for cowboys, and a blacksmith shop. These buildings formed two sides of a large corral.
>
> We also built two log houses one for Reese Anderson's family and one for my own use. These two houses formed two sides of an open square and as Indians were likely to be troublesome in that section of the country, the two houses were connected with a bastion like those used at the early trading posts.[3]

According to Stuart the headquarters of a big outfit usually consisted of a "few rude log cabins, comprising a bunk house, a cook house, a blacksmith shop, stable and corral . . .

In the early days of ranching, regardless of whether the outfit was large or small, the homes were built of logs, if timber was available, and, if not, of stone or sod. Clay was usually used for chinking and mortar, but sometimes cow manure was substituted. One of these old stone houses, that of the well-known LU Bar outfit, is shown in one of the illustrations; and the picture of the home ranch of the OX is of particular interest. A buffalo hunter named Fred Le Breche contracted to build the latter cabin for Major Towers, owner of the OX. When Le Breche came to hunt suitable material, the only logs available were so crooked that his helper wanted to give up the job. However, he sawed into the inside of the curves and straightened the crookedest logs enough to construct the walls, filling the largest cracks with small timbers and stones well chinked with clay.

Clay was widely used as a roof covering and, although it was readily available, cost nothing, and provided welcome protection from the winter cold, it had the disadvantage of sometimes leaking when it rained hard. One ranch wife recalled that

> Whoever went through the heavy rains of June 1888 can [never] forget the leaky roofs which resulted. I have often wished those experiences might be compiled into one book. . . .
>
> If I remember rightly, Mrs. Cowles could tell of sleeping under an umbrella. At the Allerton ranch, where the ceiling was of muslin, stretched firmly across, it became necessary to drain the gathered waters which had dripped through the dirt roof. So they fastened a cord in the center of the ceiling, weighted it with

29. "The Old <u>LU</u> [LU Bar] Cow Camp, North Montana, 1884."

a stone and put a tub under to catch the stream. At our house—hats on our heads and rubbers on our feet, kept those two extremities dry—and each night we moved our beds to dryer quarters and were lulled to sleep by the drip of waters which constantly ran down the inside walls of the house.[5]

The walls inside, except in cabins of roughest construction, were as smooth as hewing the inside face of the log could make them. Sometimes they were whitewashed to keep them clean—the "whitewash" often being prepared from a white shale, found in badlands areas, which was pounded up and prepared by soaking in water. Another method of "finishing" the walls was to line the inside of the cabin with muslin; and this was sometimes whitewashed. Occasionally a cretonne was used instead to provide a bit of gay color; and often the walls were papered with newspapers, pasted either directly to the walls or to a muslin or cheesecloth backing. As the papers became dirty, another layer would be applied—a cheap and convenient way of covering dirt, providing insulation, and—last but not least—sealing off the hiding places of bedbugs, which pest was by no means uncommon. One rancher noted that

After the women came along the logs of these houses were often papered with newspapers—sometimes after being covered with cheesecloth sheeting—and it was surprising how many of these papers would be read after they were plastered on the walls. . . . Someone reading an item from a New York paper plastered on the wall saw where a young man by the name of [Smith] [6] was accidently shot while hunting in a boat. This person brought this item to the

30. "Old OX Ranch near Marmarth [North Dakota]" Built in 1883.

attention of one of the members of our family, whereupon we communicated with a member of the dead boy's family and found out that they were a branch of our family. . . .[7]

Sometimes the interiors bore mute evidence of the tendency of cowboys to josh and play practical jokes at the least provocation. One rancher, recalling early days in the valley of the Tongue, wrote:

Occasionally there would be a so-called remittance man—college bred and maybe the son or relative of one of the owners of the outfit who would come out for the summer, that would feel superior to the cow hands—not all of them tried to show their superiority—but if they did the cowboys really gave them a bad time. I knew of one such who would always try to use "big words" and then follow up by explaining what he meant in more common or understandable language. So finally the boys got so when ever this individual would use a big word somebody would scream out, "Where did it go?" Somebody would point, generally, to the corner of the ceiling and somebody would whip out a six shooter and whang away at it. . . . as a result some of our old log buildings had "45" slugs peppered all over.[8]

Although dirt floors were not uncommon, the better cabins had board floors. As far as floors were concerned, the squat cabins had a distinct advantage over frame houses. One rancher's wife who lived in a frame house

. . . always rejoiced that none of my New England ancestors could see my kitchen floor, for [in the winter] it was impossible to clean it until spring sent

31. "Interior of an Old Time Ranch, Powder River."

the mercury up to above the freezing point. Again and again I would try to do it, but always the mop would freeze solid as it touched the floor. This was partly because that end of the house had not been banked up and was open to every breeze that blew; open also to the skunks which made their home under the wide hearth stone before our truly gorgeous fireplace in the living room. As a rule, they would not annoy us, but occasionally something would disturb them in the night, and then—oh, then! [9]

Considering the rough construction, it is not strange that other living things, besides humans, sometimes occupied the premises. When Lincoln Lang, whose father was one of Roosevelt's neighbors on the Little Missouri, started ranching he lived first in a wolfer's shack with a dirt floor. Two skunks burrowed under a wall and a Scotsman who lived with him, not knowing the peculiarities of the "wee dogies wi' lang bushy tails," attempted to eject one forcibly! And a family of pack rats nested in the roof and pilfered a number of small objects, including some of his teaspoons.[10] One rancher's wife remembered that when she and her husband moved into their first shack, mice ran around in the roof at night and dislodged dirt which fell down on their bed. The mice did not last long, however, as bull snakes found them.

Another pest that was not cleaned out so easily—in fact it was impossible to eradicate them short of burning the building—was bedbugs. The cracks between the logs provided ideal harboring places and, once a cabin or bunkhouse was infested, the occupants usually had trouble from that time on. There was, however, one semi-permanent remedy that permitted the occupants to sleep in peace. The bugs were eradicated from the bed and its legs set in small tin cans partially filled with coal oil (kerosene), which provided a barrier at which all bugs either balked or died trying to cross. In the summer—screen doors being nonexistent—other worse-than-unwelcome visitors sometimes slipped quietly through the open door into the welcome shade of the interior. The dry "buzzing" that announced the unexpected presence of a rattlesnake struck terror into the heart of any adult who was near, and when the housewife had a baby or small children playing on the floor that terror was compounded several times.

The furnishings of frontier homes were often as rough as the cabins themselves. Table and chairs, or stools, were often home-made, the cupboard might be equally crude, and if the stove had a broken leg it might be propped up on a flat rock. In like manner the bed might be a rough bunk built against the wall, with a bed tick filled with "Montana feathers," as one pioneer facetiously termed the native hay. Crude though it might be, a tick full of sweet-grass hay had a fragrant, pleasing smell. Many of the wives from well-to-do homes in the East brought a few pieces of good furniture with them, and these aided materially in sustaining morale.

As time passed and the country developed, improvements came to the home just as to other communities that developed on the frontier. A few of the homes would have been unusual in almost any community. Outstanding among these was the home of Pierre Wibaux, a Frenchman who left attractive business opportunities in his native land to become the owner of the W Bar and—eventually—a wealthy rancher. When Wibaux started ranching he lived in a dugout, but when his wife came he built a spacious house and furnished it with fine furniture and rugs. The yard was landscaped, planted with shrubs and flowers, and decorated with pieces of statuary after the practice of his native land. But this was not a typical ranch home.

Much of the hardship, if the inconveniences can properly be called that when judged by the standards of the times, hinged around the supply and quality of the water. The source of supply was a well, spring, or a deep hole in a stream bed—and every drop that was used had to be carried by hand. Sometimes it had to be hauled for miles. Furthermore, in many areas it was so impregnated with alkali or mineral salts that soap would not dissolve properly and white clothes came out a dingy yellow. Not only did the supply of water involve toil, but the facilities for cleansing with it were crude. Washing of the face and hands at the bunkhouse was done in washbasins placed on a wooden bench: a flour sack served for a towel. Clothes were washed by hand in a tub, and put out to dry on bushes, tall grass, a convenient fence, or sometimes on a clothesline improvised from a lariat.

A bath in the wintertime was a luxury that the ordinary cowboy did not indulge in frequently. For the rancher's family it was a major undertaking involving the use of a washtub beside the kitchen stove—and, because carrying and heating the water was a problem of no small size, one tubful served the entire family, the children bathing first and the adults last. Even in the summertime there were difficulties. A lady who grew up on Pumpkin Creek south of Miles City recalled that the Indians they knew were "friendly but most inquisitive. One big buck surprised my mother one day, looking in on her as she was taking a bath. In response to her consternation and yells, the old buck just grinned." [11] Although winter brought some difficulties, it did bring snow, and this the ranch wives melted—and hoarded even in small fruit jars—to secure a welcome change from the natural hard water.

No description of the "plumbing" at a ranch would be complete without mention of the small, humble building in the back yard. Nannie Alderson wrote:

> I'm sure mine was the most wonderful structure of the kind ever built. It was made of boards which Uncle and Baltimore Bill had whipsawed out by hand; a most delicate and difficult operation. . . . Uncle thought so much of his precious lumber that he couldn't bear to have a foot of it wasted, and so refused to trim off the ends of the boards used in the outhouse—though . . . he wasn't saving anything that way, because the long ends would be sure to warp. This they did, and curled in all directions. No roof could be put over such a crazy thing, and all that summer and fall it stood open to the sky. [12]

Another ranch wife of a later date recorded similar impressions. Hers had no stars or half-moons in the door and, while hot and stuffy in the summer, the wind whistled through every crack and knothole in the winter. She remembered that there was a diversion in the shape of a Sears, Roebuck catalogue hung by a stout cord from a nail. But she never got around to any wishful ordering: "I never dallied that long."

Not all of these ranch homes were presided over by a woman: some of them were bachelor empires pure and simple, with a male cook reigning in the kitchen. Such homes often provided little beyond a place to eat and sleep, and shelter from the elements. Therefore, most of the interest must center on the female part of the picture, even though it comprised but a part of the whole. In the area Huffman knew, the feminine fraction of the population varied widely. "There is an old and true border saying," wrote Theodore Roosevelt, "that 'the frontier is hard on women and cattle.'" No doubt Roosevelt was correct when he stated that, except for some striking exceptions,

> the grinding toil and hardship of a life passed in the wilderness, or on its outskirts, drive the beauty and bloom from a woman's face long before her youth has left her. By the time she is a mother she is sinewy and angular, with thin, compressed lips and furrowed, sallow brow. But she has a hundred qualities that atone for the grace she lacks. She is a good mother and a hard-working housewife, always putting things to rights, washing and cooking for her stalwart spouse and off-spring.[13]

Courageous and resourceful as such women were, these qualities were sometimes overshadowed—in the opinion of some of their neighbors—by their uncouth and irritating ways. At least one rancher's wife had a neighbor of this sort whose visits she did not enjoy even though she was often lonely for contacts with others of her sex.

Not all of the wives of the Montana ranchers were cast in the mold Roosevelt described. Some, women of education and talent whom their husbands brought from other sections of the country, tried to provide some softening influence in their homes to counteract the rugged nature of the country and the cabins in which they lived. Others were interesting for various reasons. Some were Indian women. Outstanding among these was the Snake woman Granville Stuart married in the early days of the gold fields. One disadvantage of Indian wives was that their relatives usually lived off their white relatives—if they could. Granville's brother James was apparently aware of this fact when, in the journal the brothers kept, he listed among Aubony's good qualities the fact that she had "few relatives." Some were girls from the red-light districts who had broken with the ancient profession. Others, secured by means of contacts made through matrimonial magazines, were known as "mail order" wives or "heart and hand" women.

Perhaps the most interesting fraction, however, were the wives of Englishmen who tried to transplant on Western ranches some of the practices to which they had been accustomed. The wife of one early rancher who located on Pumpkin Creek was amused when

> Captain and Mrs. Elmhurst stopped with us on their first trip to their ranch, accompanied by a valet and a maid, and carrying all the paraphernalia held to be so necessary to their mode of living. One very hot day Captain and Mrs.

32. "A Snug Little Home Among the Big Cottonwoods."

Elmhurst went to Miles City from their ranch on horseback. The luggage they took along was tremendous. Mrs. Elmhurst even had her bathtub (collapsible), and above all, carried an umbrella for protection from the sun.[14]

Not all the English were like this pair—neither were the Elmhursts exceptions—and an occasional American tried to imitate their "royal" ways.

Food varied with the policy of the ranch owner—and the cook. Where the owner did not live on the ranch, the staples supplied were often plain —even when variety was definitely limited at the best. The common staples at many big outfits were beans, bacon, coffee, dried fruit, syrup or molasses (sometimes called "lick"),[15] bread, and beef. Some outfits used molasses instead of sugar, and the story is told of one cowboy who, when offered white, granulated sugar at the table of a neighboring rancher, replied that he did not use *salt* in his coffee. At some outfits a can of tomatoes or oysters was a luxury, while at some of the small outfits canned goods were common. When the weather was not too hot, a beef, usually a yearling, would be killed, the carcass wrapped in a tarpaulin, and swung from the ridgepole of the cabin, a tripod, or the limb of a convenient tree. Here it hung until eaten—for meat thus cared for would not spoil if consumed within a reasonable period of time. When available and if work permitted, game was often killed, for, after all, cattle could be sold and deer, elk, and antelope could not. Sometimes game was cured to bolster the summer supplies. And, although a spread might run thousands of cattle, all the milk used came from cans—unless a woman supplied the necessary pressure for some rider to wrestle with a cow.

Where women were present, a few chickens were sometimes kept—and prized indeed were the cake recipes that required but a single egg! Sometimes a simple garden was attempted but, unless it could be irrigated, it was likely to be hard hit by the dry weather of the summer. In late summer there was often wild fruit to be had for the gathering, particularly wild plums, which made delightful jelly, and this helped to provide variety. However, there was one really serious handicap to cooking. Supplies were usually purchased but once a year—when the men went to town to market their beef. Then flour and sugar were bought in hundred-pound sacks, bacon by the side, coffee—invariably, Arbuckle coffee—in huge tins, canned goods by the case, and dried fruits by the box. If an item was forgotten, or an insufficient quantity purchased, the household went without until the next—far-distant—shopping day.

Daily life within the household was, essentially, the same as in any other household. There were meals to be prepared, and there was bread to be baked. The bread was usually sourdough bread, so named because the "starter" used to provide the yeast was a bit of dough from a previous baking. This "starter," renewed at each baking, was carefully guarded, and it was not unusual for a household to have a jar of starter that had been perpetuated for years without having been renewed from an outside source. In cold weather, when there was danger of freezing, it was even taken to bed at night! There were washings to be done—rubbing on a board in a

33. "Hat X Cow Camp on Timber Creek.   Oct 1902."

tub, with water that was often so hard that the soap did not lather properly. There were clothes to be made and mended. There were children to be reared. And, if there was enough energy after the necessary tasks had been completed, the housewife might struggle with the problem of making the cabin look a little less rough, or she might seek a bit of recreation.

Some wives broke the monotony of their daily lives by making a bit of ceremony out of their daily tasks. The principles of etiquette—perhaps to counteract the influence of the dirt floor—were often religiously practiced, even in the bachelor cow camps. Indicative of the manner in which common courtesies were observed was the practice of a rider, when approaching a strange cabin, of remaining mounted until he was invited to "Get off and rest yourself." Neither, in the days when revolvers were carried, did the rider get off his horse in such a way as to put the animal between him and the stranger he had just met.

Children lived a free and uninhibited life. As no one dictated their amusements, they developed a high degree of initiative and resourcefulness in amusing themselves that more than offset some of the obvious disadvantages of their isolated existence. Often there was much of interest to be observed. Astride the top rail of the corral beside the stable, they had ringside seats to the sort of activities that form the foundation of the now popular and widely enjoyed rodeos. One of Huffman's photographs shows a small boy entering into the activity of the roundup with every ounce of energy in his small body. Naturally they had pets of all kinds. Small animals, dogs, calves, and "tame" ponies were common. Occasionally there were fawns, both antelope and deer, but some of these had their disadvantages. Mrs. Alderson's children had

> . . . a fawn, which we fed on a bottle until he was old enough to eat grass. Eventually he grew up into a full-sized young buck, and was a rather dangerous pet. One day when Fay was playing with him at a little distance from the house he butted her down, and began pawing at her with his sharp little hoofs. . . . Mr. Zook was visiting us with his bride. When he saw what was happening to Fay he took a rifle and shot the deer from on top of her. Except for a cut on the back of her neck she was none the worse—but was very indignant at her rescuer.[16]

Sometimes attempts were made to tame even wolves and coyotes. Although pets might run the gamut of almost all kinds of living creatures, rattlesnakes excepted, there was one kind of pet that was forbidden at the home of a dyed-in-the-wool cattleman. *Lambs were positively beyond the pale.*

The problem of education—the part usually learned from books—was often difficult to solve. Sometimes there were country schools or, where several children lived in a locality, a rancher might employ a teacher. Granville Stuart hired a schoolteacher for the children at the DHS ranch, and the other children of the neighborhood were also invited to attend. In 1881, the year after his arrival on Ford Creek, he built a schoolhouse and presented it to the district. But for many scattered families there were no schools of any sort, and as the rancher usually could not afford a tutor, the problem of teaching the children had to be met—just as were all other family problems—by the home concerned. Mrs. Alderson met the problem this way:

> We had been getting the Montgomery Ward catalog since 1885. It is impossible to exaggerate the importance of the part played by this book of wonder in the children's lives. They poured over it endlessly; before they could read the pictures were there to dazzle them. . . . The catalogue is well named the "wish book" by country people.
> In time they learned to spell words out of it. They never went to school until we moved to Miles City, when Mabel was almost ten years old. All they knew up to that time was reading, as taught by Montgomery Ward, and printing block letters, which I taught them.[17]

While children provided some labor around the home after they had passed the infant stage, the ranch wife usually had no help with her work other than what she could inveigle from her husband or some cowboy who might be temporarily unoccupied. Mrs. Alderson was one of the fortunate few in this respect. She lived near the Cheyenne reservation and sometimes was able to secure an Indian woman to do her washing. One of these, a squaw with the ominous name of Rattlesnake, also brought her comely, tidy-looking sixteen-year-old daughter, Bob-Tailed Horse, to look after the baby. From Bob-Tailed Horse—whom Mrs. Alderson named "Minnie" (short for Minnehaha)—and others Nannie Alderson learned some of the basic principles of rearing Indian children—while her child became proficient in speaking Cheyenne. "Indians," Mrs. Alderson noted, "are unquestionably fond of children. They will snatch them out of mischief, give them a little shake and grunt at them, and there it ends. After that the child is simply removed from temptation, and I have never seen one of them spank a small child."[18]

Another Indian woman who worked for this housewife was one of Little Wolf's squaws. "He had two squaws," wrote Mrs. Alderson, "and he brought the one he thought the least of to wash for us." While there was nothing unusual about the squaw, Nannie Alderson recalled that, of all the "frontier folk" she ever knew, this famous war chief—who kept careful watch over her children while his squaw washed—was one of two individuals who made the "most lasting impression" on her. This contact, which came after Little Wolf had been "thrown away" by his people for the drunken murder of Famished Elk, provided an intimate picture of a great Indian.

To Mrs. Alderson, "He was a pathetic figure of a deposed king, but there was a dignity about him, despite his poverty, that was touching." He respected the orders of the Indian Department, and he often explained to her husband, supplementing his English with the graceful, expressive gestures of sign language, that, "The Indians should be friendly with the white people, and after a while they would get to be one big people." "Little Wolf never begged or stole, but his squaw . . . would sometimes make off with our towels. He would bring them back the next day, handing them to me and saying: 'Squaw hypersiba,'[19] with such pathetic dignity that I was moved." She also noted that he had courage, with a "quiet resignation to 'the inevitableness of things,'" and evidenced a kind heart and a "childlike interest in simple things—in sunlight and the beauty out of doors." And she admired his ability to appear happy "under conditions that most people would regard as impossible," and it seemed to her that his happiness was the sort that could come only from integrity and inner peace.[20]

The Aldersons gave Little Wolf a pipe, and "he would hold it in his hands between smokes, rubbing it over in a pleased way and saying: 'Heapie good, heapie good.'" This gift may have touched a deeper chord than the givers realized, for the breaking of a man's pipe was part of the procedure accompanying the expulsion from the tribe of a Cheyenne convicted of murder. This lonely outcast came to hold a deep affection for the Aldersons and when, after financial reverses on the range, they moved to Miles City, he begged them—with tears rolling down his cheeks—not to go. Years later when Mrs. Alderson, then a widow, had the post office and a little store at Birney, Montana,

Little Wolf would come twenty-five or thirty miles to visit me and my children every fall. He was a very old man by that time and blind, and his squaw would walk the whole distance leading his horse. She was the one we thought was "hypersiba" because she stole our towels, but when we saw her devotion to the old man in walking that long way, we were reminded again what a mixed thing human nature is, and how often one is compelled to give admiration where one least expected to.[21]

Although these early homes were often separated by many miles, their occupants did not let this factor deter them from making an effort to relieve the monotony that isolation imposed. Music often served as an excuse for cowboys to travel considerable distances. In the Little Missouri country, the Lang family had a piano—"the first piano the Bad Lands ever knew"— and this added much to the attraction of the "open house" for which this family became well known.

> That piano of ours had a good deal to do with it, I imagine. Anyhow it was the talk of the country, and when the people around learned that my sister was musically inclined, she was promptly elected to entertain them. About the first we knew of it was one evening when some twenty-five cowboys invaded us in a bunch with the request that she sing for them. Somehow we got them packed into the living room, chaps, spurs, guns, and all, as they stood. Through her entire repertoire the star performer had to wade to the howling [requests for] encores of her enthusiastic audience. Succeeding that, such performances became common, the men of the country being apparently music hungry. There were some good voices among them, too, and after their shyness had worn off, they were frequently induced to take a hand, so that lively concerts were by no means infrequent.[22]

The Hotchkiss family on Pumpkin Creek also had a piano.

> We shipped our piano out from the East. It was an old-fashioned square grand piano. The instrument was a great source of pleasure to us as well as to others. I recollect an occasion with some English gentry gathered about the piano one night. They sang their hunting songs. The first year that the assessor came to our house . . . he looked at the piano. . . . [and] said he would not list it as it was the only one he had found outside of Miles City. Custer County was very large then.[23]

Even the player of a jew's harp or a fiddle—as a violin was always called—was certain of an appreciative audience, and Howard Eaton[24] and his banjo were long remembered in the Little Missouri country. Eaton was a bit of a troubadour. When George Shields (for whom Huffman later guided and photographed) made his first hunting trip to Montana in 1880, he found Eaton at the Northern Pacific Railroad engineers' camp on the Little Missouri. A few days before, a hunting party from the surveyors' military escort had shot "four 'pet' wild geese" that a nearby rancher claimed belonged to him. A lieutenant was finally saddled with the "guilt," which cost him not only damages for the geese but also the cigars for the engineers' mess. "The event," wrote Shields, "was duly celebrated the night we were there, in an extemporaneous song by Mr. Howard Eaton, of Pennsylvania, which brought down the house, and some more cigars."[25]

For some housewives there were occasional trips to town. The three-day annual convention of the Montana Stockgrowers Association in Miles City each spring, provided one excuse for a trip, as this affair always ended

34. "Ranch at the 'Hole in the Rock,' head of Big Porcupine."
(This waterhole was a well-known landmark.)

35. "Powderville [Montana], June 1886."

in a ball held at the Macqueen House. Such trips were often annual affairs, however, and it was not unusual for a wife burdened with the care of a baby or several small children to be confined at the ranch for a year or a year and a half. When the roundup crew passed nearby, a wife sometimes went out to watch the work. If unencumbered by cares at home, she might stay several days, helping day-herd and camping at night with her husband in a little tent slightly apart from the chuck wagon and its bedrolls. Not only were these visits to the roundup interesting experiences for the women, but they were occasions of considerable interest to the cowboys and the roundup cooks—particularly at mealtime. Typical of these experiences, is the following related by Mrs. McLean:

On the ranch at Fallon creek—I was the only woman for miles around, and was shown much attention. From one to three delegations called to invite us to dinner at the mess-wagons.[26] I was escorted to the throne of honor—the spring seat of the wagon placed on the ground—my tin plate filled with roast beef, baked beans and hot biscuits, the riders sitting tailor fashion on the ground, their crossed legs making a table for their plates. The cook flourished his cleanest dish towel, pouring coffee, the boys farthest away taking sly glances through the spokes of the wagon wheels. On one occasion I was surprised to have one of the boys ask, "Who was that guy you ate dinner with, who had his chaps on backward?"

I answered, "That was Roosevelt of Medora." He was wearing brown corduroy, leather seated riding breeches.[27]

Although reps[28] often stopped at the cabins of ranchers when going to and from the roundups, these visitors did not fill the housewives' needs for contact with other women. So most women starved for contact with others of their own sex.

When fall brought the range work to a low ebb, there was time for dances. What these lacked in numbers and frequency, they made up in the amount of energy expended when the occasion did arise. The dedication of a new home, the opening of a new country store, the moving of a family, Thanksgiving Day—all these furnished sufficient reason for holding a dance. The occasion was planned well in advance and visitors—particularly women-folk—were invited from far and wide. It was not unusual to travel sixty to one hundred miles to these affairs—a two-day journey in a sled or wagon with an overnight stop with some family while en route. When an old lady, Mrs. Stacy recalled that

> Dances were held frequently here and there around the countryside. All the girls were much in demand. The men usually outnumbered the ladies ten to one. The first fall [1883] we attended a dance at Powderville. A Mr. Mason lived there. He had built a new store and nothing would do but that the new building had to be dedicated with a dance. Mr. Mason sent a four-horse team and wagon for mother and me. The distance was more than sixty miles. It took us all one day to make the trip. We rested all one day. By night time a big crowd had gathered, coming from far and near. Dancing began in the early evening. A lunch was served at midnight. Dancing was then resumed and kept up until daylight, when breakfast was eaten and everybody departed for their homes.[29]

And Mrs. Alderson remembered that

> Parties were held every so often in our countryside by anyone who had a room big enough—and it didn't have to be very big. . . . people would drive to them from miles and miles away, all bundled up in a wagon with babies in their arms. At most of the dances the babies were simply laid on the floor under the benches where the spectators sat. They would sprinkle corn meal on the rough floors to make them slippery, and the men tramping in and out would track in snow which would mix with the corn meal to make a kind of slush, so your skirt would be wet way above the hem, but nobody stopped dancing for that. The few women present would be danced half to death. And it lasted until morning, because you couldn't drive home anyway until it was daylight.[30]

And the music was often as rough as the "ballroom" floor for the fingers that plucked the strings of the banjo, fiddle, or guitar, twanged a jew's harp, muted the tones of a mouth organ, or—on rare occasions—traveled up and down the keyboard of a piano or organ were usually stiffened by toil. The tunes were the favorites of days long past—"Golden Slippers," "The Irish Washerwoman," "Little Brown Jug," "Rye Waltz," "Red River Valley," "Put Your Little Foot Down," "Pop Goes the Weasel," "Strawberry Roan," and others of the same vintage—and above the efforts of the musicians and the shuffling of the feet could be heard the crisp voice of some old-timer calling:

> "Balance all until y' git straight,
> Swing on them corners like swingin on a gate,
> Bow to yore partners and pull yore freight,
> All drift south."

36. "Cox Cattle Ranch. Hanging Woman Creek Near Tongue River, 1899."

But the dancers enjoyed themselves, and one old rancher, looking back regretfully, commented, "Modern transportation has spoiled us and has also spoiled a lot of our good times, I think."

In sharp contrast to these short periods of lightheartedness were other times when illness and injury gripped a member of the household. Aching teeth were a cause of discomfort, but here and there a rancher secured a pair of forceps and was prepared to take effective, though drastic, steps to cope with such trouble. While such aches were troublesome, they were minor when compared with the need for a doctor, which occasionally arose. If possible, the sick or injured person was taken to the doctor, but there were two common reasons for sending for a doctor. These were bad accidents and childbirth, and either was sufficient to send a rider—a rider who changed mounts whenever he could find a fresh one and who spared neither quirt nor spur. Indelibly etched in the memory of "Cousin Peachy" Cox, wife of the boss farmer on the Cheyenne reservation, were the recollections of fifteen hours she spent keeping a woman in labor under the effects of chloroform while a cowboy went sixty miles to Sheridan, Wyoming, and a doctor made the return trip with relays of horses arranged for by the puncher. Perhaps no one, except those women who waged that grim fight against time, can realize what the sight of the doctor's buggy coming over the hill against the light of the rising sun meant to those weary women trying to save a life.

37. "The Circle Bar <u>O</u> on Otter Creek. In anticipation of a Cheyenne Indian outbreak the fort was built on hill back of house." L.A.H.

Distance and lack of communications were not the only obstacles to be faced in such times of need. Some of the doctors who practiced in the West in the early days spent much of their time under the influence of liquor—having come West because they could not hold a practice in the East. At least one doctor in eastern Montana was often "corralled" and kept locked up by the male relatives of a prospective mother, just to insure that he would be available and sober when the time of need came.

Dr. L. F. Townsend, who came to Belle Fourche, South Dakota, fresh from college in 1898, noted that his services were in demand because he "could be depended on not to get drunk." This doctor's territory extended for a radius of about a hundred miles—as a crow flies—to the northeast, north, and northwest, and he often drove seventy-five miles to make a call. In recalling his lack of experience, Dr. Townsend remarked, "After you have driven fifty miles or so to see a patient, they expect you to help them. You have to do something or *get under the bed.*" Sometimes on these trips he would be asked to visit the patients of another doctor; and this he did, sending a note to the other doctor to inform him of any treatment or medicine prescribed.

In such traveling the wild broncos that often had to be driven, uncertainty as to directions concerning the trails, and changeable weather in the fall, winter, and spring months were all hazards to be faced. Townsend got lost in one April snowstorm, his horses stopping on the edge of a very narrow, straight-sided gully. Recalling the admonition of the operator of the livery stable not to wander in a storm, Townsend unhitched the horses and turned them loose. Then he ran the buggy over the washout and made himself a little shelter of rubber aprons in the gully. Into this he crawled with some horse blankets, raisins, and chocolate; and, pulling down his fur cap, made himself comfortable and "slept like a pig." The next morning he awoke to find four inches of snow on the ground—and the livery stable man standing near, somewhat relieved to find his customer snug and safe.[31] The lives of those who faced the hazards of lonely roads to serve the scattered homes were "no beds of roses."

In addition to the uncertainties of medical care, another worry faced the early ranch wives—Indians. Viewed from a distance of sixty or more years, this danger would seem more fancied than real. Nevertheless, fresh in the minds of these pioneers were the happenings, and legends of happenings, of a decade or two before, and the few murders and encounters that did occur seem to have been accorded a degree of importance out of all proportion to their merit. Even friendly visits were sometimes feared. One woman who came from Maine to the Rosebud Valley in 1884 wrote later:

> We lived in mortal terror of, we knew not what, chiefly Indians. . . . one day a band of Indians really came—seeing them approaching we hastily locked the door and feeling that our time had come, we crouched down behind the cook stove, the only bullet proof protection in evidence. Two of their number came to the window and pressing their faces against the pane, saw us. By this time we were paralyzed and nothing mattered much. They made motions for us to come to the door, which we did. Seeing the terror on our faces, I suppose, they mercifully laid down their guns as a signal of friendliness. Their leader said "me crow" (this reassured us somewhat as we knew the crows were friendly) and by words and signs, inquired of us if we had seen any of their ponies. We had not and they rode away.[32]

During the 1880's ranchers throughout the entire country were occasionally visited by hunting parties and groups of questionable intent, and many did not feel safe on these occasions when the preponderance of numbers or arms was with the red men. Even a decade later many of those living in close proximity to the Cheyenne reservation still felt that they were living with a powder keg. The killing of Bob Ferguson, a prominent rancher, Hugh Boyle, and a man named Hoover who was herding sheep for John Barringer, together with the uneasiness resulting from the Ghost Dance religion and the visions of the Crow medicine man, Wraps-Up-His-Tail, all precipitated flurries of apprehension which lasted for a week or two. Some of these resulted in the evacuation of homes, the gathering of some of the women and children at places like Miles City, Rosebud, and Ekalaka, and the organization of forces of armed guards.

Some of the feelings of the times are wrapped up in Mrs. Philbrick's recollections of the activities in the Rosebud Valley which resulted from the killing of Hoover by the Cheyennes in the early summer of 1897. Opening a letter left by a neighbor for her husband, she found instructions from the sheriff to move.

> Summoning the cook and her husband we gathered clothing and such valuables as seemed most urgent to protect, and with my three small children we started down the Rosebud.
>
> When we had driven about fifteen miles suddenly, coming around a curve, we met a band of Indians. Horrified, for we thought we were surrounded by Indians, we hastily admonished the children to lie down in the wagon box and requested the driver to hurry past them. As we drew nearer, Chief Two Moons who was riding in the lead said "Whoa." Our team willingly obeyed this command and he explained that they had been on the north side of the Yellowstone and asked where we were going, saying "White squaws all go to Rosebud, fraid of Cheyenne." We asked what he was going to do about the trouble. He said "Me don't know." We drove on to Rosebud where we found many families from the ranches had gathered.
>
> Two Moons proceeded up the valley, stopped at the newly organized camp [of "militia"], looked at the new rifles and ammunition and said "One sleep, maybe two sleep, me catch em Cheyenne." In a few days the three Indians who killed Mr. Hoover were turned over to the government authorities. . . . This was our last Indian scare.[33]

As the three killings by the Cheyennes all seemed to have been the result of the victim's being too close to Indians butchering a stolen beef, these murders would appear to have stemmed from defensive rather than offensive actions on the part of the Indians.

Not all of the Indian scares had their origin in aggressive acts on the part of the Indians. The stealing of Indian ponies by renegade whites was a constant source of irritation; and there were other overt acts by the whites that created bad feelings and trouble. The Alderson-Zook outfit was involved in two scares, both of which stemmed directly from irresponsible acts of its cowboys. The first of these occurred in 1884 while Mrs. Alderson was in Miles City. On March 18, the day the Alderson's first child was born, two cowboys precipitated this trouble. According to Mrs. Alderson,

> An Indian sub-chief named Black Wolf, living on a tributary of the Tongue River across the divide from us, had brought his lodge to visit on the Rosebud not far from our ranch. On a day of melting snow, he had come round begging for food and tobacco; the boys fed him, and afterwards he sat down to smoke on a pile of fence posts, some yards from our door. There was a man named Reinhart who had been working for us the latter part of the winter, getting out poles for the fences. When Hal [Taliaferro] looked out the door and saw the Indian sunning himself, he said to Reinhart:
>
> "I'll bet you five dollars I can put a hole through that old Indian's hat without touching his head."
>
> The other man of course replied: "I'll bet you can't."
>
> Hal drew his six shooter and fired, just nicking the Indian's scalp. Black Wolf of course was furious; he could not and would not believe that Hal had not meant to kill him. When they found that they could not pacify him they let

38. "Black Wolf, 1901."

him go, and rode hurredly to Young's store ten miles away to get help in defending the property, for they knew what was coming. . . . They had intended to get back inside the house and hold it, but when they got back after several hours they were too late; the Indians, the whole lodge, were in possession. Squaws and papooses were seated in a semi-circle in the front yard, while the bucks were carrying out bureau drawers and emptying the contents in the midst of them to help themselves, afterwards tossing the empty drawers against the side of the house. Hal, realizing that they meant to set fire to it, rode up to them as near as he dared, promising them beef, coffee, ponies and tobacco. But when they started shooting at him, tearing up the earth under his horse, he realized that it was no use, and the men could do nothing but ride up on top of a hill and watch while the house roared into flames.[34]

This immediately stirred up the countryside. A posse of citizens formed under the leadership of Hank Thompson, Billy Smith, the stock inspector at Miles City, and Louis King, a deputy sheriff; and this group surrounded the camp of the Indians one day before daylight. Thompson and King rode boldly into camp as soon as it was light and, largely by virtue of being known and liked by Black Wolf, persuaded the thirteen bucks who were involved to surrender. These were taken to Miles City and put in jail. In the meantime the real culprit, with the assistance of some of the settlers, eluded the authorities and hightailed it for Texas riding Mr. Alderson's top cutting horse! Two Indians, according to Mrs. Alderson—four according to "Teddy Blue," a member of the posse—were convicted of setting the fire and sent to the penitentiary.[35]

As their ranch home was gone, Alderson and Zook moved thirty miles eastward and settled in the Tongue Valley. Here, while getting their cattle acquainted with the water holes on the new range, Packsaddle Jack, a noted rider who was one of their cowboys, almost got the outfit into serious trouble a second time. A Cheyenne named Iron Shirt had his tepee near one of the water holes to which Packsaddle Jack drove cattle. When he passed the tepee, the Indian would set his dogs on the cattle—Teddy Blue recalled that the cowboy drove the cattle through the Indian's garden[36]— and, after this had happened a few times, the puncher threatened to shoot the Indian. When the cattle were disturbed again a few days later, the puncher pulled his gun and shot, breaking the Indian's arm.

Again there was a flurry of apprehension but this time when "a couple of fellows . . . rode over to the roundup [nearby] and asked for help to defend the ranch, Jess Garland, the roundup captain, told them to go to hell. He said: 'You got us into one jackpot this spring, and I won't allow a man to leave this roundup.' "[37] The next day, after the crisis had passed, Alderson persuaded Packsaddle Jack to go to Miles City and give himself up. Then he rode down to the Indian's tepee, set his arm, and made him a big present of coffee, sugar, and beef. Strangely enough, the stolid Indian reacted to Alderson's attempt to right the matter in a grateful manner, and later followed him everywhere with "seemingly doglike devotion." As the Indian always carried a gun, there was some uncertainty as to whether this attention came from a friendly feeling or a desire to kill.[38] Whether these two incidents had any bearing on the reaction of the Cheyennes who were discovered with stolen beef is not known. One old rancher was of the opinion that they may have been the real cause of the killing of Boyle and Hoover. One thing is certain, however—all the troubles with the Indians did *not* originate with the red men.

While these ranch homes were rough, and the luxuries they provided were few, there was one characteristic in which they have never been surpassed. The quality of their hospitality was superb. A total stranger passing by—no matter who he was—was welcome to food and shelter for the night. It is true that there were a few who were not that generous—but these never commanded the respect of their neighbors. They did not belong. To offer to pay for such favors was to insult the host. Friends came and stayed as long as they pleased. If the bedroom facilities were limited, three persons in a bed was the standard arrangement, and, as the saying went, they "hung the kids on a nail."

When a rancher left home, the door was never locked. In fact, there were no locks and to put a lock on anything was, in effect, to insult all who passed by. A traveler, arriving during the absence of the owner, was welcome to what food he could find—*providing* he washed the dishes and cut more wood for the stove. And rarely was this spirit of hospitality violated, even by those wanted by the law.

With customs of this sort, it is not strange that there were unusual visitors. Mrs. Alderson remembered that

> . . . four men rode in one evening across the frozen hills. They were the sheriff of Custer County, his deputy, the biggest stockman in our part of Montana— and a prisoner. I knew the last—a harmless fellow we had always thought him, who lived among the Indians, with no real job. They called him Cheyenne Charlie. . . . He had been to our house before, and I had given him an old homemade fur-trimmed cap to keep his ears warm. I think he was accused of butchering the big cattleman's beef.
>
> Perhaps because of our previous acquaintance, the poor fellow was so embarrassed at the removal of handcuffs while he ate, that I could hardly keep the tears from falling into his coffee while I poured it. One of the men said later that no one could have told from the treatment they received which was the cattle king and which the man under arrest. I thought this one of the nicest compliments I ever had.[39]

Although a stranger on foot looking for work was always viewed with suspicion, sometimes there were visitors that only the calculating eye of a man reared on the frontier was likely to appraise correctly. On another occasion,

> One evening when Mr. Alderson was home from the roundup for the night, three men rode in. There was nothing remarkable about them to my eye, except that one of their number was a fair young boy who quite won my heart, he looked so young and well raised. After supper they all played pitch for the dish-washing, and two of the strangers did it. When we were alone, Mr. Alderson said: "I don't like their looks." They had been evasive about their business, but had taken an interest in the gun rack in the hallway.
>
> I said: "Oh, but that's such a nice young boy who is with them."
>
> "Yes," Mr. Alderson replied, "I guess he's just gotten in bad company." He thought they were there to steal horses from the Cheyennes. I said: "How can you be sure?" Next morning they left, with no further incident except that they bought a gun from Alec Brown, a Kansas boy who was building fences for us that year.
>
> A few weeks later we saw in the paper that two men were caught stealing horses somewhere near the North Dakota line; that there had been a fight, and a young boy with them had been killed. The descriptions tallied, and we felt sure they were our visitors.[40]

Mrs. Alderson's experiences were not unique. A. C. Huidekoper, owner of the HT outfit in the Little Missouri country, recorded a somewhat similar experience.

39. "1899. Barringer's Ranch, Tongue River. This was in 1878 the Groom ranch where the first great herd from the south was turned loose—to perish—."

We had visitors constantly; they came and went. One day we were branding colts in the corral. . . . As we were finishing, I saw two men ride up,
especially well mounted and with pack horses equally good to those they were
riding. As was customary, they climbed the corral and watched us work. When
we had finished, I said to the strangers as I passed out of the corral, "If you
want to turn your horses out with the night herd, you better tell the wrangler."
One of the strangers said, "If you don't mind, we will put our horses in the
stable. We want to be off early." I was quite surprised the next morning when
I went to the corral to commence work, to see the two visitors seated on the
corral. After we had been branding for a time, one of the fellows said, "You
seem to be a little short-handed. Don't you want us to help out?" I said, "Yes,
thanks." They were cracker-jacks and worked like beavers all day. At night
I asked them if they wanted their horses to go out with the night herd; again
they said, "No." The next morning they left us, swinging their sombreros in
farewell. . . . I learned afterward of a sheriff from Belle Fourche that came to
our ranch in search of our visitors, that before they came to us they had stuck
up a Black Hills stage and taken $10,000 worth of gold from it, all of which
they had in their pack while they visited us.[41]

Today some of these old cabins still remain, however most of them
have either been abandoned or relegated to the role of outbuildings. As a
Montana poet put it:

> But he's gone with his smile, an' the dear little shack
> With his brand on the door won't ever come back.
> An' his latch-string is hid with the spirit an' ways
> That gladdened our hearts in them good early days.[42]

All day across the sagebrush flat
    Beneath the sun of June,
My sheep they loaf and feed and blat
    Their never changin' tune.
And then at night time, when they lay
    As quiet as a stone,
I hear the gray wolf far away;
    "Alo-one!" he says, "Alo-one!" [1]

Badger Clark

THREE

Woollies

IN 1875 John Burgess, an enterprising and venturesome operator of a sheep ranch near Red Bluff, California, heard of the gold rush to the Black Hills. As the opportunity to market a flock of woollies looked attractive he and his son put eighteen hundred head on the trail and headed east. To him the fourteen hundred to fifteen hundred long miles lying between Red Bluff and the market was not a formidable obstacle—perhaps he had never heard of the Sioux and Cheyennes, perhaps he did not consider them a serious obstacle either. Winter found him in the mountains of western Montana. There, amidst the abundant hay crop of the Prickly Pear Valley near Helena, Burgess settled down to spend the winter and his son returned to California.

In the spring Burgess resumed his journey. Following the north side of the Yellowstone, he pushed the flock eastward, and October found him—to the amazement of the soldiers—at Colonel Miles' new post.

An amusing incident occurred one bright October morning. Colonel Whistler, who was building the cantonment for winter quarters for the soldiers, saw on the bluffs on the north side of the Yellowstone, a number of animals, and he thought they were antelope. Soon, however, they moved down to the river, and were being loaded on a ferry boat and ferried to the south side, landing just near the place where the soldiers were encamped. . . . When the sheep were being unloaded, the old soldier, for he was an old man, wearing a big blue army cape, ran toward the boat crying:

40. "Sheep by the waterside, Powder River, at a time when sheep were 'pintedly' unwelcome visitors on Wyoming and Montana Ranges."

"Stop them sheep, they'll eat all my grass!" The grass was knee-deep and of course he could not stop a bunch of sheep after the leader, a big bell wether, was once off the boat.[2]

Thus did the first flock of sheep arrive in what became Miles City. Colonel Miles was much opposed to Burgess' continuing his journey, and offered to let the sheepman winter his flock on the military reservation. This offer Burgess wisely accepted and built a one-room shack and brush corral just south of the present site of the Northern Pacific depot. The flock wintered very well, furnishing a lot of good mutton for the soldiers; and when spring came, Burgess sold the remainder of the herd, 1007 head, to George M. Miles, then a quartermaster's clerk, and Captain Frank Baldwin for an even two thousand dollars. Burgess was glad to get the hard cash; and Miles and Baldwin were in the sheep business before all the hostiles had been cleaned out of the Yellowstone Valley.

The flock that Miles and Baldwin purchased had followed a pattern of movement having its beginnings with the Spanish explorers, and established in the West by "Uncle Dick" Wootton, a frontiersman with more financial ability than the majority of that adventurous breed. In 1852 Wootton, hearing that gold was plentiful and provisions scarce in California, bought nine thousand sheep and one thousand dollars' worth of supplies, hired fourteen Mexicans and seven Americans, and headed westward from New Mexico over trails he had followed as a trapper years before. With the exception of one hundred head that he killed for meat, Wootton delivered his flock intact and came back with "fourteen thousand in gold, and more than twice as much more in drafts on St. Louis."[3] Others followed the trail this trapper had blazed, among them Kit Carson who delivered sixty-five hundred head to Sacramento for a neat profit of thirty thousand dollars.[4]

The introduction of sheep into Montana followed the same pattern as in California. The first introduction, if an unconfirmed story is accepted, was in 1847 when Father Ravalli trailed sheep from Fort Bridger to St. Mary's Mission in the Bitterroot Valley; but the first definite effort to introduce breeding flocks dates from 1867 when the Jesuit fathers trailed three hundred head from Oregon over the Mullen Road to St. Peter's Mission near the town of Cascade. Prior to this, however, the gold strikes in the valleys of Grasshopper Creek and Alder Gulch, like the gold strikes in California and Colorado, provided a market for sheep, and in 1862 and 1863 several flocks were driven in from California and Oregon for this trade.

"The coming of woollies to Montana territory as a large scale business began in earnest in 1869 with the arrival of a large band of sheep from Oregon. Interested in this undertaking were John F. Bishop of Dillon and his neighbor, Richard A. Reynolds, . . ."[5] Bishop set down this record of their experiences on the trail:

About the 1st of July, 1869, Dick Reynolds and I and a man by the name of Brown started to Oregon to buy horses. Brown had a span of mules and a wagon and Dick and I had a wagon and a span of horses.

. . . .

41. "Trailing sheep, Powder River Badlands, 1884."

[This little party drove from the vicinity of Bannack southward through the mountains to Camas Prairie in Idaho, and then westward to Oregon following the route of the old Oregon Trail most of the way. After visiting Salem in the Willamette valley, Bishop and his friend turned north to Portland.]

Portland in 1869 was a small town with little more than one street along the river. Loading our team and wagon on the boat we took passage up the Columbia River to The Dalles. Having changed our mind about buying horses we looked about for a band of sheep. I sold my gold dust and took greenbacks in exchange, getting a dollar in paper for 75 cents in gold. On a ranch three miles from The Dalles we found sheep that suited us belonging to a man named Beasley. I got eleven hundred head of ewes and Dick four hundred. I paid $2.75 per head in greenbacks for my sheep.

It was about the first of August, 1869 that we got started back for Montana. A man who had gone broke gambling offered to help drive the sheep to work his passage. We crossed the Deschutes River on a toll bridge and paid $40.00 toll on the outfit. . . . From the Deschutes we took the old road by Fort Watson. Here three goats joined the sheep. We told a soldier about them and he said to let them follow if they wanted to and they came all the way to Montana.

We crossed the Blue Mountains by a toll road, paying out another $40.00, and came to Canyon City. . . . We staid over a day here and bot bolts of heavy muslin or drill and cut some stakes. We fastened a stake to the cloth about every ten feet so that we could use it for a corral at night. In the morning we rolled it up and put it in the wagon.

From here we struck across to the Malheur River and followed it down to the Snake. When we came to a small stream the sheep would usually swim but sometimes we had to throw a crude bridge across the water. We crossed the Snake at Keene's Ferry. Again it cost $40.00. . . .

Soon we reached the Boise River and were back on the road we came out on. We forded the river and had a very hard time getting the sheep across as they wouldn't go into the water. Back in Boise City again we had a 400 mile drive ahead of us without a settlement. But the only mishap we had was when I tipped the wagon over and lost most of our pail of molasses. There was small chance of getting any more.

On Lost River we came to a place where some Chinamen were camped for the night. First we knew they had a fire which was fast getting out of hand. All of us worked like mad and got it put out before it burned up the sheep and the Chinese outfit. Soon they began to cook their supper. I went over to their fire to watch them and found they had dressed off a skunk. They put it on the fire to boil and stirred in some dumplings. Each man pinched off a lump of dough and marching around the pot dropped it into the stew. What this ceremony meant I did not learn. Their supper looked good and they asked me to eat with them but I went back to our own sour dough bread and beans, and molasses.

Finally we got back to Junction, Idaho, crossed over the Main Range of the Rockies by Bannack Pass into Horse Prairie and reached Bannack on Grasshopper Creek Nov. 7th, 1869. We estimated the trip from The Dalles with the sheep at 800 miles and we made it in 80 days of travel. Ten miles a day to the tune of blatting sheep.

We drove the sheep to John Selway's ranch on the Black Tail Deer Creek for a month and then to Birch Creek where Dick herded them for the winter. He lived in a wickiup and did not suffer from cold as it was a mild winter. The sheep came through in fine shape without any hay.[6]

By 1870 flocks had been brought into the Sun River Valley and sheep

42. "Harris lamb band, Powder River, 1888."

raising slowly began to expand eastward on the plains of Montana.[7] In 1877 the Smith brothers and Henry "Little Mac" Macdonald were raising mixed Cotswold and Merino sheep in the Judith basin. Here Joseph's harried Nez Percés warriors killed one of their herders as they swept northward through the area.[8]

A very early map of Custer County,[9] which then embraced a large part of southeastern Montana, shows that about one ranch in five in the county was running sheep in 1884, and that the country was being settled up rapidly. The largest holdings south of Miles City in the mid-1880's belonged to the Meyers brothers and to W. E. "Charley" Harris. Each ran flocks of between seven and eight thousand head; and the Meyers brothers had eight or nine camps scattered along the lower part of the Powder River Valley.

In September, 1884, A. M. and A. D. Howard brought the first breeding stock to the Rosebud country. Their layout, named after their horse brand, was called the Twenty Ranch and consisted of but one-quarter section— all their grazing being done on public lands. Later, additional "homesteads" were filed on in order to insure indispensable water, and cabins were built on each. These cabins were separated by distances ranging from five to twenty-five miles, and the herders moved from cabin to cabin as the range conditions required.[10]

An understanding of sheepherding begins with the sheep—animals possessed of a multitude of idiosyncrasies.[11] Their most distinctive characteristic is the herd instinct—what one does the others will take a chance on. If the leader falls into a gully or a prospect hole, others will follow, causing a costly pile-up; or this game of follow-the-leader may take the form of jumping over a very small harmless object on the ground. In getting a flock across a stream, the problem revolves around getting the leader or a small bunch across, for as soon as the movement has been established the rest will follow.[12]

Another outstanding peculiarity is their lack of ability to protect themselves. When threatened by a very obvious danger, the flock is likely to turn into a compact mass, mill, and then scatter in several directions. If they meet something they should back away from, they are likely to stand and stamp their feet in impotent disapproval until the herder or his dog removes the source of harm. At other times they will try to evade danger by running off to one side and, if the danger fails to pursue them, they will stop and gaze curiously. However, few will leave the flock to satisfy their curiosity.

This timidity evidences itself in other ways. They dislike going over the crest of a hill, or through tall grass, where they cannot see what is in front of them. At night their distrust of the unseen is particularly strong. A dog is regarded in the same way that small boys, about to get into mischief, regard a policeman—a factor of considerable value to the herder in handling the herd. Although they are timid animals, they will fight; but the only fights that are likely to be more than ludicrous affairs are those between the rams whose horns may make cuts in the skin. If these cuts go

43. "Hot sheep in the Powder River badlands near Broadus, Montana, 1884."

unnoted and untreated during warm weather, they usually become fly-blown and harbor a crop of maggots.

There are a host of other peculiarities. Often the ewes accept their maternal duties with exasperating indifference; and even after the lamb is owned, the only approved method of identification is smelling the lamb's tail while it suckles—although that lamb may be the only black one in the lot. Usually they graze contentedly when feed is plenty, but when it is poor they string out and run hither and thither, imposing a hardship on both themselves and the herder who must try to keep them together. They travel with a cold or a high wind and against a hot one; and they dislike going either straight up or straight down a hill. They will not feed toward the sun, and they will neither feed nor travel during a hard rain. However, as soon as the rain stops, they are likely to move and start feeding—a very annoying trait if the rain ceases during the night. When hot they tuck their heads under the belly of their neighbor and refuse to move—thus a very patient man was said to be one who "could drive hot sheep." If they lie down in a small depression or on a slope with their feet on the "uphill" side, they have to be helped up, and if they get on their backs—which is likely to happen under such conditions—this help must be given quickly to prevent death. In winter they are not only afraid of, but are helpless on, a glare of ice; however, they paw loose snow very methodically and effectively to uncover feed. And they are capable of making all kinds of grunts, groans, sneezes, and other sounds for which there is no descriptive word.

Not only do sheep have to be protected against their own foolish characteristics, but against pests, parasites, and poisonous plants as well. Scabies or mange, commonly called scab, sometimes took a heavy toll of the early flocks before dipping was used as a control measure; and in warm weather all breaks in the skin have to be carefully treated with tar to keep blowflies from laying eggs in the cut. Death camas and lupine kill, larkspur is poison to young lambs, and locoweed causes the animals to jump and run in circles until they die of exhaustion. Eagles have a liking for young lambs; and magpies will peck any open cuts on the animals' backs, literally eating them alive. At lambing time the latter have a particular mania for pecking out the eyes of unguarded lambs.

In the past an unrelenting vigil had to be kept for coyotes, particularly in the spring or at lambing time; and after the buffalo herds were wiped out, wolves were a serious problem until the wolfers reduced their numbers. Coyotes would work the outskirts of a band watching for stragglers or for an unguarded moment to slip in and make a kill. If possible, a gray wolf would corner fifteen or twenty head and then slash their hamstrings as the animals attempted to run past him. Black bears would occasionally cause trouble, though they were more likely to wreck the herder's camp during his absence. These animals seemed to prefer to get into a flock and travel along with it, "clubbing" sheep with their paws as they walked along. One Basque herder told a trail driver (sheep) of an unusual experience with a black bear. Discovering the animal in the center of his band, he sent his dog to drive it out. The bear promptly disemboweled the dog with a swipe of his paw. The killing of the dog raised the fighting spirit of this Spanish mountaineer to a blind, white heat, and as he told it, "Dat make me so tam mad, I walk into de herd an' I walk right along wid de sheep, an' I catch up wid de bear. Den I take out my knife an' I cut hee's throat!"[13]

Some of the big wolves were a problem and occasionally one created a reputation for itself. One of these was Three Toes, who ranged northwestern South Dakota and southeastern Montana. In 1912 this wolf had established himself as a killer, and for the next thirteen years he laughed at traps and poison. Livestock valued at fifty thousand dollars was definitely charged against him, and in 1923 alone his kill was valued at twelve thousand dollars. Finally, in July, 1925, he lost in a battle of wits with Clyde F. Briggs, a government hunter assigned to catch him. As he was not seriously hurt by the steel trap, Briggs carefully took him alive but, like some other wild things when they realize that they are no longer free, he died of a broken heart within an hour or two after being taken from the trap.

One of the foundation stones of the sheep industry was the herder and, ironically, he was also regarded as being on the bottom of the various social strata. Sheepherding, both a profession and a way of life, required very definite abilities and characteristics of those who engaged in it. Perhaps the stigma attached to the profession was not deserved—certainly it required patience, thoughtfulness, and a very thoroughgoing sense of responsibility, all of which are admirable qualities.

The herder was entrusted with a flock of usually about fifteen hundred to three thousand sheep, and this represented a considerable investment. As the slightest irresponsibility might result in a serious loss, a high degree of loyalty to the job was necessary. Most herders, regardless of race or background, accepted their responsibilities, thus providing the profession with its share of unsung heroes who, unlike "Little Joe, the Wrangler,"[14] have never been immortalized in song. Although frightened sheep never presented a danger comparable to a herd of stampeding cattle, many a herder has been frozen to death trying to save his flock in a blizzard.

In composing his memoirs, John Clay recalled meeting, on the Sweetwater in Wyoming, a herder known as English Joe, "An old, weather beaten man . . . unshaven and unshorn, a greasy hat on his head, his clothes ragged and worn." Clay found that he had known the man when the latter had owned a farm in the lovely Cheviot Hills in the north of England. But he was a ne'er-do-well and he had drifted, a rolling stone gathering no moss. Clay recalled vividly being at the ranch house of the Seventy-One Quarter Circle in the late 1880's during a blizzard—a "howling storm" that drove down the valley with an ominous roar and a fury that fascinated him like a "snake paralyzes and coils itself around its victim." The following morning he went with a little party to hunt for English Joe. One of the cowboys found the body of the old man in a little gully "sitting, half leaning against the bank [with] . . . no signs of trouble on his face." And, as they stood there with death on one side and the weird winter landscape on the other, "the old collie . . . would first smell his master, poke his nose into his side as of yore, and getting no response, would turn around facing the [party] . . . wanting to know the reason of this strange meeting, his master voiceless, the whole world upset as far as he was concerned."[15]

Sheepherding was steady work, sixteen or more hours a day and seven days a week for months without a break. This has given rise to two sayings: one, that "no man can herd for six months without going crazy," and the second, that "a man must have been mentally unbalanced for six months before he was in a fit condition to entertain thoughts of herding." That sheep would cause a man to go crazy is said to have been a myth—but there have been a few insane sheepherders.

Herding has been pictured as a lonesome, monotonous life, difficult to endure. In the opinion of two old-time Westerners,

> Few sights are more somber and impressive than the solitary figure of a herder outlined against the sky, thousands of sheep about him and no human being or habitation in sight. For weeks he does not see his kind, and then only for a few minutes, perhaps, when a teamster brings a load of chuck to keep him for another month.[16]

On the other hand, one sheepherder wrote that it is not a monotonous task, as sheep rarely act the same two days in succession. Also, herding at one season is so different from herding at another as to constitute almost a different job. Perhaps most herders did not consider it a *lonely* life but rather one in which they knew *aloneness*.

One peculiarity of the profession was that it required that a man be forever watching—watching the flock—watching for predatory animals and birds—watching the kinds and the quantity of the vegetation on which the sheep fed—watching for any sign of a coming change in the weather—watching for a change in the behavior of his flock—watching, watching. The herder's leisure—sometimes there was considerable of it—was spent in piling rocks, various kinds of handicraft, or in reading. Probably mail-order catalogues, commonly called "sheepherders bibles," were the one class of material most widely read; however, Shakespeare and the *Illustrated London News* were not foreign to the range. And the herder had to be self-reliant, for he not only had the flock to take care of but he had to do his own cooking, washing, and mending. In matters of clothing and personal cleanliness, practical considerations of economy and comfort were usually the guiding rules.

As to race and background, herders were a motley lot. There were Scots, Irish, and English from the British Isles; there were Portuguese, French Basques, and Spanish Basques from the Iberian Peninsula; there were a few Scandinavians and Germans; and there were Americans and Mexicans. The best were Basques, Mexicans, and Scotsmen; and, as the Basques and Scots often took most of their wages in sheep, herders of these nationalities were likely to become owners. One of the important sheepmen in Montana was Ole Osnes, a Norwegian who worked his way up the Missouri by rustling wood and firing boilers on the steamboat *General Terry*. The captain was so impressed by the lad's pluck that he recommended him to Henry Macdonald, who hired him as a herder. Osnes, being

44. "A typical sheepherder."

canny and thrifty, saved his money and invested in sheep, finally building his holdings into one of the largest layouts in Montana.

In addition to the normal sort of herders, there were fugitives from justice, henpecked husbands, broken men, habitual drunkards who could not hold a job in town, floaters, and other odd pieces of human flotsam. Naturally, these strange pieces of humanity were often more interesting than the normal. An Irish priest, tortured by the memory of a murder he had committed, drifted into Macdonald's camp and found a job as a herder. The flock he was tending lay in the path of Joseph's Nez Percés in 1877, and, as previously noted, the Indians killed him. Macdonald had another unusual herder—Louis David Riel, the Canadian half-breed, who led two rebellions of the Metis in Canada. But Riel was a dreamer and a writer of poetry, and Macdonald had to let him go because he sometimes forgot his flock. Another herder, Archer B. Gilfillan, wrote a delightful and instructive book about his profession.

45. "Nigger Bob" Levitt's saloon in Ismay, Montana.

In general, however, the uncommunicative herders proved to be the most interesting. Typical of these was an old herder whom a Miles City newspaper man chanced to meet in Ismay, a "wide-place-in-the-road" in the northeast corner of Custer County. A small group of Miles City businessmen had visited the little town and, while awaiting transportation for their departure, Albin Buchanan visited "Nigger Bob" Levitt's saloon[17] to bend his elbow. "Buck," not being the sort who liked to drink alone, invited a disreputable-looking sheepherder to have a drink with him. One drink led to another until the two were in the condition commonly known as "well oiled." Finally the old herder—remembering the days of his youth—backed up to the bar and began to recite the poetry of Robert Burns in a flawless manner, even to a Scottish accent. For a while "Buck" was speechless, but he finally recovered and, between poems, asked, "Where did you learn that stuff? You must have gone to college!" "Yes," replied the herder with a bit of pride coming to the surface, "I graduated from Yale in the class of '76 with Judge Milburn."[18] But he did not reveal why he was herding sheep, and Western courtesy forbade the asking of that question.

Although the herder has never become the subject of legend, his *alter ego*, comrade, and friend—the sheep dog—has accumulated so much that fact and fiction have become inextricably entwined. Many are the stories of dogs that took care of flocks on the death of the herder, saved the sheep from dangerous situations, and hunted for missing animals. The devotion and companionship of the dog meant much to the herder, there being an unusually strong bond between the two. As noted in the case of the Basque who killed a bear with his knife, this bond sometimes caused men to go to extreme lengths to protect or avenge their dogs. One saloon-keeper at a stage stop in the valley of the Powder remembered a cowboy who was drinking at his bar when a herder and his dog came in. Commenting that, "This is no place for dogs," the cowboy pulled his gun and shot the dog.

46. "Sheep by the waterside, Big Dry, Montana."

As he fired, the herder drew his gun. Seconds later both men lay on the floor—dead.

A few dogs developed into "one-man" dogs. One such, missing his master away on a Christmas vacation, returned to the wagon where he stayed for three days and nights with the temperature well below zero. Another, when his elderly master suffered a stroke, grabbed the trailing reins of the herder's horse and led the animal to him, thereby allowing the stricken man to secure the saddle blanket for a covering. Then the dog curled up beside the man and helped provide warmth until help finally came, thus, in the herder's opinion, saving his life.

While many sheep dogs were mongrels or curs, most were descended from the small, long-haired, black-and-white Border collies that were imported from Scotland or Australia where, in turn, they had been brought from Scotland. Such dogs were smaller, broader-headed, and quicker than the larger show type of dog. Their ability to herd was inherited, and they were usually trained by working with an experienced dog. Even with an older dog to show the younger ones, such training took kindness, genuine affection, and infinite patience. Although one dog was all a herder needed —that one being indispensable—two were desirable so that one would provide companionship for the other, but three, just as with small boys when there is work to be done, were worthless.

While much herding was done on foot, a horse was considered a big help for herding in the summer, for then the flock could be allowed to spread more and still be kept under control. However, it was difficult to use a horse the year round as it could hardly be put on a picket line in the winter. Unlike the cowboy, the last thing a herder wanted was a spirited horse or one that exhibited any tendency to stray. As one herder put it, the ideal horse was one interested only in eating.

The early herders lived in tents in the summer and dugouts or cabins in the winter. The sheep wagon did not come into general use until the mid-1890's, and the first one is credited to James Candlish, a Canadian who followed the Union Pacific Railroad construction across Nebraska and Wyoming to Fort Steele. Later he opened a wagon and blacksmith shop in Rawlins, Wyoming, where, in 1884, he designed and built a "house on wheels." It was not until about eight years later, however, that a firm in Casper, Wyoming, began to manufacture these portable homes for the trade.

The sheep wagon was a modified prairie schooner—the wheel base being shortened, the box widened to extend out over the wheels, the canvas cover increased to several layers and pulled taut and smooth, and a door put in the front and a window in the rear. Essentially, it was more than a modified wagon: it was a specially constructed job from the ground up. The door in front was built in two halves like a barn door, thus allowing for partial ventilation while keeping the dog either in or out; and the window in the back was hinged at the top so that it could be easily raised or lowered by means of a rope and pulley. This made it easy to control the temperature and keep the little dwelling comfortable. Inside the door on one side was the stove with the dish cupboard behind it and a short bench,

47. "Drifter sheep wagon and band on winter bed ground."

and on the other side was a longer bench running back to the bed. Each bench had a trap-door opening into the grub boxes that were suspended on the sides of the wagon box between the wheels. At the back was a built-in bunk and above it a shelf or two for personal belongings. The space beneath the bed was used to store bulky articles or to keep the dogs out from underfoot; and hinged to the bed, or designed to slide in and out, was a table that could be put up when needed.

With several layers of canvas on top, to keep either the heat or the cold out, and a double floor, it was a very comfortable little home the year around. But it had its shortcomings. In spite of the railing in front of the cupboard shelves, the tin dishes were likely to get scattered about, and the kerosene can and the syrup bucket spilled when the wagon was moved to a new site. And in extremely cold weather about the only way the herder could keep his potatoes and other perishables from freezing was to put them in bed with him at night and wrap them in his bedding during the day. This gave rise to the practice of judging the severity of the cold by counting the number of nights a man had to sleep with his groceries.

Moving was accomplished by the camp tender who visited the various camps of the sheepman at regular intervals bringing supplies and mail, and taking care of any business the herders might have. Food varied with the ability of the herder to prepare it—some of them were excellent cooks— and the supplies the owner saw fit to supply. Food had to be adequate to sustain an active life in the open, and there was usually a preference for

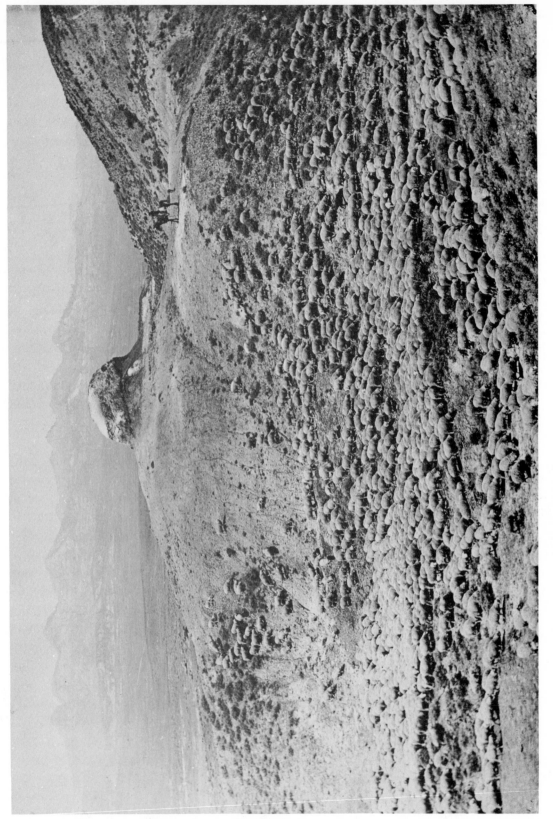

48. "Sheep grazing, Cap Butte, Powder River badlands, 1886."

things that were both satisfying and easy to cook, such as beans, oatmeal, biscuits, dried fruit, "sow belly," game, sometimes hominy, and, of course, there was coffee. The dogs were fed on the scraps and any rabbits shot during the day.

According to one sheepherder, if the day went according to the way it should, the herder got up at dawn and cooked a simple but substantial breakfast. Then he pushed the flock off the bed ground and, keeping them under control with the dog working as he was supposed to, grazed them slowly to water which was reached about noon. After watering, the flock lay down for an hour or two, giving the herder an opportunity to eat his lunch, smoke his pipe, and perhaps read a story if he had a book or magazine. Then the sheep grazed back to the wagon and, in the glory of a prairie sunset, the herder preceded the sheep back to camp and cooked his supper while the dog brought the flock in to the bed ground.

However, if the herder overslept, he usually found himself bolting his breakfast and putting up a hasty lunch while the herd left the bed ground —usually in the wrong direction. Then the dog might mistake his signals and turn the flock the wrong way a time or two before the flock could be lined out in the proper direction and, later when the herder relaxed his vigilance and took a bit of time off to eat, something might frighten the sheep and cause them to scatter, at which time the dog might decide to fake a sore foot. Then after getting them under control again, the herder would have to close-herd them back to camp, usually arriving after dark with all his chores to do.

Since sheep will not graze during the heat of the day, a summer day divided itself into two working days. The herd usually left the bed ground shortly after sunrise and grazed until the sun became uncomfortably hot, when they strung out and went to water. After drinking, they huddled in little groups in any shade they could find, or stood at the edge of the water with their heads under each other's sides and near the wet sand and away from flies and mosquitoes. Then, in the middle of the afternoon, they were headed toward camp and started on the return trip. At the end of summer the wether lambs and the old ewes were sorted out and driven to market. While this lessened the load on the herder later, the first days of this drive were usually particularly trying as the cut was likely to be difficult to handle.

Fall herding was the most enjoyable of all, for the weather was neither too hot nor too cold, there was plenty of feed, and the sheep grazed contentedly. Unfortunately, the herder knew then that the time was not far away when he would have to dig sheep out of snowbanks after the snowstorm, and be faced with the problem of wearing sufficient clothes to keep warm during periods of inactivity and still not have so many that he would perspire too much when walking.

For about three weeks during the latter part of May when the lambs were dropped, everyone on a sheep ranch was extremely busy. Some of this work was due to having to watch the ewes at time of lambing, but much of it stemmed directly from the difficulty the mother and her offspring had in learning to recognize each other. While a colt stayed with its mother

49. "Percy Williamson's Ranch. An odd little place tucked away in a sand blow-out on the breaks of the Missouri. August 1904." L.A.H.

after birth and a cow always knew where she left her calf, a ewe and her lamb paid little attention to each other except when it was time to suckle. Therefore special care had to be taken to see that the mother recognized and accepted her offspring immediately after birth, sometimes a difficult task, and to see that they learned to recognize each other among increasingly larger numbers lest the lamb become lost and turn into an orphan or a "bummer."

Although there were various ways of conducting lambing operations, the principle involved in each was the same. The ewes were divided into flocks known as "drop bunches." Each morning the ewes that had lambed during the night were separated and held with their lambs, and those that lambed during the day were handled in the same manner, this process being repeated until the entire bunch had lambed. Each little band was kept by itself for a day to allow the ewes to become acquainted with their lambs without becoming confused by having to select the lamb from a large number. Then one band was combined with another, and then another, thus training the mother to recognize her offspring under increasingly difficult circumstances. In the early days this was accomplished by driving the drop bunch slowly along a stream, leaving bunches of ewes and lambs spaced along the valley. Later lambing pens were used to facilitate handling and to provide shelter from inclement weather. One of the photographs reproduced here shows the old-time system, and another shows the wagon used in connection with the lambing sheds.

50. "Old time lambing camp, Powder River, 1886."

51. "The lamb wagon—1886."

Shearing took place about the middle of June. This work was done by parties of professionals who started in the Southwest in the spring and followed the season northward. These crews were composed of about six to twelve men, one of whom assumed the responsibility of taking care of all business matters. The shearing was done in a series of small pens with a shearer in each pen. A certain number of sheep were placed in each pen by the owner and, when these were sheared, another lot was driven in, thus providing a tally of the number sheared by each man as well as a means of checking each for careless work. The handling of the flock was done by the owner, a task that was accompanied by considerable confusion, dust, bleating of sheep, barking of dogs, and strong language. The fleeces were rolled, tied with soft twine, and put in a sack about seven feet long. This sack was suspended in a. frame and about three hundred pounds of wool packed in by a tramper who started at the bottom and, strangling, coughing, and sweating profusely, tramped his way up to the top.

In shearing, the shearer set the sheep on its rump and held its head and shoulders close to him with his left hand. Then, with the shears in his right hand, he opened the fleece, usually on one of the shoulders, and proceeded to clip the sheep in a very precise manner, with no waste motions,

52. "Early day sheep shearers at work in a bower."

every stroke of the shears being designed to work best on the part of the body being clipped. This was hot, hard work and, as the shearer was paid by the head and was docked if he became careless, required precision and endurance. Although early estimates of hand shearing varied from eighty to one hundred and fifty animals per day, eight hundred was considered a good day's work for a crew of ten. Strangely enough, this is one task where the old-time method is still preferred by many, for hand shears left a little more of the fleece than power clippers, thus providing more protection against spring storms and lessening the danger of blistering by the sun.

Although the trailing of cattle was an activity that has received considerable publicity, little attention has been paid to similar movements of sheep. Trail driving was extensive, and it has been estimated that the sheep driven east to market from the Southwest, California, and Oregon numbered well over "fifteen million head . . . in the more than three-decade trail era."[19] Illustrative of the distances covered during this movement was the observation of one cowboy who remembered that in 1882, while on the trail from Oregon to Wyoming with a herd of cattle, he saw a flock of nine thousand "woolybacks" that had been driven from New Mexico to Oregon and, as the owner could not make a satisfactory sale there, was then en route to Cheyenne, Wyoming. Montana also saw considerable trailing of sheep. There were seasonal movements from the wintering grounds to summer ranges and back again; and certain buyers who specialized in purchasing

53. "Freight teams laden with wool."

in Oregon and Idaho trailed across Montana by a route that followed along the Missouri River to the wheat fields of North Dakota and, finally, to the feed lots and markets at St. Paul. Plodding along in the dust behind a flock of four or five thousand smelly sheep moving at a snail's pace of three or four miles a day, facing hostile cattlemen seeking to prohibit passage across their range, and giving a cold shoulder to farmers with exorbitant claims for damage to their crops, did not make these movements spectacular; but the careful planning, perseverance, and patience of the herders and the owners' foremen did make them successful.

Antagonism between the sheepmen and the cattlemen developed early. The first recorded friction dates back to the winter of 1869-1870 when John Bishop and Dick Reynolds wintered a flock in a mountain valley near Bannack. Although this was a tame affair it developed according to a pattern that became common. According to Bishop,

> There was a settler on . . . [Birch Creek] who had two or three cows. He wrote me a letter saying that unless I took the sheep away he would scatter the sheep and kill the herder. I warned Dick and took him a six-shooter. Dick, tho a gentle mannered man, wasn't afraid to take anybody's bluff and nothing came of the matter.[20]

Such openly hostile relations were not uncommon when cattle and sheep came into competition on the plains a decade or two later. Huffman indicated something of this hostility when he noted on one of his photographs that it has been taken "when sheep were 'pintedly' unwelcome." However, this feeling never reached the violent pitch in Montana that it did in several other places in the West.[21]

This bitter feeling was built around both fact and fiction. The fictional part was based on the fact that a sheep has a gland between the two halves of the hoof that secretes a foul-smelling fluid. While there is no doubt that cattle and horses not accustomed to this odor did not like it, this dislike may not have been as deep-seated as it has been claimed. At least it seems to have died a natural death as more and more cattlemen took to the raising of sheep. The fundamental trouble was that sheep were very destructive to an overstocked range. They cropped the grasses down to the ground and their sharp hoofs destroyed the roots, thus ruining a range for years.

As cattle could not live on a range that had been closely grazed by sheep, it is not strange that cattlemen took steps to protect themselves. Robert S. Ford, a pioneer cattleman in the Sun River Valley and upper Missouri country, attempted to organize the cattlemen into an association designed to keep sheepmen off their ranges.[22] However, in Montana the opposition to sheep was never organized in a formal way but rather crystallized as the occasion demanded.

Not all of the friction resulted in actual violence, although some incidents came close to it. One rancher related this account of such an occurrence:

> Philbrick in the Rosebud country tried to edge over into the Tongue valley with his sheep. The ranchers objected even though it was open range. They drove a bunch of horses into the flock of sheep and tried to drift them out of the country but this did not work too well. Finally, the rest of the ranchers stayed out of sight and sent Tom Horton down to talk with the herder. He was an even tempered man. Horton had a Winchester across the saddle and he rode up close to the herder to talk with him. When he turned his horse away, the barrel hit the herder and knocked him out. As *whipping* a man with a gun was a penitentiary offense, suit was brought but Charlie Landis was named as the man. When A. H. Terrett was put on the stand to testify he was asked if Charlie Landis hit the man. He replied, "No," and, before he thought, added, "Tom Horton did it." The judge threw the case out of court.[23]

However, there were times when a flock encroached on the range of a cattleman that this smoldering dislike did flare into explosive violence. In 1904 Montana cattlemen were reported to have killed five hundred sheep belonging to George Crosby, a Wyoming man, in retaliation for grazing in Montana just south of the Pryor Mountains. On August 25, 1905, ten masked men rode into a sheep camp late one evening in the Big Horn Basin not far from the Wyoming-Montana line. They shot, dynamited, or clubbed about four thousand sheep, shot a team of horses, burned the herder's and camp tender's wagons, destroyed all supplies and equipment, tied the dogs to the wagon wheels where they scorched to death, and warned the herders to leave the country and never come back. The accusation was that these herders had moved their flocks so slowly that the grass was entirely consumed along the trail they were following to the Big Horn Mountains.

When asked about these times, one old rancher wrote:

In the old days the cattlemen and sheepmen did not get along very amicably, in fact they just did not love each other. I can remember three sheep wars. [In] one, masked men and masked horses rode out to a band of 2500 sheep. One man entertained the herder, the rest took the sheep to a corral and killed them with clubs. Only twelve sheep got away. O. C. Cato, an old cattleman, was sheriff at the time. Selway, the owner of the sheep did not think Cato was trying to catch the cow men and told him so. Cato replied, "Just give me time. I have a scheme that will catch all of them. I went out to the corral, looked the situation over thoroughly, found all the clubs, and now have them in the office at the jail. And the very first man that comes in and claims one of those clubs I intend to arrest him."

The men who killed the sheep were all sworn to secrecy and had taken an oath if any one of them ever talked the others would kill him. The mystery was never solved but there used to be a lot of joshing done about it. One night at a dance, Mrs. [William Smith[24]] said to me, "You are a mightly little fellow to handle one of those big clubs killing those sheep." I said "Why Mrs. [Smith], I did not handle a club. It kept me busy carrying water to [William]."[25]

Another recalled that occasionally a rancher would drop in at the sheriff's office, look the bloodstained clubs over, and joshingly remark, "Well, you can't do anything to me. My club isn't there. Whose club is that? Must belong to [so-and-so]. He's the only one big enough to handle a club like that." Dan Squires, who was herding the sheep at the time, later went to work for the LO outfit; and John Childress, the foreman, recalled, "Dan wouldent talk about it." This incident had a most unusual ending. At a later date fifteen thousand dollars was sent to a bank in Miles City in an "anonymous" letter for deposit to the owner of the sheep. It was assumed that Selway, who often staked small operators starting on a new range, was actually the owner of the sheep Squires was herding for John Dant. So the money was deposited to Selway's credit but, according to the cashier, he refused to accept it. "That money," the bank employee recalled, "is still unclaimed as far as I know."

When the writer of the letter was pressed for details regarding the other two incidents, he replied: "In regard to the other sheep wars I spoke of some of the men on both sides are still alive and it would be much better to let sleeping dogs lie." Interesting as these details might be, it is best, even at this late date, not to revive bitter memories of those times.

Your grub is bread and bacon
And coffee black as ink;
The water is so full of alkali
It is hardly fit to drink.

They wake you in the morning
Before the break of day,
And send you on a circle
A hundred miles away.

All along the Yellowstone
'Tis cold the year around;
You will surely get consumption
By sleeping on the ground.

Work in Montana
Is six months in the year;
When all your bills are settled
There is nothing left for beer.[1]

From a Cowboy song

FOUR

With Coats Of
Arms On Rawhide

Part I: Men with a Vision

A MAN *on a horse*—far back into the dim past of history he has always
attracted attention; and no character in American history has captured
popular interest to a greater degree than the cowboy of the high plains.
Cow was king in eastern Montana during the 1880's and 1890's. Therefore
it is not strange that life on the range should have been a favorite subject
of Huffman's, particularly since he was once a small rancher and had many
acquaintances among ranchers and cowpunchers. As cowboys and ranch
life have become encrusted with a great deal of fiction, Huffman's photographs are all the more interesting for their lack of concocted glamour.

There were *cows* in Montana before there were cowboys—although it
was the cowboy who applied this generic term to everything from a suckling
heifer calf to a ten-year-old bull. Ranching began in 1850, not on the
Plains where it flowered in full glory forty years later, but in Beaverhead,
Stinkingwater (now the Ruby), and Deer Lodge valleys among the mountains. The first "ranchers" were trappers and traders who bought poor,
footsore *bulls* and other stock from emigrants on the Oregon Trail. These
they drove north to the mountain valleys to recuperate, and brought back
to the trail the next year to trade for others in need of rest and feed;[2]
but it was not until the gold rush developed in the early 1860's that there
was a local market and the raising of cattle primarily for meat began.

54.   "Dunn—The Hat X horse wrangler, Aug 1904." ‾

Nelson Story is credited with bringing the first trail herd from Texas. This herd of about six hundred head[3] was purchased in the vicinity of Dallas and was trailed in over the Bozeman Trail in 1866. In the same year Conrad Kohrs stocked a ranch in Deer Lodge Valley with a breeding herd. Kohrs' ranch had been acquired the previous year from Johnny Grant, a son of a Scottish employee of the Hudson Bay Company. Kohrs' action in improving this herd with Shorthorn bulls probably represented the first constructive cattle-breeding effort in the state, and launched him on his career as the greatest single figure in the cattle industry in Montana.

Kohrs may have had the local gold field market in mind, for the following year he formed a partnership with John Bielenberg, a relative, to sell meat. Of the Kohrs and Bielenberg meat business no memories of unusual interest remain, but the use to which a meat saw from Bielenberg's butcher shop was put was long remembered. A local doctor, interested in examining the damage caused by a bullet that entered the head of a man killed in a gunfight and lacking the necessary tools to open the skull, borrowed Bielenberg's saw to make the required cuts. Probably this would have excited no interest in this rough-and-ready community, but it was

55. "Saddle bunch listening at cocktail time."

remembered that it was hung back in its usual place on the wall—without cleaning.

Thus stock raising began in the mountain valleys to supply the needs of the nearby gold fields and the Salt Lake City markets, and by 1870 the industry had pushed eastward to the Sun River Valley on the western edge of the plains. Robert S. Ford, the first to bring cattle to the prairies, recorded—in a little book labeled on the cover, "R. S. Ford—Herd Book—July 1, 1870"—the details of their purchase in Colorado and of the drive to Sun River. Of the 1,412 cattle, seven cost fifteen dollars each; twenty-five, seven dollars; and the balance, ten dollars a head. In the tally—four head killed by wolves, nine recovered of ten head that were stolen, three killed for beef, and the others that died or strayed and were recovered—is a mute record of the troubles of this drive. Likewise in the entries noting the places he stopped—Fort Lupton, Fort Halleck, Fort Steele, Green River, Soda Springs, Snake River, Beaverhead, and Crow Creek—is recorded the route followed by this drive. This, it will be noted, followed the Plains just east of the mountains in Colorado, crossed Wyoming to the westward side of the Continental Divide by the route followed by the Overland Stage line, and thence northward and eastward through the passes and mountain valleys, reaching the prairies, as it were, through the back door.

At Ford's winter camp near the mouth of Sun River, he and his riders had to watch constantly to keep the cattle from mixing with the drifting herds of buffalo and becoming lost.[4] Ford, Kohrs, John Cox, Nelson Story, John T. Murphy, and others pushed their herds out onto the Plains in the years that followed, but the buffalo and hostile Indians provided a barrier that discouraged all except a venturesome few.

This was a broad, wide-open country stretching from the Black Hills and the Big Horns on the south to the Canadian border, and from the Missouri River on the east to the Rockies on the west. It had always had desirable range possibilities, but it took three "developments" to make the country attractive to the cattlemen. First, of course, was the cutting down of the size of the Indian reservations and the elimination of the threat posed by the Sioux and Northern Cheyennes who opposed fiercely any encroachment on their favorite hunting grounds. It was not until these Indians had been displaced and confined on reservations that any rancher, except the daring few who nibbled at the extreme western edge of this Plains area, would risk putting cattle on the prairies. By 1879 this problem was almost a thing of the past.

The second difficulty was transportation. Although trailing several hundred miles to the ranges was practical, moving fat cattle over long distances to market was not desirable. When the Northern Pacific Railroad began to build westward from Bismarck, the solution to this problem was in sight. By the fall of 1881 this line had reached Miles City—the *Dodge* of Montana—and as it continued on up the Yellowstone Valley it brought to an end the isolation of this area and its dependence on the steamboat and the creaking wagons of the freighter. Although many cattle were trailed to the northern end of the Black Hills and shipped from Belle Fourche, the Northern Pacific did provide the necessary facilities for moving cattle to market.

The third barrier—the great Northern Herd—was equally formidable. It was practically impossible to occupy the ranges as long as great herds of buffalo roamed at will. Not only did these animals compete for the grass, but their uncontrollable movements—sometimes in stampedes that swept across large areas—were a serious threat. Horses and cattle "swallowed up" by a moving herd were almost never recovered. It was the "wasteful" slaughter of the hide hunter that removed this last remaining obstacle. By the summer of 1882 only a few harried survivors remained; and the flood of cattle that had been steadily moving northward since the close of the Civil War surged into this empire of grass.[5]

One of the first indications of the value of this country for stock came when a bunch of Diamond R *bulls*, turned loose in the deep snow late one fall, were found not only to be alive the next spring but—much to everyone's surprise—in excellent condition. If George Miles'[6] memory is correct, this happened near Fort Keogh in the winter of 1876-1877; and General Miles, on being informed, prophesied, "When we get rid of the Indians and buffalo, the cattle and sheep will fill this country."[7] However, the optimists were to find that it could be a forbidding country at times. Huffman noted, in filing the negative of Barringer's ranch, "This was in 1878 [1880?] the Groom ranch where the first great herd from the south

56. "C. Horse Camp."

was turned loose—to perish." Another rancher, who trailed twenty-five hundred head from New Mexico in the fall of 1885 and turned them loose twenty-five miles north of Miles City, rounded up three head the following spring. Even when stock was accustomed to the country, there were losses— and the disaster brought by the winter of 1886-1887 to cattle on the over-grazed ranges has never been forgotten!

Except for small herds to fill beef contracts at the army posts, and a bunch of milk cows that saloon-keeper Charlie Brown is said to have kept in the valley of the Tongue near Miles City, there were almost no cattle in the five-hundred-mile stretch between Bismarck and Bozeman in 1880. Three years later the entire country—with the exception of what Huffman called the "Big Open" between the Yellowstone and the "Big" Missouri— was dotted with ranches. These great stretches of badlands and open prairie were occupied more slowly, and it was not until the XIT stocked a ranch in the heart of this country in 1889 that it began to lose its wide-open aspect.

In the Montana-Dakota border country the southern cowmen, born and raised in the business and with a canny eye for the best grazing lands, are said to have asked friendly Indians where they killed the fattest buffalo so that they might locate their steers on the same range. One of the early settlers in this area remembered that

The first real ranch to be located north of the Black Hills was the Hash Knife of Texas, they picking a spot at the head of the Little Missouri River about eighty miles south from where the Milwaukee Railroad now crosses that stream. Colonel Simpson had picked this spot in 1880, and from then on his

57. "Working a Little Bunch in the Hills."

trail herds from the Pecos River of Texas had been turned loose to fatten on Dakota grasses. It was all his as there were no cattle outfits between him and the Canadian line. Next outfit from the south to settle on the Little Missouri was the OX of Towers and Gudgell, with a ranch on Little Beaver just above where Marmouth now stands. Then came the 777 of Berry and Boice. . . . Just across the Montana line was the Mill Iron ranch. . . .[8]

The first cattle to come into the badlands around the village of Little Missouri—later swallowed up by its near neighbor, Medora—were two hundred head of Eastern cattle shipped in by Wadsworth and Hawley in 1882.[9] These, branded with the Maltese Cross, were acquired about a year later by Theodore Roosevelt and formed the nucleus for his ranching venture. Of the ranchers in the badlands along the Little Missouri, an old cattleman wrote:

> The cattlemen with ranches [near the Northern Pacific] . . . were . . . Northern men who had followed the track laying crews into this frontier country seeking excitement, adventure and such opportunities as might be offered. Now, . . . with optimistic cattle talk on everyone's tongue, it was generally thought to be an opportune time to enter into the ranching business. There followed the forming of companies, partnerships and operations by individuals who sought favorable locations for establishing ranches. They were new at the game and made mistakes, but they accepted hardships and dangers in a self reliant way, and with indomitable will helped open up and settle a fine big country. [Among them were "Wadsworth, Prescott, Danz, Lang, Huidekoper and Eaton, and finally Theodore Roosevelt. . . . In the little town of Medora was the Marquis de Mores of visionary ideas."] [10]

Contrary to what might be expected, Huffman's pictures indicate that the stock brought onto these ranges, in the main, were not the longhorned, rangy animals that made up the first trail herds out of Texas fifteen years before. Much of the early stock, of good Shorthorn and Durham breeding, was trailed in from Oregon, Washington, and Idaho. The foundation stock for these trail herds were animals having beef- and milk-producing qualities, so-called dual-purpose cattle, which had been taken into the Pacific Northwest by emigrants from the Midwest. Compared to the Texas cattle these animals had better conformation, were more docile, while still possessing the ability to rustle for themselves. They had feet equally as durable on the trail, and were of more uniform color, the Texas herds containing many off colors as duns, creams, brindles, "brocha-faces,"[11] and buckskins.

The Texas ranches and the overstocked ranges of Colorado, New Mexico, and northern Arizona also constituted an important major source of cattle. Two classes of cattle were brought in from the south—breeding stock and stock cattle destined for the market in the not distant future. In the beginning years it was observed that both horses and cattle increased noticeably in size when moved from southern to northern ranges. Thus, steers brought to the northern ranges as yearlings and allowed to run until matured would average two hundred pounds more than others from the same herd grown out on southern ranges. In the 1890's many Texas ranches sent their steers north as yearlings or two-year-olds to be "double-wintered" and finished for market at a ranch in the north. The "Three Sevens" of Berry and Boice was devoted entirely to such operations.[12]

Over in the Little Missouri country, many of the inexperienced cowmen,

> Instead of obtaining a fair grade of southern steers, raised on grass and accustomed to rustle for a living, . . . [made] initial purchases . . . of assorted lots of farm animals from Minnesota and Iowa. Bought and gathered at shipping points on the new railroad, or in some cases trailed overland, these poor grade cattle were finally turned loose to take chances in the Bad Lands. Fortunately there were a succession of good seasons so no heavy losses occurred until the catastrophe of 1886-87. . . . As an example ["my own family"] bought 2000 young steers in Minnesota . . . [in the summer of 1886] at $14 per head which were turned loose in the Bad Lands to rustle for themselves. Tragically, there were one hundred that survived.[13]

While the growth of the cattle industry in eastern Montana is not a subject that can be treated casually in one or two short paragraphs, Granville Stuart's journals provide a thumbnail sketch of what happened throughout the northern range in the 1880's. On the Fort Maginnis range where Stuart located the DHS in 1880, there were twelve outfits three years later, and on the nearby "Cone butte and Moccasin range" were an equal number. Writing only of the movements of large herds, Stuart set down that

> In the summer of 1883 Conrad Kohrs drove in three thousand cattle and placed them on the Sun river range, and D.A.G. Floweree drove three thousand Texas cattle in and threw them on the Sun river range. The Green Mountain Cattle Company drove in twenty-two hundred and located on Emel's creek. The Dehart Land and Cattle Company came in with two herds of three thousand each and located on the Rosebud. Griffin Brothers and Ward drove in three thousand head and located on the Yellowstone. J. M. Holt came in with three thousand head and located on Cabin Creek. Tusler and Kempton brought in three herds of twenty-five hundred each and located on Tongue river. Ryan Brothers brought in three herds of three thousand each and located on the Musselshell. John T. Murphy and David Fratt drove in six thousand head and located on the Musselshell. Poindexter and Orr increased their herds in Madison county. Lepley brought in two thousand head, Green three thousand head and Conley twenty-five hundred and placed them on a range near Fort Benton. These cattle were nearly all Texas cattle and came up over the Texas trail. By the first of October there were six hundred thousand head of range cattle in the territory and these together with the horses and sheep was as much stock as the ranges could safely carry.[14]

This may have been all the ranges could "safely carry," but each succeeding year for several years saw a further crowding of the ranges until the stage was set for the never-to-be-forgotten winter of 1886-1887.

The business was both fascinating and profitable—at least in the early years. Ranchers figured their yearly profits at 100 per cent—easily calculated—each cow had a calf! Very few bothered to count the losses due to severe winters, storms, parched summer ranges, hostile Indians, and the rustler

58. Roundup Herd—Powder River Valley in the mid-1890's?

with his running iron. Even trailing could bring fabulous profits and cattle sometimes sold at the end of the trail for as much as twice their original cost. Unfortunately for the "blue-sky" artists, there was a saturation point both in what the ranges could carry and in what the market could absorb.

The business brought together cattlemen who knew cows from A to Z but who had only the slightest idea of the value of a dollar, Eastern businessmen who did not know a branding iron from a stove poker, and men like Conrad Kohrs, John T. Murphy, T. C. Power, John Holt, Henry S. Boice, and Pierre Wibaux who understood both cows and dollars. There were canny Scotsmen like John Clay, younger sons of titled English families, impractical visionaries like the Marquis de Mores, and "little men" who by frugal living and industry acquired enough property to live out their years in comfort.

Of all the cattlemen one of the greatest was Conrad Kohrs. A Dane by birth, he went to sea when he was fifteen and, on one voyage, caught yellow fever in Havana, where his shipmates left him to die. Recovered, he wandered to Iowa in 1854, then to the California gold fields, and finally, in 1862, to Montana. Here he mined and in 1865 started in the cattle business. In 1883 Kohrs, acting for Kohrs and Bielenberg, and Granville Stuart, acting for himself, bought out the interests of the Davis brothers and Hauser in the DHS. This transaction, which involved twelve thousand cattle valued at four hundred thousand dollars, launched the Pioneer Cattle Company. As a cattleman Kohrs had his ups and downs, but in the opinion

59. "Con Kohrs and other old timers."

of a contemporary he had a magnetic personality, a great wealth of common sense and splendid judgment, a kind heart, and a definite sense of fair play. He was a great figure, and the color of his personality lay in his vision and the quiet manner in which he worked toward his goals.[15]

Other cattlemen had, to some degree, many of Kohrs' characteristics and abilities. One of these was Henry S. Boice—considered by one old rancher as "one of the most outstanding rangemen of all time." As a man his appearance is said to have been deceiving. As previously noted, the Three Sevens specialized in finishing out Southern cattle. Boice, as manager of the outfit, made a practice of buying feeder cattle at Holbrook, Arizona. The story is told that when he first contracted with the Arizona cattlemen they took this quiet, low-voiced, pleasant man—who dressed like a well-to-do Eastern businessman and had uncalloused hands—as a "bird to be plucked."

Boice contracted for a herd of two-year-olds—to be all good stuff, full age, and no scrubs or cripples. When he returned a few months later to take delivery, the first herd inspected was well padded with under-age animals and as many undesirables as the ranchers thought they could get away with. Boice, wearing a little felt hat, low shoes, and colored socks, drove out to the herd in a livery buggy, climbed on a horse, and rode leisurely through the herd without saying a word. The jubilant cowmen winked at each other behind his back, feeling that they had sized their customer up correctly. The manager of the Three Sevens climbed off the horse after inspecting the herd, and made a short, devastating little speech consisting of one sentence: "When you get a few hundred yearlings, and about forty cripples, runts, stags, and big jaws out of that herd, send me word at the hotel and I'll come back and see what you've got." The illusion that Boice was a bird to be picked vanished immediately, for one of the earmarks of an expert cattleman was the ability to ride through a herd and come out on the other side with an accurate estimate of just what it contained. Boice had done just that.[16]

Another colorful cattleman was Pierre Wibaux, owner of the W Bar and the son of a French textile manufacturer. While preparing to enter his father's firm, he heard of the business opportunities on the prairies of the United States and, against his father's wishes, decided to investigate. His father staked him with ten thousand dollars—deemed sufficient to allow the young man a fling at his folly—and with this sum Wibaux left his native land. Unlike many others Wibaux laid his foundations carefully. He worked in the mud of the Chicago stockyards and learned the rudiments of market values: and during his first year on the range he lived in a dugout on Beaver Creek and for five years he worked on the range as a common hired hand. When the disastrous winter of 1886-1887 struck and other cattlemen folded up and quit, Wibaux pulled his belt a notch tighter and bought the remnants of others' brands and new herds from the South to restock his ranges. In the end he emerged as one of the largest ranchers on the Montana-Dakota prairies. "Estimates on the number of cattle he owned at one time vary from 40,000 to 200,000."[17]

Wibaux and his French wife were popular on the range, and neither they nor their neighbors ever forgot the Christmas dinner served the first year he and his bride spent on the range. While dinner was being served, water from melting snow dripped through the dirt roof of their log shack and rats and mice scampered and squeaked above the muslin ceiling. The picture of Mrs. Wibaux presiding at one end of the table in a "strictly modish Paris gown" and Pierre sitting at the other in "faultless black and white," was a far cry from later years when Wibaux had a big house with servants, and a French gardener to tend the flowers and shrubs on the lawn![18]

No mention of early-day ranchers would be complete without reference to Theodore Roosevelt, who came to the Little Missouri country in 1883. He owned three brands, the Maltese Cross ⊞ , the Elkhorn ⋌ , and the Triangle △ , all of which were small, and after the winter of 1886-1887 he made no attempt to restock but closed out his holdings. In the few years he operated, Roosevelt spent much of his time in the East and never really learned the business from the ground up. When on the range he accepted no favors and did his best to do his share of the work, but he was at his best when working in the meetings of the stockgrowers, where his ability as a leader and an organizer was very evident. Judging him as a cattleman, one old-time cowman said of him, "He didn't know a thing about cattle; he could not catch his own horse out of the cavy. Roosevelt took part in

60.   "Marquis De Mores 1886."

only one roundup—that of 1885, and here he was simply in the way. He was willing to help but a nuisance anywhere you put him. He didn't have a cowman in his outfit, though he had some who made pretty good hands."[19] No doubt there is a great deal of truth in that comment; nevertheless he is remembered as a vigorous, two-fisted, friendly man who was respected even if he was not a top hand.

Among those whose abilities ran to the promoting of blue-sky ideas was Antoine-Amedée-Marie-Vincent Manca de Vallombrosa—a Frenchman otherwise known as the Marquis de Mores. De Mores met the daughter of a wealthy New York banker at Cannes, France, married her, and came to New York where he was given a place in his father-in-law's bank. While in New York, he learned about the cattle industry and decided there must be a future in the Western country and cows. The marquis had no desire to operate a ranch—he thought he saw a future in packing operations conducted close to the source of supply.

In April, 1883, after making a careful examination of the situation, he founded a town where the Northern Pacific Railroad crossed the Little Missouri River, and named it Medora after his wife. Here he built a packing plant that operated spasmodically for a few years and finally ground to a halt in November, 1886, not, however, until large icehouses had been built at four points along the railroad, and extensive promotion work had been done in Eastern cities to sell Medora-killed beef.

61. Marquis de Mores' packing plant at Medora, North Dakota.

The packing plant, owned officially by the Northern Pacific Refrigerator Car Company, was not the only one of the marquis' schemes. He shipped fresh salmon from Portland to New York; he experimented with vegetable gardening under irrigation; he organized the stage line that connected Medora with Deadwood for a year before it folded; and he had ideas of promoting dairying and the manufacture of butter and cheese, and of opening a pottery works. The marquis had much energy and many ideas, all of which cost his father-in-law an estimated three hundred thousand dollars to one million five hundred thousand dollars in the end. In 1887 he and his wife returned to France, and in 1896 the marquis was killed by a party of Touareg natives in North Africa. Today all that remains in Medora is the brick chimney of the packing plant, the brooding chateau on the gray bluff above the Little Missouri, and a confused story of whether or not he and Roosevelt had a disagreement that reached the stage where Roosevelt offered to shoot it out with him—with rifles at twelve paces.[20]

Granville Stuart's name is written large in the history of the early range days, not because of his ranching activities, although he was a prominent rancher, but because of his vigorous support of law and order on the range. Prior to his ranching days Stuart had seen much of the life on the frontier. When only fifteen he had gone with his father and brother to the California gold fields. In 1857, having failed to make a valuable find, he and his brother started back to Iowa to visit their father who had rejoined his

62. "Marquis de Mores Residence, Medora, N. D."

family. A serious illness prevented his traveling farther than the vicinity of the Great Salt Lake, and here his brother and a mutual friend stopped and nursed him back to health. Here the forlorn little party fell in with Joe Meek, a former mountain man who was trading skins and buckskin clothing to the emigrants and buying footsore stock. Both the Mormon War and the lack of funds and supplies complicated the problem, and in the end the three travelers turned north with Meek's party to winter with the Indians in the Beaverhead country. The rumor that a half-breed had found gold in the mountain country fascinated them and, after returning to the Oregon Trail where they made a small stake trading for worn-out stock, the Stuart brothers and their friend returned to Montana to trade with the Indians—and prospect for gold.

As the mining activity increased, the brothers, mindful of the lessons they had learned in California, let others hunt for the pot of gold at the foot of the rainbow while they spent much of their time trading food, clothing, and other supplies to those who blindly pursued fickle Lady Luck.[21] When the prairies opened for settlement at the end of the Indian wars, Stuart, A. J. and Erwin Davis, and Samuel Hauser entered into a partnership known as Davis, Hauser and Company. This company was founded with a capital stock of one hundred fifty thousand dollars and registered its brand as the D5 , known as the DHS. As noted, the Davis brothers and Hauser sold out their interest in 1883 and the outfit became the Pioneer Cattle Company with Conrad Kohrs as the guiding light.

Although Stuart went through the rough schooling of the frontier, he was a dreamer and a philosopher as well as a practical man. He liked to read, appreciated good music, was a close observer of nature, and had no small ability as an untrained artist. Perhaps it is not strange, therefore, that after seeing the carcasses of cattle strewn everywhere along the streams and in the coulees after the snow melted in the spring of 1887, he wrote in his journal: "A business that had been fascinating to me before, suddenly became distasteful. I wanted no more of it. I never wanted to own again an animal that I could not feed and shelter." The Pioneer Cattle Company lost 66 per cent of its cattle; and Stuart left the battle of getting the outfit back onto its feet to Kohrs and others.

Part II: The Stranglers

The history of the open range is a story with many facets. Of these none is more fascinating than the activities of those who bore the grim title of *The Stranglers*. The members of this group were efficient men who did not talk openly about their deeds. Some of the names became known several decades later, but at the time the general public knew only that the individual who seemed to be the central figure was Granville Stuart. Years later his son-in-law recalled that "there was a lot of bitterness in the country against Granville Stuart after the raids. But he never denied anything, nor did he tell who was with him. Once I heard a woman accuse him of hanging thirty innocent men. He raised his hat to her and said: 'Yes, madam, and by God, I done it alone.' "[22] It is strange that this friend of Huffman who could not bear to continue in the ranching business after seeing cattle starve during the winter of deep snow should have been the leader of men who enforced their orders with pieces of rope and blazing Winchesters. But Stuart had been through it all in the days when Plummer's gang of "Innocents" made life uncertain in the gold fields—he knew what to do and how to do it, and he was not the sort to shirk a civic responsibility.

The salutary lesson the early Montana vigilantes taught the outlaws of Virginia City and Bannack lasted for about a decade. Then, in the late 1870's and early 1880's, a new assortment of toughs and thieves gathered in an area of rugged badlands along the Missouri between the mouths of the Judith and the Musselshell rivers, and in the territory encompassed by the lower parts of the Yellowstone and the Little Missouri rivers. Many were rough characters who passed as traders, wood hawks,[23] buffalo hunters, and wolfers but who really made much of their living dealing in stolen livestock and the illegal sale of rot-gut whisky to Indians. Others were said to have been members of guerrilla bands, notably Quantrill's, who had drifted onto the plains at the close of the Civil War. And mixed with these were some of the scum of the frontier as well as sons of good parents who had gone wrong.

Perhaps the most serious form of rustling was the stealing of organized gangs. It was thought that some of these were well organized and had spies planted at strategic locations, for there was a tendency for them to operate arrogantly and brazenly, confident of the security provided by their numbers and by the rugged badlands in which the hangouts were sometimes located.

Other stealing was the result of the work of whisky peddlers. These "human ghouls" traded whisky to the Indians, taking in payment anything of value they had—which was often horses. After the Indian sobered up—if he lived through the violence that invariably accompanied a drinking party—he would attempt to improve his impoverished state by stealing other horses. These animals, in due time, were traded for more whisky, and the vicious cycle would be repeated. In this way stolen stock was accumulated by the whisky runners who, if they did not trade the stock themselves, would dispose of the animals at "questionable" *settlements* located at Rocky Point (later known as Wilder), Wolf Point, or the mouth of the Musselshell River. It was at the latter place that "squaw man" Billy Downs—who had acquired a favorable reputation by making good a debt incurred by some crooked partners—became involved in such questionable dealings.

Stock gathered in these operations would be held in a well-hidden spot until the brands could be worked over, and then it would be driven to some distant point and sold. Many rustlers disposed of their loot in Canada—then stole from Canadian ranchers and brought this stock back to sell in Montana. It was an efficient business without any lost motion.

Of course, there were other kinds of thieves. Stuart noted that

> Near our home ranch we discovered one rancher whose cows invariably had twin calves and frequently triplets, while the range cows in that vicinity were nearly all barren and would persist in hanging around this man's corral, envying his cows their numerous children and bawling and lamenting their own childless fate. This state of affairs continued until we were obliged to call around that way and threaten to hang the man if his cows had any more twins.[24]

Conditions went from bad to worse until about the only way a rancher could be certain that the horse he put in the stable at the end of the day would be there the next morning was to spend the night in the manger with a rifle. Losses of cattle on the range increased until, at the close of the fall roundup in 1883, some ranchers estimated that the loss from rustling was at least 3 per cent. This, added to the toll taken by the gray wolves that had lived off the buffalo herds, was more than the ranchmen could stand.

The problem was a frustrating one in several respects. For one thing, the country was big and new and it was almost impossible to enforce even the few laws that were then in existence. To secure a settlement of claims against Indians—which sometimes involved both horse stealing and wanton killing of cattle[25]—ranchers turned to their congressmen. Bills for the payment of such damages had a way of starting out with proper approval and then, somewhere along the line, bogging down and never being paid. Appeals to Indian agents were often futile, for many of these individuals were either misfits who could not, or would not, see the problem, or they were members of the nefarious "Indian Ring" who were interested only in the opportunity for graft, which their position made possible. The one bright spot in the Indian problem was the cooperation of British authorities and the Canadian Mounted Police. This was excellent.

Army officers were prone to take the stand that troubles with the Indians were outside their jurisdiction, and sometimes handled such problems in a manner beyond understanding. From the home ranch of the DHS near Fort Maginnis, Stuart made some exasperating observations. On one occasion when horses stolen by the Blackfeet were brought in to this post, General Terry, then commanding the Department of the Missouri, directed that the stolen property be sent—with military escort—to the Crow Reservation. These animals were never returned to their rightful owners. A second lot of stolen animals were disposed of in like manner—except that two thirds of the animals, which were in an exhausted condition, were shot along the road by the soldiers before they reached their destination. The third such consignment, when out of sight of the post, was met by the local stock detective and two cowboys: and the lieutenant in charge decided that facing the Winchester in the hands of the detective was something his orders did not cover. He transferred the custody of the stolen property then and there. With obvious satisfaction Stuart made this entry in his journal:

> This was the last attempt of the military to hold horses stolen from white men by Indians.
>
> From this time on, bands of roving Indians found on the range, with or without permits from their agents, were promptly escorted to their reservations and warned never to come on the range again. Those caught in the act of stealing horses or killing cattle, or with stolen property in their possession were punished just as the white thieves had been.[26]

The early cowmen were not lawless men even though they had the vigorous, "two-fisted" qualities necessary for survival on the frontier. Cooperative effort to control stealing was practiced from the very beginning of ranching on the Plains. The first ranchers in the Sun River country, led by Robert S. Ford, organized a force known as the Sun River Rangers, which rode the ranges to combat the activities of renegade Indians and horse and cattle thieves.[27] And in 1881—only a year after the flood of cattle began to pour onto the Montana ranges—the ranchers began to form protective associations.

One of the first details of business attended to by the Stockgrowers Protective Association of which Granville Stuart was a member was the hiring of a stock detective.[28] The duties of such individuals were to watch the ranges, spot trouble, and—when necessary—take steps to protect the livestock of their employers. The first detective employed by the group of which Stuart was a member was William "Floppin' Bill" Cantrell. He had been a woodchopper along the Missouri and, not wishing to be found in the company of the outlaws who frequented the area, had come to the DHS asking for work. Stuart hired him for the local association; and he rendered effective service as a range detective and later as a stock inspector.

Stuart was elected to the Territorial Legislative Assembly in the fall of 1882. Here he tried to further the cause of law and order by sponsoring legislation designed to properly regulate the rapidly mushrooming livestock industry. While some good was accomplished, several measures failed to pass because of opposition by the miners and other interests: other bills were vetoed by an ignorant and overly officious territorial governor.

Some of these difficulties were made even worse by malicious and maudlin gossip and publicity. On one occasion Stuart read in the Chicago *Times* that a woman and her baby had been run out of their home on the Yellowstone by cowboys in a particularly inhuman manner. When he checked the case, the woman proved to be the wife of a whisky peddler who had been kicked off the Crow Reservation by the agency police, and her husband had *high-tailed*[29] it for sanctuary across the Canadian border.

This, then, was the situation the ranchers faced as they united and formed the Montana Stockgrowers Association. Across the line in Dakota the cattlemen faced similar problems and they, too, took steps to cope with stealing. Among these men were several who are noted on these pages.

Well over half a century later one tight-lipped rancher who was well acquainted with what happened set down a brief outline of these events:

> . . . it seems proper that an account should be given of a justifiable but grue-some happening that occurred in connection with the livestock operations in the Bad Lands of our Dakota country. . . . no authoritive information has ever been given, as the strictest secrecy has always prevailed. After sixty-five years, a little summary of events, without going into details, should be of historical interest. . . . not one word has ever leaked out pertaining to the summary handling of the outlaws in extreme eastern Montana and along the Little Missouri River in western Dakota. . . .
>
> The initial meeting of . . . [the] cattlemen was held in the fall of 1883 in the bunk room of a two story log house . . . on the Little Missouri River about six miles south of Medora, with the following men present—A. C. Huidekoper,[30] Marquis de Mores, Henry Boice, Eaton Brothers,[31] Wadsworth Brothers and Theodore Roosevelt. The stockmen of eastern Montana also held a meeting in Miles City on October 12th of the same year. No decisive action was taken at either of the meetings, but arrangements were made for a general meeting at Miles City the following spring which became the first conventional gathering of the Montana Stockgrowers Association. . . . Marquis de Mores, Henry Boice and Theodore Roosevelt . . . [attended] as representatives from Dakota Terri-tory.[32]

The spring meeting of the Montana Stockgrowers Association was a turbulent one: and Granville Stuart, president of the Association, found himself in hot water when, as the presiding officer, he tried to discourage certain action that he had favored in private conversation. He wrote in his journal:

> The second annual meeting . . . convened at Miles City on April 20, 1884. There were four hundred and twenty-nine stockmen present. . . . Everybody seemed to have a grievance. . . .

The matters for consideration were overstocking the ranges, . . . Texas fever, . . . and how to stop "rustling."

The civil laws and courts had been tried and found wanting. The Montana cattlemen . . . had $35,000,000 worth of property scattered over seventy-five thousand square miles of practically uninhabited country and it must be protected from thieves. The only way to do it was to make the penalty for stealing so severe that it would lose its attractions. When the subject was brought up some of the members were for raising a small army of cowboys and raiding the country: but the older and more conservative men knew this would never do.

I openly opposed any such move and pointed out to them that the "rustlers" were strongly fortified, each of their cabins being a miniature fortress. They were all armed with the most modern weapons and had an abundance of ammunition, and every man of them was a desperado and a dead shot. If we had a scrap with them the law was on the side of the "rustlers." My talk did not have the conciliatory effect I had expected and seemed only to add fuel to the fire. The younger men felt they had suffered enough at the hand of the thieves and were for "cleaning them out" no matter what the cost.

The Marquis DeMores, who was a personal friend of mine and with whom I had had some previous talks on the subject, was strongly in favor of a "rustlers' war" and openly accused me of "backing water." The Marquis was strongly supported by Theodore Roosevelt, who was also a member of the Montana Stock Growers' Association from Dakota. In the end the conservative members of the association carried the day and it was voted that the association would take no action against the "rustlers." In some way the "rustlers" got information about what was done at the meeting and were jubilant. They returned to their favorite haunts and settled down to what promised to be an era of undisturbed and successful operations.[33]

Stuart's handling of this situation shows the touch of a master's hand. The temper of the cattlemen had been sounded out and crystallized; and a fine piece of deception had been set up to cover plans for stern retribution which, in all probability, were taking form in private at the very time the ranchers went on record as being *officially* against vigorous action.

A few weeks later "At the close of the [spring] roundup there was a meeting of a few stockmen at the "D-S" ranch. They and some men employed by the Stock Growers' Association had been watching the operations of the rustlers."[34]

And over in Dakota, there was also a meeting of the ranchers but

No direct action resulted from this meeting as it was too free and open a gathering and, without doubt, some interlopers were present, whereas secrecy was essential. . . . No more publically heralded meetings took place, but a few of the larger operating stockmen did hold clandestine gatherings at isolated ranches.

Without mentioning names suffice it to say that the men responsible for the events to follow were a small group of cowmen of that strong and practical type who had already successfully pioneered the west, quiet in speech and demeanor but quick to assume justifiable action when convinced of its need. It can also be stated that neither de Mores or Roosevelt were in on the deal, but a well known stockman from Montana, with former vigilante experience, was called upon and played a prominent part.[35]

63. "Granville Stuart, 1883."

The men who had vetoed an open declaration of "war" a few weeks before were now ready to strike, with Granville Stuart directing the operations. Plans had been carefully made, intelligence on the rustlers had been compiled and—it is said—lists of names prepared, and a small force of competent, dependable, close-mouthed men had been selected.

In the rugged badlands along the Missouri below Cow Island were a number of thieves who drew the attention of the group that met at the DHS ranchhouse. Some of these were small operators, but there was one gang in which the vigilantes were particularly interested.

The captain of this gang of outlaws was John Stringer who answered to the sobriquet of "Stringer Jack." He was a tall handsome young fellow, well educated, and of pleasing personality. His distinguishing features were his piercing grey eyes, white even teeth, and pleasant smile. He came to Montana in 1876 and hunted buffalo along the Missouri and Yellowstone rivers and was a conspicuous figure around the wood yards, trading posts, and military cantonments. He did not drink to excess but was an inveterate gambler. When the buffalo were gone he turned his attention to rustling cattle and stealing horses and established his headquarters on the Missouri river at the mouth of the Pouchette.[36]

From now on a cloak of secrecy covered—and still covers for the most part—the events that followed. Aided by a few well-placed observers, the "Stranglers" struck effectively, ruthlessly, and without warning. Stuart personally led the raid on Stringer's gang; and he set down in his journal one of the very few firsthand accounts of what happened when the "chips were down."

Fifteen miles below the mouth of the Musselshell, at an old abandoned wood yard, lived old man James,[37] his two sons, and a nephew. Here also was the favorite haunt of Jack Stringer. There was a log cabin and a stable with a large corral built of logs, connecting the two buildings. One hundred yards from the cabin in a wooded bottom was a tent constructed of poles and covered with three wagon sheets. At the cabin were old man James, his two sons, Frank Hanson and Bill Williams. Occupying the tent were Jack Stringer, Paddy Rose, Swift Bill, Dixie Burr,[38] Orvil Edwards, and Silas Nickerson.

On the morning of July 8, the vigilantes[39] arrived at Bates Point. The men were divided into three parties. Three guarded the tent, five surrounded the cabin and one was left behind with the saddle horses. They then waited for daylight. Old man James was the first to appear. He was ordered to open the corral and drive out the horses. This he did but refused to surrender, backed into the cabin and fired a shot from his rifle through a small port hole at the side of the door. This was followed by a volley from the port holes all around the cabin and in an instant the whole party was in action.

Two of the vigilantes crawled up and set fire to the haystack and the cabin. The men inside stationed themselves at port holes and kept up the fight until they were all killed or burned up. The cabin burned to the ground. The tent was near the river bank and almost surrounded by thick brush and it was easier to escape from it than to get out of the cabin. Stringer Jack crawled under the tent and reached a dense clump of willows from which he made his last stand. Dixie Burr had his arm shattered with a rifle ball but jumped into an old dry well and remained until dark. Paddy Rose ran out of the tent, passed back of the men engaged at the cabin and concealed himself in a small washout and after dark made his escape. Nickerson, Edwards, and Swift Bill reached the river bank and crawling along through the brush and under the bank, succeeded in passing above the men at the cabin and hid in some brush and drift wood. Orvil Edwards and Silas Nickerson were the only ones that escaped without wounds. After the fight at the cabin the men went down the river and spent the day looking for the men who had escaped but failed to find them.

.   .   .   .

There were one hundred and sixty-five stolen horses recovered at Bates Point and one hundred and nineteen at other places.[40]

Other evidence indicated that twelve thieves were present when the fight began. Of the five known to have escaped, Paddy Rose was the only one who succeeded in getting out of the country.

A few days before the Bates Point, or James wood yard, fight the vigilantes visited the trading post at the mouth of the Musselshell, which was just up the river a short distance. Here Billy Downes and California Ed were asked to account for "twenty-six horses in the corral, all bearing well known brands . . . dried meat found in the house . . . [and] a stack of fresh hides folded and salted ready to be shipped down the river, all bearing the brand of the Fergus Stock Co." The two admitted stealing Indian ponies, but failed to explain the horses in the corral; and they claimed the dried meat was buffalo meat, although there had been no buffalo on the range for more than two years. Such explanations being unacceptable, the two were requested to ride away with the Stranglers.

The horse on which Downes rode away returned one bright morning—riderless—and shortly afterward a steamboat nosed around the bend just above and stopped to take on wood. The "roosters," [41] other members of the crew, and the passengers were not long in discovering the reason for the tense attitude of the few people who were about, and why the woman they saw "crouching in the doorway of the 'saloon'" had "shaking limbs and streaming eyes." Rufus Zogbaum, an artist who was on board, prepared what is probably the only illustrated account of vigilante activities by an outsider who was also a witness.

As the steamboat prepared to continue on down the river toward Bates Point, he noted

Smoke has been seen rising over the trees down the river, vague rumors of a fight below seems to fill the air, and the feeling of excitement communicates itself to our little group of passengers, and as the boat swings out again into the swift yellow current, and continues on her voyage downstream, we gather at her low rails, looking out curiously and anxiously ahead at the high, sandy, tree-covered banks on either side. Rounding a long point of land running out into the river, a call from the pilot house attracts our attention to a blackened, smoking heap of ashes on the left bank—all that is left of a ranch that had stood there—and a short distance farther we slow up a little at the still burning ruins of another house. "It's the Jones [James] boy's ranch," says the mate. "By Jiminy, the cow-boys is making a terrible clean sweep of the kentry!" That they have not been long gone is evident. Two half-charred wagons stand in the "corral," the wooden fence of which is brightly burning, the flames licking the edge of a great woodpile, that even as we pass bursts into flames. In a small field of waving corn joining a potato patch the carcass of a mule is lying, while right on the bank, the red blood still flowing from a hole in its head, a large dog—a hound—is stretched lifeless. Near a pile of debris, which may have been a kitchen or other outhouse of some kind, for a pot or two and a tin camp-kettle are hanging from the low fire-seared branches of a tree hard by, a few chickens, shrilly cackling, are huddled together. No other sign of life is visible, and as we proceed, the quiet of the wilderness is broken only by the snort of our steampipes and the thump, thump of our great wheel beating up the muddy waters. Suddenly there is a movement among the "roosters" on the deck below; they are gazing with bated breath and blanched faces at something on the river's bank. Follow the direction of their gaze, and peer into the dense thicket where, above the matted willows growing up from the black ooze, that dead tree raises its white, barkless branches like skeleton arms, as if in fearful exultation over the dreadful fruit it bears. Almost hidden from our sight by the tangle of underbrush and low trees, something is hanging there motionless and still, something formless and shadowy in the gloom of the jungle, something indistinct, but fearful in its mystery and silence, a silence rendered yet more appalling by the hoarse croaks of the black-winged ravens, ill-omened carrion birds, circling above the thicket, and fluttering on the top-most branches of the blasted tree.

"Look! Look! down thar by them cotton-woods! that's them! that's the cowboys!" Half hidden in a mass of wild rose-bushes, backed by the gray trunks and graceful feathery foliage of the poplars, a group of men and horses is standing. . . . As the current takes the boat inshore, and we approach nearer and nearer, they present an interesting tableau. Most of them have dismounted and are standing at their horses' heads waist-deep in the weeds and wild flowers, bronze-faced, resolute looking men, unconsciously picturesque in costume and attitude; bright-barreled Winchesters swing across their high pommelled saddles, on which is bound the scanty baggage of the cowboy, while a few pack-mules quietly crop the grass a few paces in their rear under the care of their driver. They are evidently under some discipline for no one else moves as a tall, handsome, blond-bearded man, flannel-shirted, high-booted, with crimson silk kerchief tied loosely, sailor fashion, around his sunburnt neck, advances to the water's edge; and with courteous wave of broad-brimmed hat hails the boat. Clang! goes the gong; the big wheel stops. The stranger politely requests information about the purchase of some supplies, and inquires as to the news up the river.[42] Many on board recognize him for a man of wealth and education well known in the territory, but nothing is said as to the errand of himself and his men in this distant wild region. During our parley his men remain quietly at their posts, and when their leader, his questions answered, returns toward them, and we move on again, we can see them mount and ride off over the hills in a straggling, dust-enveloped little column.[43]

Four of the outlaws who escaped from Stuart's men made a little raft the following afternoon and floated down the river. They were discovered hiding in a swampy bottom near Fort Peck; and from a nearby bluff Zogbaum watched soldiers and Indian scouts flush them from their hiding place and take them, "wild-eyed and haggard, covered with mud and dirt, their brier-torn clothing hanging in shreds . . . one of them with a bullet-torn arm bound in blood-stained bandages," to the guardhouse. They were also wanted for stealing government horses and killing a soldier in an attempted holdup of an army paymaster.

Notice of their arrest was sent to Fort Maginnis and Samuel Fischel, deputy U.S. marshall, started at once to get the prisoners and take them to White Sulphur Springs. At the mouth of the Musselshell a posse met Fischel and took the prisoners from him. Nearby stood two log cabins close together. A log was placed between the cabins, the ends resting on the roofs, and the four men were hanged from the log. The cabins caught fire and were burned down and the bodies were cremated.[44]

The disposing of fifteen or eighteen rustlers by operations from the

DHS did not end the activities of the vigilantes. According to one rancher, who got his information "personally from the fireman on the engine that pulled the train,"

> a special train on the Northern Pacific Railroad [consisting of one or two horse-cars and a coach or two], carrying a "committee" of vigilantes and their horses, was taken eastward from a point near Billings, stopped at various places along the road where the "law enforcers" left the train to ride off and attend to the business at hand, returning to journey on to the next place and so on down the line, finally abandoning the train at Medora, Dakota, the job having been finished.[45]

This work required considerable saddle stock, which the larger ranches furnished "upon request with no questions asked." While the Marquis de Mores was not allowed to accompany any of these secret forays, he was asked to support the work. One of his foremen,

> Goodall took no part in the Vigilante proceedings, at least no active part. While on the roundup in the spring of 1884, he recalls that one Elf Cole of Powder River, who was generally known to be an active member of the Vigilantes, had a conversation with Goodall in which he requested that Goodall deliver to the Stock Yards at Wibeaux, fifteen good saddle horses, and with this request Goodall complied. Very little was ever said by the Vigilantes and, consequently, the conversation of Cole with Goodall was very short. The fifteen horses were promptly delivered, and one of Goodall's wranglers, or cow men, who helped to drive the horses to Wibeaux, asked Goodall who was going to get them, and he replied that he was not interested in who was going to get the horses. His duty was to deliver them. That being done, they both went on back to Medora.
>
> Goodall recalls too, that Cole wanted Goodall's best saddle horse for the boss, probably meaning Granville Stewart [Stuart], and gave directions that the horse should be left in the livery barn at Medora. With this request Goodall also complied, and left in the livery barn a white saddle horse known as "Snowball," and the best horse in his entire string. Shortly after midnight, after the horse was left as indicated, a friend of Goodall's . . . saw someone riding Goodall's horse pell-mell across the bottoms of the Little Missouri. . . . This horse was afterwards seen with the Vigilantes at Fort Buford, and at Schafer Springs in McKenzie County, and in the spring of 1885 all of the horses were back on their accustomed range.[46]

Of the happenings in the extreme eastern part of Montana and the western part of Dakota, the following is all that has been set down by anyone who could do more than make a conjecture:

> Absolutely no leakage of news occurred [before the vigilantes struck], but somehow the entire country seemed permeated with a sort of ominous threat similar to that of the quiet before a storm. And then the real storm did break with terriffic force, coming like an avalanche in a sudden, secret and terrible way, with the lifeless bodies of well known rustlers hanging from the limbs of cottonwood trees near or at the very doors of their cabins and dugouts. The entire action was swift and thorough and showed a master hand in organization and in the making of a clean sweep throught the entire country. Rumor had it that mistakes were made, but apparently there was a carefully prepared list

of the most prominent rustlers and these were put on the rope first, with others following as evidence of their guilt appeared. . . .

The deadly nature of this work, the secrecy of it, and the uncertainty of who might be next put such fear into the hearts of any remaining rustlers still alive that they soon quit the country and wholesale cattle and horse stealing became a thing of the past.

. . . who were the reckless, fearless and hard riding ones that did the actual job? The circulating gossips had it that a tough gang of Oklahoma cowboy killers had been brought in for the cleanup, but this is not so. The work was done by a few range detectives and the quiet top hands of some of the larger cow outfits. The outlaws called them the "Stranglers" which they undoubtedly were. The total number of outlaws hung and shot in extreme eastern Montana and western Dakota was sixty-three.[47]

Of the mopping up that followed this first sweep, Roosevelt recalled

One . . . fight occurred north of me early last spring. The horse-thieves were overtaken on the banks of the Missouri; two of their number were slain, and the others were driven on the ice, which broke, and two more were drowned. A few months previously another gang, whose headquarters were near the Canadian line, were surprised in their hut; two or three were shot down by the cowboys as they tried to come out, while the rest barricaded themselves in and fought until the great log-hut was set on fire, when they broke forth in a body, and nearly all were killed at once, only one or two making their escape.[48]

Such activities usually do not receive unqualified approval by those who are onlookers, and these were no exception. The vigilantes were accused of using strong-arm methods to extract information from some who were not guilty of stealing, of burning hay belonging to sheepmen, and of trying to drive small ranchers out of the country. Roosevelt himself commented that the "vigilantes in eastern Montana shot and hung nearly sixty —not, however, with the best judgement in all cases."[49] Nevertheless, the editor of Medora's *Bad Lands Cowboy* published this comment on April 2, 1885: "Whatever can be said against the methods adopted by the 'stranglers' who came through here last fall, it cannot but be acknowledged that . . . it seems as though a very thorough cleanup has been made."[50]

Although Roosevelt was a spectator on the side-lines during the vigilante roundup, he did become a minor participant on his own initiative the following spring. At the Elkhorn ranch Roosevelt had a "clinker-built" boat they used when the water was high, in which he planned to make a hunting and "exploring" trip down the Little Missouri and on to Mandan during the "spring rise." One morning late in March, not long after an ice jam had gone down the river, the boat was missing—stolen he felt certain by

. . . three hard characters who lived in a shack, or hut, some twenty miles above us, and whom we shrewdly suspected for some time of wishing to get out of the country, as certain of the cattle-men had begun openly to threaten to lynch them. . . .

The three men we suspected had long been accused—justly or unjustly—of being implicated in cattle-killing and in that worst of frontier crimes, horse-stealing: it was only by accident that they had escaped the clutches of the vigilantes the preceding fall. Their leader was a well-built fellow named Finnigan, who had long red hair reaching to his shoulders, and always wore a broad hat and a fringed buckskin shirt. He was rather a hard case, and had been chief actor in a number of shooting scrapes. The other two were a half breed, a stout, muscular man, and an old German, whose viciousness was of the weak and shiftless type.

Roosevelt resolved to go at once in pursuit, for "it is in the highest degree unwise to submit to any wrong without making an immediate and resolute effort to avenge it upon the wrong-doers, at no matter what the cost of risk and trouble. To submit tamely and weakly to theft, or to any other injury, is to invite almost certain repetition of the offense." As it was impossible to travel by horseback, two of his cowboys—originally from Maine—fashioned another boat. Into this Roosevelt packed supplies "to last us a fortnight or so," and, with his two ex-Maine woodsmen, pushed off on the trail of the thieves.

In the afternoon of the third day they came up with their unsuspecting quarry and captured them without difficulty. Then their troubles began. The weather was too cold to permit tying the men securely, so one of the party had to stand guard constantly.[51] It was impossible to return against the current and an ice jam delayed going on downstream. Finally, with provisions low, the party got as far as the vicinity of the Killdeer Mountains where Roosevelt "was able to hire a large prairie schooner and two tough little broncho mares, driven by the settler himself, a rugged old plainsman, who evidently could hardly understand why I took so much bother with the thieves instead of hanging them off-hand."

Roosevelt

. . . took the three thieves to Dickinson, the nearest town. The going was bad, and the little mares could only drag the wagon at a walk . . . it took us two days and a night . . . [and] was a most desolate drive. . . . I soon found the safest plan was to put the prisoners in the wagon and . . . with the inevitable Winchester . . . [trudge] steadily the whole time behind the wagon through ankle-deep mud. . . . At night, when we put up at the squalid hut of a frontier granger . . . it was even worse. I did not dare to go to sleep . . . [and] sat up with my back against the cabin-door and kept watch over them all night long. So, after thirty-six hours' of sleeplessness, I was most heartily glad when we at last jolted into the long, straggling main street of Dickinson, and I was able to give my unwilling companions into the hands of the sheriff.[52]

The identity of those who were active in 1884 have never been made public. Cowboy gossip and old letter files[53] indicate that Stuart, Kohrs, Fergus, Ford, Adams, Bryan, and others were leading figures. When queried regarding names, one old rancher wrote, "I am sorry to appear disobliging but I feel I should not go any further in the publication of facts appertaining to vigilantes in eastern Montana and western Dakota. . . . It is past history and might bring unpleasant reflections." Another old cowboy did name a half-dozen men who rode with vigilante parties. After he had finished, his wife remarked, "Do you think you should tell him that? They may have had relatives some place." In keeping with the spirit of the men who did this work, those names which are known have not been set down on these pages. The secrecy with which this deadly work was conducted put such fear into the hearts of the rustlers that those alive soon quit the country and *wholesale* stealing became a thing of the past.[54]

But rustling did not stop. The only thing that changed was the manner and scale in which operations were conducted, and the type of men who did the stealing. Little ranchmen and cowboys-turned-ranchmen who swung a *long rope* caused most of the trouble. As in the case of Stuart's neighbor, their cows were likely to have twins and triplets; they picked up mavericks whenever they could do so without being observed; they "sleepered" calves;[55] and the bolder ones altered brands with a running iron, hot wire, or acid. Some butchered animals and sold the beef—or "slow elk" as it was called. Horses might be hidden in some out-of-the-way spot until the brands could be worked over—heavy nuts tied in their foretops or front hoofs rasped down to the quick discouraged traveling back to the home range. And of course now and then someone stole a little bunch and tried to move them completely out of the country.

While Montana never had an overdose of this kind of theft as did Wyoming—where the cattlemen, apparently trying to imitate Stuart's solution to a somewhat different problem, "invaded" Johnson County in 1892—such losses presented an ever-present problem. After Stuart wiped out the big, organized gangs, the ranchers never let the situation get out of control. Men caught stealing seldom did it again. "The last we heard of Indian Dick," wrote an old cowboy, "he was decorating a cottonwood tree on Cow Island. The Vigilantes had hung him up to dry."[56] Canada Dave —a very good cowboy—drew his pay at the LO and rode off across the Powder River Hills. One day the story drifted back that Dave and five others had been caught up near the Missouri driving a band of horses with fresh brands. The men who caught them could see no good reason for trying the men in court. A. C. Huidekoper trailed some horse thieves six hundred miles before he ran them down in a saloon in Miles City where, he wrote regretfully, "the law had to be respected. If we could have caught them in the open, it would have been cold lead or a neck-tie party."[57] The law was not always certain—and it took too long.

At least one man hunt had an unusual ending. One of the large outfits in the Judith River country was the P Lazy N owned by T. C. Power and G. R. "Bill" Norris. Power's son recalled

An amusing incident happened to Bill Norris before his marriage. We had employed a Texas cattle man for some time who brought up trainloads of cattle purchased by the company in various years from Texas. His brother, who was a wild-eyed Texan, came up to visit his brother and Norris took quite a fancy to him and had him appointed cattle inspector for that district. They spent the evenings in the office of the company having a few drinks and, during one of these evenings, one of the ranch men came in and told them that two men had sneaked in and had taken 10 or 12 horses out of the home pasture and gone up the Judith River.

64. "Montana Man-Hunters . . ."

Norris and his Texan friend went up there, left their horses a little ways from where they knew these men were camped, and sneaked in on them, captured both and also got the horses back. They tied these two thieves on to their own horses and went back to the building where they had some shackles, and tied them to the big pillars that held up the roof. Then they went back to the office and got good and thoroughly drunk and went to sleep there.

The horse thieves got loose and brought Norris and his Texan friend out and shackled them to the big post to which they had been shackled, went out and got their horses and the stolen horses also, and went on their way, and they nor the horses were ever heard of afterward.[58]

In addition to doing police work on their own, the ranchers employed —through the Montana Stockgrowers Association—livestock inspectors. These men worked in various ways, from checking the brands on shipments at the markets to riding the ranges. One of those who did this type of work in eastern Montana was Billy Smith, whom Huffman photographed in Miles City with a group of "Montana manhunters." Smith was considered to be a very cool, level-headed man but, as Huffman commented about Smith and the others in the group, "These men could write interesting stories, but they are not built that way. They were men of action."

One of the men whose name has been mentioned in connection with rustling activities was Sim Buford Roberts. While there is no conclusive evidence that Roberts was a rustler—it is said that he was in court several times but never convicted—he is an interesting figure, for it was against men of his type that the finger of suspicion was sometimes leveled. Those who knew Roberts have described him as a very pleasant man of "considerable presence," "a wonderfully good cow-man who knew his stuff," a good foreman, an excellent trail boss, and a cool man with a gun when the chips were down.

According to some notes Huffman made during an interview with him on June 8, 1926, Roberts was born twelve miles south of Paris, Texas, in 1859. In 1876, at the age of seventeen, he helped drive a trail herd out of Old Mexico for Doc Simmons [sic], and later worked in the vicinity of Fort Griffin for Colonel Simpson, the well-known cowman. Then he went back again and came up the trail in 1877, and again in 1878. The fall of 1878 found him in the valley of the Platte helping gather beef and working for "Balsay & Bruce who had a contract to run beef (scalawags[59]) to White Clay Sioux." Here he had an adventure with Dull Knife's Cheyennes when they were near the end of their famous retreat. He told Huffman that he was sent to the Indian agent at Fort Robinson with a note about cattle deliveries, and that he fell in with Dull Knife's hostiles. "I did not know hostiles—held me—on Bordeaux. Thought I was a scout—close call. Met Bill Rowland[60]—convinced them—turned me loose. Reno's command took them soon after.[61] Told me they didnt want to kill north of the Platte." Roberts worked for these contractors long enough to help deliver the scalawags, "one to this lodge, two to that," and to watch the Sioux turn out to shoot their beef. Then, although he was offered a winter job, he "wanted to ramble." So he took a pack horse and headed north and "in '79 worked for 79 outfit breaking horses."

Bill Roberts, Sim's brother, was foreman for John T. Murphy, owner of the 79. Not long after Sim arrived, Bill was killed by a cowboy in a gunfight. This killing Sim avenged as soon as an opportunity presented itself. Later Roberts was foreman for Murphy, and for Briggs and Ellis. Then he became a small rancher, choosing for his brand the $ mark. This brand, because of the possibilities of working other brands over into the pattern of the $ sign, was in itself a subject for suspicion. From this time on a confused picture of the man develops.

According to one account[62] several accusations of rustling were made against Roberts, but no case was proven in court. The story is told that Murphy hid marked coins in the briskets[63] of 79 cattle—and received some back from Roberts with a note suggesting that he be more careful with his money. He shot Nate Young, a witness against him in a trial at Big Timber, and claimed self-defense. Perhaps it was—but the only evidence was Roberts' account. There were said to have been other shootings. At one trial Roberts obtained permission to go armed and sat in the courtroom with a rifle across his knees. On one occasion unknown parties tried to bushwhack him while he was riding on a hayrack, but he whipped up the horses and escaped.

In the late 1890's Roberts moved to a small ranch in the Rosebud country. As long as he lived, there were people who liked him and there were others who, while admitting with one breath that he had a very pleasant personality, would refer to him in the next as a "notorious thief." The story is told that on one occasion, when Roberts had reached the age where he had "mellowed" a bit, Whit Longley, foreman of the FUF near Forsyth, once introduced a rancher-friend to Roberts in this manner: "I have always admired a man who is at the head of his profession, even though he be a horse thief. Mr. T——— meet Mr. Roberts." Roberts acknowledged the introduction—and laughed heartily.

According to the findings of the local courts Roberts was an honest man. Yet there were rustlers who were like him—top hands on the range and likable men to meet. Some used a long rope and a running iron in the days when they were accumulating a herd—and then went straight. Some, like author Will James, did a stretch behind the bars. Some were unlucky and got caught red-handed by ranchers who knew how to use a Winchester.

Part III: Hired Men

Although ranchers with money were the foundation of the cattle business and the rustlers provided a bit of color, the dominant figures on the range were the hired men on horseback. Commonly called cowboys, they were also known as riders, waddies, buckaroos, ranahans, or any one of a hundred other allied or similar names. Some were frontiersmen, some were Indians,[64] some were men born to the business on the southern ranges and who came north with the trail herds, some were Negroes and Mexicans who found the North more to their liking than the South where they had been born, some came from God only knows where.

As with the sheepherders, it was the small minority who added color to the group. Remittance men and "soldiers of fortune" from the British Isles were not uncommon. An early settler in the Tongue Valley discovered that a cowboy who had taken a liking to his daughter was the grandson of people he had known well in Scotland. Some who had burned their bridges behind them slipped easily into a society where it was impolite to inquire about the past. Sometimes there was a revealing slip of the tongue such as that made by a liquor-wrecked wrangler who, on overhearing strangers discuss an English university boat race, exclaimed, "Thank God, we won!" One of the strangers, an Easterner unfamiliar with the code of the West, asked why *he* should care so much, and the wrangler, caught unawares, blurted out, "Why, man, once I stroked that crew!"[65] And there were many like Jim Culver who arrived at the Lang ranchhouse more dead than alive after an adventure in the icy waters of the Little Missouri. Lang liked him and hired him. He was a young man of about twenty, fearless, of good morals, and with an unusual amount of energy and initiative. When a mean horse side-flopped and killed him two years later, all that was known about him was—*he said his name was Jim Culver.*

65. "Henry Tunis on his Favorite Mount [*circa* 1896]."

Although many cowboys were known by their proper names, others were not. Their names reflected the custom of the times which ruled that it was very impolite to inquire about the name by which a man chose to be identified. One old rancher, in looking through Huffman's pictures of cowboys, came to the picture of Henry Tunis. "Well," said he, "that is the first time I knew what his first name was. We just called him 'Tunis.'" Yet the rancher had worked on several roundups where Tunis had repped, and had shared his bedroll with him. Occasionally a name came from some incident, as did "Muddy Bill's," who was once bucked off into a mudhole. Others were identified by the brand for which they worked as was Three Sevens Charlie who worked for the 777 outfit, which was located not far from Roosevelt's ranch. He was remembered particularly because he engineered a holdup of a Northern Pacific passenger train solely for the fun of it—according to one story, so that he and his friends could commandeer the stock of fruit and candy of the news butcher and distribute it to the girls on board. This cowboy prank created a small furor!

Some names like Chicago Kid, Yankee Sam, Texas Jack, Dutch Henry, and "Montana Bill" Roberts indicated a geographical location. Of the latter, John Childress, a foreman of the LO, commented,

Yes, I know Montana Bill. I was the one who gave him that name. I was working for the XIT outfit in Texas at the Yellow House Ranch Division when he came there and went to work. And he was *always* talking about Montana. So I gave him the name of "Old Montana Bill." You see he came from Montana to Texas, hence his conversations were mostly about Montana.

Personal characteristics were responsible for names like Fatty Hamilton, Lazy Dick, Itchy Jake, Six Shooter Bob, and Windy Jack. When he first came to Montana, Charlie Russell, then in his middle teens, was called Kid Russell; "Nigger Bob" Levitt, as might be expected, was a rabid Southerner; and Phonograph Charlie "talked all the time." Other names doubtless reflect some incident long forgotten. There was a Cyclone Ed, a Tepee Dick, a Loose Twist, a Sliver, a Beaver Slide, a Never Slip, and a Chippy Colorow. What their names meant one can only guess.

Like most professions the range had its own slang and characteristic expressions, all of it highly descriptive, and much of it full of dry wit, for the cowboy was a *real* humorist. For example, a snorty animal, either horse or cow, was sometimes called a *snuffer* from the characteristic blowing or snorting just before acting mean. A cow hunting trouble was said to be *on the pick* (or *prod*). A horse with unusual stamina was called a *rimrocker* because, on the circle[66] at the roundup, the rim rock (if present) represented the greatest distance a rider would have to go to gather cattle—hence the implication that such a horse could go as far as there was any need for him to go. The night herder of the *remuda* was called the *night-hawk* after the bird of the same name which rarely flies in the daytime. As the cowboy had but little respect for the fighting qualities of Mexicans, a struggle in which one side was forced to retreat might be referred to by the loser as a *Mexican standoff*. Once a cowboy acquired a saddle that fitted him to his liking, he had to be in dire straits before he would part with it; one Montana schoolboy is said to have identified Benedict Arnold as the general who *sold his saddle*.

Not only was the cowboy's conversation sprinkled with peculiar terms, but his entire speech had a salty flavor all it own. On the whole it was characterized by three qualities—brevity, vividness, and wit. Who but a cowboy, after noting the shaking of the excess flesh on a fat lady walking down the street, would liken what he saw to "two shoats fightin' under a wagon sheet!" Some of his expressions cannot be put into print, although his profanity had a Homeric quality with the emphasis on humor and not on filth, as is indicated by his describing, in the vernacular of brands, the ⟍⚬⟋ not as the Flying O but as the Flying Ass Hole.

On a trip to watch the Spear outfit run wild horses near Tullock Creek, Huffman set down in fragmentary notes some of the comments which he heard. As the hours were long, Huffman asked one cowboy when he slept. The reply was, "In the winter, same as you." Bart Maxwell, in describing the sensations of riding a fast horse across some particularly broken country, said, "Comin' 'crost them roughs on Concho or Bird Ketcher shore makes me feel *two pounds liter'n a straw hat* every time they clears one of them ledges or washes." Later, on a hot day, he commented, "Hot! Wouldent this be a fine day t'd die. Feller'd never notice the difference." Another remarked of the baldheaded cook, "The cook haint got ery hair 'tween him'n heaven." And of the bantering between the men, Huffman recorded one very early rising "when the cook called, 'Roll o-u-t. Roll o-u-t.' Keks says, 'you bald-headed, lop-eyed old son of a bitch I orto k-i-l-l you. Its only twenty minuets past two.' And the cook replied, 'Me? When did I get up? Jest a little past 'leven.'"

Often when the cowboy wrote letters, he omitted punctuation and sprinkled capital letters carelessly here and there, thus adding additional color which did not in the least detract from his vivid, clean-cut expression. One old rancher, perhaps not one of the very best riders but a very competent one nevertheless, wrote as follows of being thrown—at an age many regard as *old*.

I will tell this one on me. When I was 57 years old I was breaking a bunch of half thorough-breds which were 6 and 7 years old   they had never been off the range and Boy they were wild   the Lord threw his arms around me and I got along fine until one morning just as I mounted a rooster ran a hen just in front of the bronc   he went into the air struck the bridle with his front foot and knocked it off.   he then swallowed his neck up to his shoulders and proceeded on up to where the lights of Jerusalem shone   there we parted company and the bronc came down alone.[67]

Like all human beings, cowboys differed one from the other but, as a class, they had certain rather definite characteristics in common. It is true that among them were some tough nuts who respected neither God, man, nor the devil. However, these individuals were not typical. Nor was it true that they were all young men, for some followed the business well past what is considered the normal period for living a strenuous life.

A sense of equality was one of several personal characteristics typical of the men of the range. The story is told that while waiting for his baggage, a young Englishman, just arrived in Miles City, spoke impatiently to the old baggage man at the Northern Pacific depot, "My man! I am [so and so], and I wish my bags jolly quick!" The porter speaking in the spirit of the country, replied, "That is nothing against you, but in this country you will get your bags when your turn comes." Another prominent quality was honesty—interpreted, of course, according to the code of the times. Hell Roaring Bill Jones of Medora, when he came to collect his pay for digging some post holes, would not take pay for one he had failed to dig as deeply as the others; and the N Bar foreman once fired a hand because he rode out of Miles City without paying his bill to a prostitute. While on the circle at a roundup in the Little Missouri country, a rep found a mare which had gotten away while being broken. This shifty character stole the saddle from the animal, hid it, and later tried to point the finger of suspicion at another rider. He was trapped in his lie by the roundup foreman who then promptly kicked the man off the roundup. "Not in the length or breadth of the Bad Lands," wrote one who witnessed the incident, "could the culprit obtain work thereafter."[68]

Strangely enough, pride in the integrity of one's word was not limited to those who lived within the law. A rancher in the Tongue Valley was called to the cabin of a small cattleman who was about to leave and go "on the dodge." The following conversation took place:

"Mr. T———, I want to sell my cattle—range count." [69]

"How much do you want, Mr. B———?"

"I want $25.00 a head, and there are 500 head."

"Mr. B———, are you sure you have that many? I did not think there were so many."

"Mr. T———, *I said* there were 500 head."

"Very well, I will buy your cattle."

The rancher paid the "wanted" man for five hundred head, and when the cattle were gathered at the next roundup there was a full count and some over.

With honesty as a cardinal virtue it is not strange that men had a sort of feudal loyalty toward the brand for which they rode. A man was a *Three Sevens man,* a *CK man,* or whatever the brand happened to be, and they were trustworthy even when faced with death trying to guard stock drifting in a blizzard, or riding full speed to turn a stampeding herd in the inky blackness of night. Neither is it strange that they were polite, generally soft-spoken, and given to levity in tight spots.

Because they had to be experts in their business, and often worked under conditions where each had to be self-sufficient and to make decisions for himself, they were proud. And being proud, they were sensitive, egotistical, and sometimes vain. Charlie Russell recalled that "cowpunchers were mighty particular about their rig" and that one of the best hands he ever knew was called Pretty Shadow. "This sounds like an Injun name," he explained, "but it ain't. It comes from a habit some punchers has of ridin' along, lookin' at their shadows." [70] And they were clannish, just as soldiers who have been under fire appear clannish to troops who have never been blooded.

Their work required that they be watchful and remember small details—on what parts of the range certain animals were most likely to be seen, the peculiarities of certain horses, particularly the mean ones, and the reaction of stock to certain weather and range conditions. Typical of their capacity for minute observations was the incident one rider related to Huffman:

I was settin' watchin' ants onct 'n I noticed carcasses of a heap of dead ones layin' 'round the hill. Purty quick a middlin' sized black spider comes down offen a twig of a sage brush and dashes at a lope after one of the ants and so help me bob if it did'nt look ezactly like he roped him and hogtied him in spite of a swarm of ants that hurried around. Where the swarm had him busy he tied this roped one to a little stake and loped up a bush, me still watchin', and when they all had gone back to work he slips down and bites this ant just in the right place to kill him quick. Then cuts the rope and hoists him on his back when he cuts fer a hole and disappears.

On the whole they were neat in appearance and, although their clothes

66. Two cowboys *circa* 1895.

might not be ironed, they tried to keep clean. Most of them were self-respecting and law-abiding according to the code of the times. Bravery and pride in carrying their just share of the daily work were commonplace. Some saved their money and invested in a small outfit of their own. Others had not the slightest sense of the value of money. These would squander several months' wages during a spree of a few days in town—and come back to the ranch in debt for a few clothes to wear until the next payday. In some respects the characteristics that have been noted depend on the observations of the individual who set them down. "Cowpunchers," wrote Charlie Russell, "were . . . careless, homeless, hard-drinking men." An old rancher, writing of a slightly later date, said, ". . . old cow hands were often men of high honor and intellect . . . often self educated by reading everything they could get their hands on."

Of all the traits of the cowboys those most universally possessed, and certainly the most striking, were wit and love of humor. Perhaps because they had but little recreation that was not self-made, they were continually playing practical jokes on each other, joshing and telling funny stories. Many of these, products of the moment, have been forgotten but perhaps the following will indicate the nature of this wit. As one Westerner put it, cowboy humor was sometimes close to grimness and often related to the sardonic.

The sort of "jobbing" that was continually engaged in is illustrated by a couple of incidents Teddy Blue related to his biographer. Once, while in Nebraska with a trail herd for the FUF, the cowboys made a dummy man and, as a Union Pacific passenger train pulled into a station, they hauled it up to the crossbar of a telegraph pole and began to shoot at it. The bullets cut the rope letting the dummy fall, and the show ended with Blue galloping away with the dummy bouncing along behind on the end of the rope. Consternation reigned in the train; and it was not long before the cowboys' boss, the sheriff, and the coroner arrived. "The sheriff demanded the corpse at once. . . . I can hear yet how [the boss] laughed when they turned it over. Well, it ended in a big laugh all around. . . ."

One boss for whom Teddy Blue worked tried to reform the boys. He refused to allow *The Police Gazette* on the ranch and, when they came to Miles City, he tried to keep them out of the saloons. One day as this individual was sitting in the hotel lobby—keeping an eye on the door to the saloon—Calamity Jane came in. Teddy Blue, who knew her, asked her to make love to the boss. Calamity, not being one to let her friends down, sat down on the man's lap, put her strong arms around him, pinioning his arms to his sides, kissed him, and inquired why he had not been to see her any more. In the meantime the boys stood near making "appropriate" remarks. When Calamity let the old man go, he sputtered, spit, wiped his mouth, and left the hotel—and that was the last the boys saw of him that night.[71]

Sometimes these pranks had dangerous possibilities. There was a small rancher who lived near Medora who would recite poetry when in his cups. One day the boys, having loosened the cinches on his saddle, helped him on his horse, and when it came time to leave the saloon and go home, then stood by to watch the fun. The man paused for a parting selection, which was "Barbara Frietchie" on this occasion, and as he came to the closing words—"skip along—I'm d-e-a-a-d"—he spurred the horse and he and the saddle went backward over its rump as he voiced the last two words in a "long, drawn-out, despairing cry." The performance brought howls of glee from the assembled crowd.[72]

More often, however, these jokes were of the innocuous variety. Henry Tunis, a Three V man, did not bring a bed on one occasion when he repped[73] with the SL wagon on the roundup. The horse wrangler, a young chap with a good bed, was comfortably situated in the tepee of another puncher. So it was suggested to Tunis that he "throw in with the kid," which he did. The next day as the roundup was moving, two cowboys rode up one on either side of the young horse wrangler and started a casual conversation. This, in the due course of time, turned to a discussion of Tunis. Finally, one cowboy said confidentially to the other, "You know, he's as lousy as a pick." Thus was the idea planted. The wrangler immediately began to "crawl and scratch" and several days passed before he figured that he had been jobbed.

Those who did not measure up to the code of the times were particularly likely to be made the butt of jokes. One of the first jobs Charlie Decker had when a young man was that of *whipper* with a trail team. On one occasion while coming through Nebraska, the wagon train encountered a bad storm, and the men wanted to stop at the house of a settler named Henry Tusler. Unfortunately for the freighters, Tusler was not the hospitable sort and the travelers spent a miserable night in the open—a night young Decker never forgot. A few years later, after Decker had come to Montana, Tusler shipped a trainload of cattle into Miles City. As he did not have hands available to receive the shipment, he hired some cowboys who were loafing around town to take the cattle out and graze them. Among them was young Decker. Many years later when relating the incident, Decker would shake his fist and chortle, "Gosh dang, I thought I knew him. We grazed them cattle alright—we scattered them *all over* the country! He never caught up with them cattle until the fall roundup!"

Decker also told of another prank he helped play on a Tongue River rancher named E. C. "Cold Water" Howard.[74] Howard was a "close" individual who did not "throw in" with the community and would not allow cowboys to stop overnight at his ranch—which was something of a sin where food and shelter were given freely to travelers regardless of who they were. One day Decker and another came by Howard's place with a bunch of cattle they had gathered on the circle for a roundup. Spotting the calf of Howard's milk cow staked beside the road, they threw the little animal in with their bunch and were ready to proceed when Howard, observing what had happened, called out for them to leave the calf. Deaf to the old man's call, the cowboys proceeded up the road with the cattle. After calling again, the owner came in person—very much irritated. After making Howard identify his property—which further increased his anger—the cowboys informed him that the roundup boss had given strict orders to bring *everything* in and that they would get into trouble if they did not comply. Then Howard cut the calf out, the cowboys turned it back, and, needling the owner more and more, the cowboys slowly drifted their little bunch to the roundup ground. Decker, in telling of the incident would end up roaring with glee and observe, "He was the maddest old man you *ever* saw!"

Sometimes range humor was the result of a lightning-quick reaction. The following story has been attributed to Charlie Russell. Horsewrangler Russell rode in to the chuck wagon one day just as the cook had the misfortune to burn himself on a skillet. When the *old woman* threw the skillet on the ground and began to swear, Russell promptly pulled his gun and shot a couple of holes through it. The cook's feelings of exasperation immediately turned from the skillet to Russell. "What's you do that fer?" he demanded. Russell replied immediately, "Damned if I'm going to let any skillet get the best of one of my friends."

Sometimes cowboys spent as much time making up humorous stories as they did planning practical jokes. However, as John Lomax observed about some of the cowboy ballads he collected, "a number of the most characteristic cannot be printed for general circulation." Such humor had an earthy quality quite different from the cheap barroom jokes often told in more sophisticated society. Some indication of this quality is contained in Russell's story, "Piano Jim and the Impotent Pumpkin Vine." The version given here was written down after Russell's death by his friend, Irvin S. Cobb.

Charley loved to talk about his old friend, Piano Jim, who had been a gun-man, a faro-dealer, a barkeeper, a bouncer, a sure-thing gambler and finally, falling on evil days, became the "professor" in a honky-tonk. Now when Piano Jim was getting on in life, he grew tired, Charley said, of the smells of stale beer and sour sawdust and Hoyt's German Cologne and decided to go straight. For proof that his reformation was complete he married the leading retired elderly prostitute of Western Montana whose name as pronounced by Jim who stuttered badly, was "N-n-nellie." So he and Nellie pooled their accumulated wages of sin and went off to the Flathead Valley, a green oasis in the very heart of the glacier-trimmed Rockies, and bought two fertile acres by the lakeside and put up a green-and-white bungalow and moved in. And Jim laid out the flower garden and the vegetable patch and Nellie made the window curtains and watered the rubber-plant and they settled down to enjoy the simple pastoral life.

Now all through his wanderings across the old Range, in the midst of alkali desert and scrub, Jim had carried a delectable vision of his youth—a boyhood picture of a Tennessee cornfield in the fall of the year when the frost fell and turned the pumpkins into vast golden orbs. He craved to reproduce that picture.

So he planted two rows of horse-corn and between the rows planted one prime pumpkin seed and he watered it and he fertilized it and cultivated it as it germinated and sent up a tender green shoot which in turn became a lusty vine which went weaving in and out among the young stocks of growing corn. So Jim piled on more manure and dug up the weeds. In due season the vine put forth buds and the buds turned into big saffron-colored cusps of bloom. Under the warm suns of the springtime the blossoms withered and fell away—but no little round green bulbs followed. By mid-summer the vine still stubbornly refusing to put forth fruit, Jim grew desperate. He began to fear that never would his pet produce those fat sweet globes of his imaginings.

In this emergency he decided to call in a specialist for the patient. So he went down the valley and rounded up a German, a practical dirt farmer. Being appealed to as an expert, the German responded to the call. He drove up to Jim's place and got down on his knees along side of the balky thing and broke off a leaf and tasted it and sniffed at it and rubbed it with his fingers. Then he arose and to the anxious amateur he said:

"Chim, I dell you vot here is der trouble. Here is der trouble dot you haf got a female pumpkin vine. Now uf you vant pumpkins, you must go ulso and get a male pumpkin vine and blant it close beside der female vine and den dey vot you call pollenize and maybe den by-and-by you get pumpkin. Oddervise nodt! So Chim, vot you must do is go und get a male pumpkin und—".

"S-s-sucker!" commanded Jim, "l-l-listen. All my l-l-life I've been a r-r-rotten, no-good, l-l-low down s-s-son-of-a-bitch, but I'll be t-t-teetotally God-dam' if at the age of s-s-sixty-four I'm goin' to start p-p-pimpin' for a p-p-pumpkin!" [75]

There have been various descriptions of what the cowboy wore. Charlie Russell indicated that

The puncher himself was rigged, startin' at the top, with a good hat—not one of the floppy kind you see in pictures, with the rim turned up in front. The

67. "A Typical Trio."

68. "Honeycut on White Star, Aug 1904."

top-cover he wears holds its shape an' was made to protect his face from weather; maybe to hold it on, he wore a buckskin string under the chin or back of the head. Round his neck a big silk handkerchief, tied loose, an' in the drag of a trail herd it was drawn over the face to the eyes, hold-up fashion, to protect the nose an' throat from dust. . . . Coat, vest, and shirt suits his own taste. Maybe he'd wear California pants, light buckskin in color, with large brown plaid, sometimes foxed, or what you'd call reinforced with buck or antelope skin. Over these came his chaparejos or leggin's. His feet were covered with good high-heeled boots, finished off with steel spurs of Spanish pattern.[76]

Other contemporaries of Russell add that the hats were usually light-colored Stetsons; sometimes the pants were bibless overalls, a prototype of the present-day levis; that often the black silk handkerchief was considered more of an item for dressing up instead of an item for everyday wear; and that the boots covered the calf of the leg and came almost up to the knee. As to chaps, one Montana rancher recalled, "The first chaps were made of heavy leather and did not snap on and did not have flaps as did the later ones [that is, they were simply leather pants with the seats cut away]. They were oily and kept your legs dry, buckled at the waist to hold them up. In the older times we never saw the Angoras, they came later."

Although Russell was meticulous in his attention to detail when he put the cowboy in his pictures, nevertheless he managed to invest him with considerable glamour. Huffman's photographs present the cowboy as a working man on horseback. His hat shows unmistakable signs of wear and individuality; his shirt was sometimes dirty and sweaty; and often his vest

69. " 'Montana' bedrolls." (Pumpkin Creek Pool—spring of 1895.)

had seen better days. Except for the lack of color and the smell of sweat and horses, these photographs show the cowboy as he actually was.

A very important part of the cowpuncher's personal property was his bedroll. He was rarely without it and, when away from the bunkhouse, it also served as a trunk. In making up his bed the cowboy first laid out flat a tarpaulin, which was usually about six by fourteen feet. This was always called a *bed tarp*. On one end of this he spread half of his bedding, which usually consisted of quilts, known on the range as *sougans*. These were almost square, and "trying to find the long way of a sougan" was a range joke of long standing—cowboys sometimes remarked that this was what made sheepherders crazy! In the center of the bedding a lightweight double blanket sheet was sometimes spread and the other half of the bedding placed on top. If the roll was to be used by one man, the side of the canvas would be folded up over the edges of the sougans: and then the other half of the tarp would be brought up to cover the entire bed. In bad weather this end would be pulled completely over the occupant's head to keep out rain or snow.

Considerable bedding was often required to keep warm in Montana; and the large rolls that resulted were known in warmer areas—particularly in Texas—as "Montana" bedrolls. As bedding got damp, and sometimes downright wet, during a rainy spell it was necessary to spread it out to dry

70. "The SL Wrangler and Red Nut" or "Cowboy Henry and His Top Horse [1897?]."

on the next sunshiny day. The little "Biddle tepees,"[77] which Huffman's photographs indicate came into use during the latter days of the open range, were a big improvement to personal comfort in bad weather.

Into his bed went the personal effects of the owner. His spare clothing was packed in a grain sack—known as a *war bag*—and this was kept inside the roll. In addition to his bedroll and war bag, a puncher's incidentals were few—a slicker, perhaps a six-shooter, sometimes a razor, and a few personal trinkets.

The tools of his trade were also few in number—a saddle and blanket, bridle or hackamore, a lariat—or rope as he usually called it, and a few odds and ends such as a picket rope, a pair of hobbles, and sometimes a quirt. Just as it is possible to sometimes date a photograph by the style of chaps the rider is wearing, just so it is possible to fix an approximate date by looking at the saddle. Early saddles often used a Visalia tree, as the basic framework was called. This tree had a high fork that terminated in a long, slender saddle horn, and only a moderate swell. While it was a tree of rugged design, the lack of swell was a handicap when one rode a mean horse. This shortcoming was sometimes alleviated by attaching bucking rolls or by tying some object, like a tightly rolled slicker, across the saddle just in front of the seat. Such saddles had a long skirt that helped them stay put on the horse's back, and part of the tree also came behind the cantle. In later years the design was sometimes modified to provide a tree with more swell and the saddle horn was made squat and flat-topped.

"Ox-bow" stirrups were common in the early days. As the rounded bottom of this pattern was hard on the feet, men used long stirrup straps and "rode with their knees." Later the stirrups were widened and flattened on the bottom, making it possible to ride comfortably with a shorter strap. These variations in length were not great, for the Western rider rode deep in his saddle and his seat never approached that used with what he derisively termed a "postage stamp" saddle.

Saddles also varied in their rig but this was basically a regional preference. The Texan preferred a double rig, which employed two cinches, and was sometimes called a rim-fire saddle. Riders from west of the Continental Divide were often influenced by California styles and might prefer a single cinch. If the cinch was placed slightly to the rear of the stirrups, or at the most even with them, the rig was called a center fire; but if it was placed slightly forward of this position it was known as a three-quarter rig. It is not strange, therefore, that Lee Warren (the broncobuster featured in some of Huffman's photographs) who was born in Idaho should write, "I all ways used a center-fire saddle."

Bridles varied according to whether a throat latch or an earstall was used to secure it to the head, type of bit used, the material from which it was made, and the ornamentation. Some animals were ridden with a hackamore, which was, essentially, a halter with a bosal in place of a bit and with a pair of reins. When a hair rope was used for the reins, or for a lead or tie rope, it was called a mecate or, in the slang of the range, a *McCarty*. The lariat, normally about fifty feet in length, was usually a hard-laid Manila rope but occasionally was made of braided rawhide.

While they did not belong to him personally, each rider had his own string of horses, usually numbering from six to a dozen animals. This number contained an assortment of animals varying from newly broken to well trained and from rough to gentle. Topping each string were one or more cutting horses. Such horses were able to cut out a cow with no guidance other than to be shown the animal once—work that required that they be able to "turn on a dime" and have trigger-quick brains to enable them to outguess the most wily old steer or cow. These were the elite and the heroes of many a campfire story. Next in importance was the animal used as a night horse, which must have a quiet temperament and be sure-footed. The remainder of the animals were sometimes called circle horses. They were the unskilled labor used for the tiring circle rides at the roundup and most of the routine work around the ranch.

Only geldings were used in a *remuda*—mares having the usual female reputation of being unreliable, unstable animals. Their tails were kept thinned out and shortened by pulling by hand until they only reached the animals' hocks. A long-tailed horse was the mark of a farmer or a town gambler. And of course the rider was responsible for keeping his animals' feet in condition by trimming their hoofs and shoeing when necessary.

Strange as it may seem in an occupation that required large numbers of saddle horses, each horse had a name. Some names indicated the rider's opinion of their desirability. Who would trust Rattler, Rowdy, Old Fistula,

71. "Corn Cob Cutting Out a Big Roan Cow."

72. Pulling a horse's tail to proper length.

Sunfish, or Hellcat? Other names such as Corncob, Buck, Lily, Brown Jug, Old Spider, Paint, Neptune, San Bass, Sandy, Red Ear, Yellow Belly, Red Nut, White Star, Baldy, Bull Pup, Bird Catcher, Slick, Ginger, and Comet indicate that a number of qualities varying from speed to color markings prompted the cowboy when he attached that name to a particular animal. Although the horses were geldings, they often bore such names as Beth, Pansy, Dolly, Irene, and Dimple, for sometimes the men named their mounts after their girl friends, or girls whom they admired and to whom they had never been introduced! Once a cowboy was given a string, he was supposed to be able to pick them out from a large band. One horse wrangler, on viewing some of Huffman's photographs of *remudas*, remembered horses that he had herded well over half a century before!

Not all the men on a ranch did their work on horseback; perhaps the most important one did his work on foot. Because of his touchy ways, this individual acquired an unenviable reputation as evidenced by the range saying that "Only a fool argues with a skunk, a mule, or a cook." One man wrote

> If ever there was an uncrowned king, it is the old-time cook. He had to be good to qualify as a wagon cook because he had to be both versatile and resourceful. He was the most important individual in camp, and even the boss paid him homage. He was conscious of his autocratic powers, and his crankiness is still traditional.[78]

Although roundup cooks were autocratic, they were accepted in the society in which they worked. One old cowboy recalled, "There never was a roundup cook that didn't have the name of being a grouch," but with the next breath he added, "but they were pretty good fellows." And he remembered kindly the days when, as a young man, he had been a horse

73. "Roundup Cook and Pie-biter at Work."

74. An old-time chuck wagon, about 1885.

wrangler. When he happened to bring the horses in a bit early at noon, one cook would often call, "Come here, young man, I've got something for you," or he would remark as he laid out some tidbit, "Here, you'd better have some of this." And another often helped him set up his ropes at noon even though it was not a part of the cook's work. There can be no doubt that a good cook was an artist and a "jewel beyond price"—and the amount of wages paid to him was exceeded only by that paid the foreman.

While there were all kinds of cooks—white, Negro, Chinese, good, bad, dirty, clean, and indifferent—no one kept a poor cook except in a case of necessity, for poor food eventually made a grouchy crew. On the other hand, if a cranky cook served good meals, his personal idiosyncrasies might be largely overlooked or even catered to within the bounds of reason. Some were rough characters. Huffman sometimes told of one such character who "went on the prod" and ran the cowboys out of camp. When the foreman[79] heard of it, he rode casually up to the cook's fire, dismounted, and—with a six shooter in one hand—proceeded to insult the cook by helping himself to a snack without so much as a "by your leave." The cook moved to a spot where he was temporarily out of sight. As he ate, the foreman remarked, speaking to no one in particular, "The cook? Where is the son of a bitch? He wooden' shoot nuthin." As Huffman observed in regard to this incident, it sometimes took a strong man to run an outfit in the early days.

Not only did this individual have duties as a cook and a teamster, but his detached position in the bit of society in which he was placed brought to him other duties as well. If wagers were placed, he was often the stakeholder and, likewise, he might be asked to act as banker if a cowboy had some spare change he was afraid of losing. At other times he doubled as a doctor, dentist, veterinarian, barber, father confessor, and, because he used a shovel in digging his fire trench, undertaker when there was a bad accident.

75. "LU Bar Cook Making Bread, [July 18, 1904?]."

On the range, the cook's world centered around the chuck wagon. This was an ordinary wagon with a small cupboard securely fastened in the extreme rear end of the wagon box. The remainder of the wagon box served as a storage place for supplies—flour, beans, rice, sugar, etc., in double sacks to prevent loss; jugs of vinegar and "lick" or "long sweetnin'" as molasses was called; sometimes sides of bacon or slabs of sowbelly, potatoes, part of a carcass of beef wrapped in a heavy tarpaulin; occasionally some "air tights" as canned goods were called; boxes of dried fruit; one-pound sacks of Arbuckle coffee; and other miscellaneous items. Here were stored also various pieces of equipment ranging from Dutch ovens to branding irons and, under its canvas cover, was a snug place to sleep in foul weather —a privilege reserved exclusively to the cook. Sometimes an untanned beef hide was stretched, hammock fashion, underneath the running gears. Into the *cooney,* as this receptacle was called, went extra cooking utensils—to give forth an ungodly jangle of sound when the wagon was moved—and sometimes pieces of wood when fuel was scarce.

In the early days the cooking was done over an open fire. It takes but little imagination to picture the cook's difficulties when working with wet wood on a rainy day, or when the wind blew smoke in his eyes, scattered his fire, blew the heat away from his pots and Dutch ovens, and deposited

76. "SH SH Roundup Outfit in Camp, 1886."

dust, sand, and ashes in the food every time he lifted a lid. Later there was
a long fly of canvas stretched from the wagon to cover the working area, or a
tent and small portable stove. These went a long way toward lessening the
cook's troubles.

The statement that the cook was an uncrowned king was no figure of
speech. In the area between the tail of the wagon—which he always set
headed into the wind—and his fire, he reigned supreme, and woe unto the
puncher who dared to intrude into this little domain or to take undue lib-
erties in the vicinity of the chuck wagon. His utensils were few and far from
fancy. Most of the open-fire cooking was done in Dutch ovens, a large
kettle or two, and a large coffeepot of at least two gallons' capacity. The
Dutch ovens, which figure in a number of Huffman's pictures, were large
cast-iron pots with tight lids. The rim around the edge of the lids kept
hot coals from rolling off, and the whole was an excellent, versatile cooking
utensil. There was a dishpan for mixing bread and other similar tasks,
and a large container called a camp kettle for heating water to wash dishes.
Further than that, ingenuity had to substitute for any other utensils.

It is not surprising that a roundup cook acquired the reputation of
being cranky. His working hours, if nothing else, were enough to spoil all
except the most sunny disposition. "On the roundup," recalled an old

77. "The Roundup on the Move, [1897?]."

rancher, "breakfast would usually be over by 3:00 or 3:30 in the morning." So, sometime before that hour, the cook would have to rise, build a fire—sometimes the night-hawk did this job for him—and prepare a substantial breakfast of meat, hot bread, dried fruit, and coffee for ten, twenty, or thirty men. Now and then a cook added variety to the customary chow call of "Grub p-i-l-e," "Come an' get it," or "Grab a root an' growl," by some novel device such as rubbing two Dutch oven lids together, thus producing sounds calculated to wake the dead. On one roundup, unusually early rising evoked the comment from one cowbody that "a man didn't need a bed. All he needed was a lantern to catch a fresh horse." Under such conditions one might wonder if it was worthwhile for the cook to go to bed at all!

By five o'clock the dirty dishes would be washed and things packed for a move of ten or fifteen miles. If the next roundup spot was on a well-defined trail, this move might be uneventful; but when it led across trackless country, anything—runaways, upsets, breakdowns, bogging in quicksand at a ford—might delay arrival at the spot designated by the roundup boss. All of this to the cook-now-turned-teamster—sometimes with a pan of dough for the next meal under his watchful eye—might be something of a problem! Before the day ended there would be two more meals to prepare for the hungry crew and after these were over—and the coffeepot placed beside the remains of the fire for the night-hawk, the dough made up for the next day's bread, and the lantern hung on the camp pole to guide the night-hawk and men coming in off night guard—then and not until then, was the day's work of this man over.

Food varied with the outfit and the ability of the cook. If it was clean and reasonably well cooked, no one was likely to find fault, at least audibly within the hearing of the cook. Criticism was likely to cause the cook to get peeved, and he had a number of subtle ways of making his displeasure known, such as putting pebbles in the beans and making weak coffee, that were disagreeable to all.

Obviously, there were no standard menus. Breakfast has been indicated. The noon meal usually had a greater selection of foods, but the emphasis was on items that could be cooked in a Dutch oven or a kettle, such as roast beef, boiled potatoes, a pot of beans, brown gravy, light bread or biscuits, and coffee—there was always coffee, the stronger the better. Dessert might be stewed dried fruit, spiced cake made without eggs or butter, dried fruit pies, or rice and raisins. The evening meal was similar except that there might be beefsteak fried in deep fat, short ribs cooked with onions, or some dessert other than stewed dried fruit. Whatever else may be said of these cooks and their open-air kitchens—they were excellent meat cooks.

There is some question as to whether Northern outfits had better food than those in Texas and the Southwest. To quote the opinion of one who worked in both Montana and Texas:

I think the northern outfits fed better than the southern but those trail

78. " 'Mexican John' XIT Cook."

herds didn't have *too* much to eat—sow belly, spuds, dried fruit, coffee, and sour dough biscuits, yes and frijoles & lick. There wasnt much difference in the meals [as] those trail outfits didn't have too much beef because they were not on their home range and didn't have anything fit to kill for beef while other outfits managed to have beef some way.[80]

A trail boss was expected to end his drive with as many head as he started with, or as near that number as possible. Therefore, the only animals that it was permissible to butcher were strays that were far from their home range and which, naturally, did not come out of the trail herd.

Although the number and variety of cooking utensils was limited, many cooks made up what they lacked in equipment by the use of their ingenuity. Pies, with the crusts ornamented with the outfit's brand, were cooked in Dutch ovens. So was gingerbread, and ginger cakes with raisins in them. Hot rolls with brown sugar and cinnamon sprinkled on top provided a special treat. Some desserts had characteristic names all of their own. Rice and raisins cooked together was called "spotted pup." A pudding in a sack, cooked by steaming in a big kettle so that it was moist but not soggy, was known far and wide as "son-of-a-bitch-in-a-sack" and, served with hot fruit sauce, was another favorite dessert. And any food that had the quivering qualities of jelly was sometimes known as "shivering Liz."

79. "Killing a Beef on the Roundup [1897?]."

Butchering on the roundup, as the long shadows in Huffman's photograph clearly indicates, was usually done near sundown. The animal, usually a yearling or a two-year-old, would be shot or knocked on the head, on a clean, open spot. Then it would be butchered on its hide and the carcass split or quartered with an ax. The meat would then be hung from the branch of a tree to cool out. If no tree was available, the brake lever of the wagon and the camp pole were used. The latter was a stout tent pole that was kept in the chuck wagon and on such occasions leaned over one side of the wagon box with the bottom end secured in the corner on the opposite side.

In the morning the meat was cooled and ready to use—no aging for two weeks or more at controlled temperature and humidity, now considered desirable for good flavor! The carcass would be taken down in the morning, rolled in a heavy canvas, and stored in the chuck wagon. There it would be kept, protected from the hot air of the day and any rain which might fall. Strange as it may seem, meat so handled did not spoil, and with a hard-working crew of meat-eaters to feed, a beef did not last long. Some roundup crews were a bit fastidious in their tastes. Steaks and rib roasts were preferred and, if there happened to be a settler nearby, the less desirable part of the forequarters were often traded for vegetables and eggs.

Sometimes humorous incidents occurred. Although liquor was strictly forbidden on the roundup, now and then a bottle was smuggled in. The story is told that one cowboy, on hearing shooting in the vicinity of the

chuck wagon, rode into camp to see what was happening. The cook—
"Nigger Bob" Levitt, the Negro-hating Southerner previously noted—was
stirring navy beans in a pot with the barrel of his Colt, and then expelling
those beans that adhered to the inside of the barrel by shooting at a nearby
rock. When the cowboy inquired regarding this strange procedure, Levitt
informed him that he was testing the beans to find out when they were
soft enough to eat!

Part IV: The Day's Work

In the days of the open range the cowboy's calendar was quite simple.
In the early spring when the cattle were weak from the winter and the
cows heavy with calf, riders had the unpleasant task of riding the range.
Here the work involved pulling bogged animals out of mudholes, and
rendering such veterinary aid as the means at hand permitted. There were
also preparations to be made for the spring roundup. The major part of
these activities centered around the *remuda*—the horses had to be gathered,
sometimes new ones had to be broken, there were tails to be pulled, and
hoofs to be trimmed and sometimes shod. As the time approached, the
chuck wagon was pulled out and readied. Wheels were greased, any mice
nests cleared out of the little cupboard, and the supplies were double-
sacked and prepared for the jolting they would receive.

The spring or general roundup got under way in May after the details
had been arranged at the spring meeting of the stockgrowers at Miles City.
This continued until the range had been combed and the spring calf crop,
plus any mavericks found, had been branded. This task completed, each
rancher turned his attention to a miscellaneous assortment of jobs ranging
from haymaking and fence-building to breaking horses. Sometimes these
were done by labor hired especially for that particular job. In the early
fall the beef roundup got under way. This one gathered the stock that
was to be sold; and when this herd had been trailed to market, the major
part of the season's work was over.

Not all the cowboys would return to the ranch after the cattle were
shipped. There was little work in the winter, and no rancher could afford
to pay for the privilege of feeding idle hands. So the extra help was paid
off and these turned their attention to other tasks such as odd jobs around
the saloons and livery stables, trapping and wolfing, mining, and *riding
the chuck line.* The latter activity consisted of drifting from ranch to ranch,
moving on each time before the welcome wore too thin. But regardless of
what occupied their time during the winter months, when spring came
they were ready to ride again. Of course, not infrequently, they might
have to bail saddles and personal gear out of some pawnshop before they
could really go to work.

Each ranch retained some help for the winter work. Some of these
were stationed, two men to a cabin, in line camps at the edges of the outfit's

range to turn back any cattle that drifted in the winter storms. Others rode the ranges watching the stock, directing the use of snowplows to uncover feed, and sometimes bringing in weak cattle to be fed from the usually meager supply of hay. Perhaps it should be noted also that this was the season of the year when the cowboy was supposed to catch up on his lost sleep.

Although there were other severe winters, no mention of winter work can omit noting that of 1886-1887. There were several causes for the disaster of that winter. The ranges were overstocked; and although the old-timers argued the fact at length in the 1886 meeting of the Montana Stockgrowers Association, the Southern cattlemen and the newcomers refused to see the potential possibilities. Rainfall was slight in the late spring, and the springs, water holes, and little streams on the divides dried up, thus forcing the cattle into the valleys of the larger streams where there was flowing water. More cattle poured onto the ranges during the summer, and prairie fires made inroads into the already meager supply of pasturage.

Fall brought ominous omens—heavier coats of fur than usual on the animals, earlier migration of the birds to the southward, and at last the white owls of the arctic. Indians and trappers, wise to the ways of the wild, shook their heads. The top of the first snow melted slightly and then froze, preventing stock from feeding on the covered grass. The middle of December brought a blizzard that lasted three days. Then the weather cleared until January 9, when the knockout punch started. Granville Stuart wrote in his journal:

> On that day a cold wind blew from the north. It began to snow and snowed steadily for sixteen hours, in which sixteen inches of snow fell on a level. The thermometer dropped to twenty-two degrees below zero, then twenty-seven degrees, then thirty degrees, and on the night of January 15 stood at forty-six degrees below zero. . . . This storm lasted ten days without abating.[81]

The young and the unacclimated stock went first. Native cattle made some attempt to shift for themselves, but there was nothing to eat except the tips of sagebrush sticking out of the snow and the bark from willows and the small branches of trees. One rancher noted that he saw woody pieces up to the diameter of a lead pencil in the manure. In some cases, all the way from Helena to Medora, cattle came into the towns searching for something to eat and some of these even ate tarred paper from the walls of shacks. One official of a Miles City bank wrote: "The willows along Powder River, Rosebud and the Big Horn were the graveyards of seventy percent of the cattle in eastern Montana. Any old dugout or log shack that was open was the grave of all the starved cattle it could hold."[82] Other cattle huddled wherever they could find a bit of protection from the wind and slowly dropped one by one, to be covered by the drifting snow. The only animals to live comfortably were the wolves and coyotes.

Of the DHS range where the cattle were seasoned and the riders did their best to bring the cattle through, Stuart wrote:

80.   Eight of the winter's toll.

It was impossible to tell just what the losses were for a long time as the cattle had drifted so badly in the big January storm.[83] We did not get some of ours back for a year. Our entire losses for the year were sixty-six per cent of the herd. In the fall of 1886 there were more than a million head of cattle on the Montana ranges and the losses in the "big storm" amounted to twenty million dollars.[84]

Stuart noted also that, "Herds driven up from the south and placed on the range late in the summer, perished outright. Others lost from seventy-five to eighty per cent of their cattle." However the storm was a godsend to many ranch managers who had underreported their losses to the owners in previous years. "It is told of one truthful manager in an adjoining county," wrote a reporter in *The Yellowstone Journal,* "that he reported a loss of 125 per cent, '50 per cent steers and 75 per cent cows.' "[85] The survivors were weak and poor and many of these mired in mudholes and were lost even after the coming of spring. The only ones to come through with moderate losses were the little ranchers who had some hay to feed, thus setting the pattern for successful ranching operations in the future.

When the snow melted, thousands of carcasses bobbed along with the cakes of ice on the foaming flood waters of the streams—a grim procession that continued for days. One cowboy in the Little Missouri country remembered in later years that it was only necessary to stand on the river bank for a few minutes and watch the never-ending stream of dead bodies to realize in full the depth of the tragedy the past few months had brought.[86]

Any letters Huffman may have written to his father about the blizzards of this winter have been lost. His letter of December 22 is concerned with William T. Hornaday's visit and the buffalo that the latter had just collected for the National Museum. The next letter dated June 28, 1887, contains some comments on range conditions and the effects of the winter on the finances of Custer County. As one of the county commissioners his concern is easily understandable. He wrote:

> . . . We have had but one light rain since last of May and do not expect any more.
>
> Ranchmen who were so encouraged with the outlook a month ago are now witnessing the same old process of kiln drying and are correspondingly gloomy. . . .
>
> Things in general are at a complete standstill—we are now on the eve of an entire change of methods of conducting the great industry of this country and the sudden change has and is financially annihilating our solidest men.
>
> We have a county debt of nearly $300,000 drawing 7% considered only a Vajatle [sic] when our annual assessment was 5 to 7 millions and growing fast but at one hard sweep it has fallen to less than 3,000,000   It makes a fellow do some hard thinking to know how to make $50,000 pay when it took $110,000 to pay last year. Theres no use to kick   we all get our share of these things if we live long enough—Our ranges are better than since 80 and we will not have to send our money all out of the country for baled hay next winter.   the crop promises to supply home needs.
>
> I hope that you will not think that I have grown indifferent that I do not write oftenr or at more length   I find little time and dislike to write unless upon pleasant themes

In another letter dated September 25, 1887, he returned briefly to the subject again:

> My time has been so much taken up of late viewing Roads and Bridges throught the Co and sitting on boards of equalization I have found little time for my own affairs.
>
> . . .   .
>
> Our assessor—with the aid of two wooden headed commissioners rounds up $4,600,000 worth of taxable wealth if 5,000,000 worth did die last winter Our county was never before closely assessed—

Thus the winter of 1886-1887 passed into history.[87] Some ranchers were forced to take their losses and quit. Others, with an eye to the future, pulled their belts a notch tighter and dug in for another start. But to the hired man on horseback, it was not a winter associated with red figures on the account ledger. His memories were of riding all day—without any dinner—in snowstorms and cold that was thirty and forty degrees below zero, *cows* that were nothing but ambling skeletons held together by tightly stretched hides, and of little snow-covered mounds.

81. "Putting on a Hackamore."

There is a range saying that "There ain't no hoss that can't be rode, an' there ain't no man that can't be throwed." Perhaps it is this uncertainty, along with the violent action, that has made horse breaking the fascinating activity that it was—and still is. Each cowboy took pride in being able to top all the horses in his string, but this pride did not necessarily extend to being able to master unbroken animals. This job was usually left to a professional bronc buster and, in the ranch calendar, such activities often came either before or just after the spring roundup.

Busters used various methods of breaking horses. Some were able to gentle a horse by working with him easily and slowly. A few were apparently able to exert a strange quieting influence on a horse; Indians, in particular were able to break horses so that they were not likely to buck—or even try to buck.[88] But professional riders who made a living by breaking animals at so much a head merely cinched a good saddle tight, climbed on, and stayed on top by sheer strength and ability.

Of these individuals who apparently exerted a strange quieting influence over a horse, Huffman sometimes related a story told him by an old trail boss. The central figure in the story was Stutterin' Bob who, after shooting up a dive in Cheyenne, had gone on the dodge and lived for a time with a band of Crees and breeds. When he could no longer stand the life in an Indian tepee, he stole a horse from the Indians and drifted southward where, on the Powder, he encountered old Twodot Satchel and two herds of Swinging A cattle. The drifting cowboy asked the trail boss for a job. The latter, having a strong dislike for squaw men, breeds, and Indians and catching a whiff of "tepee smell" on the cowboy's clothes, pretended to offer him a job and a couple of "gentle" horses from his own string. These "gentle" horses were outlaws that the boss kept for unsuspecting riders. Twodot's successor, a cowboy named Andy, related the events that followed:

Next thing we see is this wild man leadin' old Zebra out of the bunch with this hackamore of his. Now, Zebra, he's one of these splay-footed, old hellyans that'll stand kinder spraddled, thoughtful, and meek-like for saddlin', never making a flounce until his man starts swingin' up; then of a sudden he breaks out er-rocketin', hoggin', sun-fishin', and plowin' up the yarth for about seven jumps, when he changes ends, caterpillers, goin' over back quicker'n lightnin'. The way the outfit begins to line up watchin' him cinch that old center-fire tree on old Zebra confirms his suspicions. He gives Twodot a savage look like a trapped wolf, tucks the loose coil of that hackamore rope into his belt, and just *walks* onto that hoss; never tries to find the off-stirrup, but stands high in the right [left?] one, a-rakin' old Zeeb up and down, and reachin' for the root of his tail, and jabbin' him with his heel every jump until he goes to the earth, feet upwards like a bear fightin' bees. Old Bob ain't under there to get pinched none, though, not on your type; he's just calmly puttin' a pair of rawhide hobbles on these front feet and a-wroppin' old Zeeb's head in that rag of a coat of his'n, that seems like he shucks before he hits the ground. I'll never tell a man what that long-legged, stutterin' maverick does to a bronc. Zebra ain't the last horse, though, that I see him mesmerize, ontil they'd foller him around crow-hoppin' in the hobbles like a trick mewl in a circus. Less time than I'm tellin' you, he has them hobbles off again, and is ridin' old Zebra round as quiet as a night hoss.
    The laugh is on old Twodot; and he's that ringey he breaks out intimatin' Bob of some dirty breed work, like slippin' a handful of gravel or a string of buckshot into old Zeeb's ear, and a chow-ow-in' that he never *did* see no squaw-herdin'—— that rides fair. At that Bob climbs down, sayin' quiet like, "Eat that Injun part and that name or I'll ride you." Old Satchel goes after his gun, but Bob is too quick. He has him plugged through the wrist, and sends another barkin' his scalp that downs him like a beef before he ever gets into action. That's how I got *my* start in life, runnin the old A outfit.[89]

However, such handling as this was the exception rather than the rule and, generally, horse breaking, like prizefighting, required that the rider accept a large amount of bodily punishment. Huffman, in writing of this activity, noted that

"Weak head and strong back for a horse fighter" is an old and common saying; and likewise it had not infrequently chanced in the old days that the gentlemen could, with certainty, almost unerringly, at any time or place, be spotted by his swagger, his unfailing weakness for wearing heavy bear-skin or llama leggins, even in the hottest weather, and his spurs.[90]

Not all were of the swaggering type, however. Although nothing is now remembered about Andy Spellman, whom Huffman photographed saddling a big white horse, he at least lacks the hairy chaps of a swaggering

82. "Saddling the Wild Horse, 1894. Andy Speelman, Ekalaka, [Montana]."

professional. That he was a good rider appeared obvious to one rancher who, after looking at the photograph, observed, "A man who could take a big horse like that outside of the corral, saddle him, and ride him without assistance was a sure-enough rider." Nor did all bronc snappers follow this work exclusively. Looking back forty or fifty years, Lee Warren—whom Huffman photographed breaking horses—wrote: "I did every kind of work for those big outfits. Was common cowboy, straw boss, horse wrangler, rode the rough string, broke broncks, nite hawked. Was considered a good hand, and a good rider."[91] Judging by Huffman's picture of the man, and the recollections of another for whom he worked, Warren was a top hand and a fine rider. He was also a modest man, and the woman he married made him quit snapping broncs before he became all stove up.

On July 19, 1904, while Huffman was with the camp of a roundup crew along the Big Dry, Sandy B, a rep from the Bow and Arrow—or Bow Gun as Huffman called it—stopped overnight on his way back to the ranch. He had been "moonshinin'[92] the breaks below Hell and Crooked Creek, with a bunch of breeds from Poplar River way for ten days." As the rep left he told Huffman that his outfit planned to break a bunch of horses soon, and invited him to "come out and see a touch of high life and bring your snappin' machine." That Huffman did.

83.   "Lee Warren [right] the Buster, and his 'hazer,' Sept 1904."

. . . so it fell out that one raw windy September evening I pulled up at the Bow-Gun, one of the old-time cow camps of the north country, built nearly twenty-five years back, and now sadly fallen to dilapidation and decay.

Foreman Bob made me welcome. He and his crew were enjoying a rest between the general and the beef round-up, and lending a hand with the broncs. The old place seemed deserted until the cook, a tall, bony, four-eyed[93] rooster, let out a yell that searched the crannies of the old place and echoed back from the buttes, "It's a-l-lright with m-e-e!" The cry brought foregathering from the one-time "buckaroo" house and sundry tepees pitched beside the dry washout, the hungry crew of the Bow-Gun, fifteen strong, to file by the lay-out box, where each man supplied himself with an outfit—plate, cup, knife and fork—and straightway to load the same with ribs of beef, pot-roasted, hot biscuits, stewed corn, and the ever present "Blue Hen" tomatoes, and to top it, a portion from the Dutch oven, of pudding with rasins galore, and sauce too *à la* Vanilla magoo, and strong black coffee, of course.

As Foreman Bob and I supped elbow to elbow in the firelight, listening to the chaff of the crew, I asked him which was Lee Warren, who was to begin on the following morning to ride the wild Bow-Gun horses at the rate of six or eight a day. Pointed out, he proved to be about the least conspicuous, least loquacious man of the bunch. Short to stubbiness, and dressed like a farm-hand; declining the proffered weed with thanks, saying he'd never learned to smoke.

Supper over, we gathered in the bunkhouse for a memorable evening of

84. "The Bow Gun ranch on South Sunday Creek near Miles City, Sept 1904."

85. "[The] flying noose . . . falls true."

songs and stories. No herd to hold, no guards to stand, so no one seemed in haste to seek his blankets. The four-eyed one, too, joined us when his work was done for the night; and there was a man with a voice and a laugh—such a voice and contagious laugh you never could forget, once you'd heard it. A man could top my string of the best nag in it if I could fetch a laugh like that. And the one story—I'm sorry it's unprintable—that old four-eyes springs on us put's it out of everybody's reach for that session. So we unrolled our beds and turned in.

. . .   .

In the cold grayness the wrangler tiptoed in among the silent sleepers, wakened the cook, mounted old "Specks," the gray horse, and was off to round-up his night grazing band.

Then the voice, clear as a bugle: "R-o-l-l o-u-t, R-o-l-l o-u-t, while she's hot." It was steak, stacks of griddle-cakes, and coffee; after which Foreman Bob, addressing Warren, said: "Lee, tell Lem [Lem was the horse wrangler] how many you want, and the boys will run them in for you when you're ready." Warren "reckoned" six would do to sample them at the jump-off. . . .

While we waited for the horses, Warren took stock of his outfit. Just a plain, ordinary, single-rigged cow-saddle, bridle, and lariat, spurs, quirt, and some short pieces of grass rope for the cross-hobbling. Presently the voice, its owner elbow-deep in his bread pan, announced, "Hy-ar they come a f-o-g-g-i-n'."

Swiftly across the wide flat, flanked by a half a dozen well-mounted riders, the little band swings in a wide circle, leaving adrift behind it a long ribbon of dust. The big gate is flung open, and the day's work is corralled. An inner gate swings, another swift rush and the six beautiful beasts are bunched, snort-ing and trembling, in the round corral. . . .

Warren, as he looks them over with critical eye, uncoils the rawhide, adjusts the hondo and loop. At his first step of approach they break away. Round and round they circle, in vain effort to dodge that flying noose, which, at the second cast, falls true, and the bright bay leader of the bunch, Oscar Wilde (a name that Warren flung to him with the first throw that he so neatly dodged, and Oscar he will be to the end of his days in the Bow-Gun saddle bunch) is in the toils, leaping, bucking, striking savagely at the thing that grips him by the throat, now held taut by Lee and his two helpers, who, when his first desperate lunges are past, take a turn of the rope round the snubbing-post set deep in the earth.

86. "The First Pull at Latigo."

"Easy, easy now! Snub him too sudden and he kinks her [his neck]. Steady now!" He is facing the post, feet braced and wide apart, straining at the rope until in his final, blind struggle for breath, he throws himself. Quick as a flash, Warren has his knee on Oscar's neck, grips him by the underjaw, tilts his head so that his nose points skyward. Instantly the turn is thrown from the post. The noose slackens, is slipped off, passed bridle-wise over his ears and, by a dexterous and simple turn made fast curbwise to his underjaw.

For a full half-minute Oscar has found that dust-laden air so good that he has relaxed, forgotten to fight. Deftly and quickly, Warren hobbles his front feet together and slips on the bridle. Oscar bounds to his feet, but quickly finds that his struggles to free himself only result in a succession of falls that cause him to hesitate, until, in some mysterious way, he finds his near hind foot too, caught in a noose and made fast to his near front one. He's cross-hobbled now and ready for the saddle.

Here the skill and patience of the broncho rider are put to a severe test. He must hold his horse by the reins and rope, lay the saddle blanket, then with a one-hand swing place that forty-pound saddle where it belongs. Dazed, cross-hobbled as he is, the horse resents the blanket to the twentieth time, often, and may frustrate as many attempts to reach with the latigo strap that swinging cinch ring, and often he will slip from under the saddle a good many times before it is caught and the first hard pull cinches the saddle firmly in place.

Oscar has been in the toils fifteen minutes—no doubt it's seemed longer to him. His hobbles are now being removed—often quite as exciting a task as putting them on. They are off, those hobbles, but Oscar does not know it. His attention is distracted by a pain in his ear. Lee has it twisted firmly, gripped in his strong left hand. Strange, but true, nine times out of ten, the wildest

87. "Broncho cross hobbled and saddled."

outlaw will stand motionless for a minute or more if you get just the right twist on his ear.

Cautiously, tensely, without the shadow of hesitation, Warren swings lightly to his seat. The critical moment has come. For five breathless seconds after that ear is released Oscar stands frozen, wide-eyed, nostrils distended, muscles strained until under the rear of that saddle-skirt there's room for your hat 'twixt it and his back.

In response to the first pull at the rein, by one or two quick, short, nervous steps he discovers that his legs are once more unshackled. Up he goes in a long, curving leap like a buck. Down goes his head, and he blats that indescribable bawl that only thoroughly maddened, terrified bronchos can fetch, something uncanny, something between a scream and a groan, that rasps the nerves and starts the chill, hunted feeling working on your spine.

The Voice, drawing water at the well, sends a hail: "N-o-w he t-a-k-e-s her. S-t-a-y with him, Lee. S-t-a-y with him," as round and round he leaps, reined hard, now right, now left, by his rider. Again and again he goes high, with hind feet drawn under, as if reaching for the stirrups. Fore-legs thrust forward, stiff as crowbars, driving hoofprints in the packed earth, like mauls, as he lands; yet light and tight, seeming never to catch the brunt of the jolt, sits his rider.

Now the little horse begins to sulk, backs suddenly, and rears high, as if to throw himself backward. If he should succeed, should he rid himself in that way, of his rider, he would surely try it again. His first lesson might end in failure, and he'd have made a good start toward becoming Oscar the outlaw.

But Lee has another card looped to his wrist, one that he is loath to use, that stinging rawhide quirt, which now decends fore and aft, round his ears, and raising welts on his quivering flanks at each stroke. Oscar is quickly dis-

88. "His attention is distracted by a pain in his ear."

tracted from rearing and backing. Again he sulks, refuses to respond to word, rein, or quirt.

Now for the first time it's the steel—the spurs—and the horse chooses doing the circle, the thing of the least punishment. Oscar has been in the corral forty minutes. Sweat runs from belly and nose, and in little rivulets down his legs. Warren swings off gently, then quickly up again, mounting and dismounting rapidly half a dozen times, each time, with his gloved hand, patting the blowing horse on flank, rump, and neck.

Almost in one motion, saddle and bridle are off—flung together at the post. Oscar's first lesson is finished. The gate swings, he dashes through to the outer corral, while Foreman Bob, where we're perched on the fence, says to me: "Old Lee knows when to quit. He's careful; never baked a horse for us yet. Keeps his temper. *That's* where most of us loose out in that game. Feller we had here last summer—good rider, stout as a mule—loses his, and his job. Bakes the first one he tackles. Fights him an hour saddlin', then sifts him outside; throws him the gut-hooks and quirt until the hoss is plumb baked, overhet. Falls dead there a hundred yards from the ranch. Third time's plenty soon to ride 'em outside.

. . .   .

It is eleven o'clock now. Warren, bare-headed, shapeless, sooty as a smith with dust and sweat, is up on "Stripes," his sixth and last horse, when the Voice sings, "B-o-n-e-h-e-a-d-s, b-o-n-e-h-e-a-d-s, take it away," which announces the best meal of the day—roast beef, boiled spuds, fresh bread, cinnamon rolls, and, to trim it, quarters of thick, juicy, blackberry pie.

. . .   .

It was the third and last day of my stay at the old ranch. Warren, rising from breakfast asked—of no one in particular—"Who all is going to haze me?" Which was to say that Oscar, Flaxey, Stripes, and their fellows of that day's

89. "Broncho's first slicker lesson."

work are to-day to get their first gallop outside—with a hazer, a rider mounted on something wise to the game and swift enough of foot to stay alongside, heading them from washouts, dog-towns, and miles on miles of breaks and cut-banks, any direction from the Bow-Gun, where's such footing as one takes with caution on well-broken mounts.

Now he dispensed with hobbles and helpers, roped, bridled, and saddled the horses unaided, mounted them, circled the corral a turn or two, gave the gateman the word, and out they went like a shot, buster and hazer neck and neck, off up the flat like a whipping finish in a quarter-race. Four rides with a slicker lesson or two, and these dare-devil riders call them "plumb gentle," and each man gets his share of the new ones for immediate use in his string.

"Of course," mused Lee, as we lounged by the cook's fire that last evening; "of course, if a buster was getting fifteen bones a head instead of five, and all the time he needed, say thirty instead of five days, for a bunch like this one, horse fighting would be safer, less exciting, less picturesque, as you'd say. We would do our work, too, in a heap safer way for horses and men; but will it pay? is the question. Whether it's bustin' a bronc or a bank, bosses won't stand for a fifteen-dollar finish on a thirty-five dollar horse." [94]

This was the last string Warren snapped before he was married.

Trailing, another fascinating range activity, was of two general kinds. One of these involved the moving of stock cattle over long distances, and the other, the taking of the beef herd to market. In many ways these two activities were similar; in others they were quite different. Also, just as there was no one method of handling a trail herd, just so there were no routes that were rigidly followed to a given destination.

Cattle trails were determined, just as were other trails, by topography and sources of water. Although cattle could go where bull trains could not, trail bosses used valleys and passes in moving through mountainous country, they avoided terrain cut up by numerous canyons and coulees, and, above all, they did their best to choose a route insuring adequate water where it was needed. So, while there were a few routes that were used by most of the drivers, others worked out routes to fit their own specific needs.

Many of those who blazed their own trails were moving consignments for army posts and Indian reservations. Such a movement is chronicled in Andy Adams' piece of historical fiction, *The Log of a Cowboy*. This herd followed well-established trails from the Rio Grande to the western edge of the Black Hills, where it turned northwest across the headwaters of the Powder and the Tongue to swim the Yellowstone at Terry's Landing, and continue across country to its destination. Huffman told Neil Clark about a similar movement along the Yellowstone in—probably—1880 or 1881:

> One day several of us were setting in the Officers' Club at Fort Keogh playing a game of freeze-out with a two dollar limit, when somebody ran in with the news that an immense herd of cattle was on the trail. We all jumped for our horses: in those days any excuse was a good one if it gave us a chance to get on a horse and go somewhere. The herd, we found, belonged to John R. Tingle; he had brought it over the mountains from Virginia City, and was headed for Abraham Lincoln.
>
> John R. Tingle's cattle were about the first to come into our country in any numbers. He lost the greater part of them, because the drive was too long and hard, and the country was not well known to the trail drivers.[95] But he made the break, the time was ripe, and others speedily followed.[96]

Most of the cattle trailed into Montana arrived over one of two general routes, one from Oregon and the other from Texas and Colorado. Oregon cattle came east over the trail along the Snake River to the Continental Divide just west of the Yellowstone National Park. Here the Targhee, Raynolds, Monida, and Medicine Lodge passes provided access to the valleys of the Madison River, Ruby River, and Red Rock Creek. Many of the herds came over the Monida Pass, went down Red Rock Creek to the Bannack-Virginia City road which they then followed to Virginia City, and thence by way of the Bozeman Trail to the plains of the upper Yellowstone Valley.[97]

Cattle that came in from the south traveled a route called the Texas Trail by some, and, by others, the Northern or Montana Trail. This route varied as did its name. Early trail herds came from Dodge City to Ogallala and then on to the headwaters of the Little Powder—some of them swinging to the west, and others to the east, of the Black Hills. Later, settlers pushed the trail farther westward so that during the last of the trailing days herds came north from Amarillo, across the eastern edge of Colorado, and on to the Little Powder via Lusk, Wyoming. The last herd came up in 1896, and the trail boss had "one continual row from start to finish" with homesteaders who claimed recompense for various and assorted damages.

The route of the Texas—or Northern—Trail in Montana did not vary as did the southern portion. It came down the Little Powder and Powder to the vicinity of Powderville, then northwest across Mizpah Creek to

Pumpkin Creek, and then down this stream and the Tongue to Miles City. Herds bound for points farther to the north and west crossed the Yellowstone above Fort Keogh and traveled up Sunday Creek, across Little Dry to Big Dry, and then followed Big Dry to the divide. If going further west, the herds headed down Lodge Pole Creek to the Musselshell River, which was considered the end of the trail.[98]

A trail crew consisted of a boss, cook, horse wrangler, night-hawk, and eight or ten cowboys. The cook had a chuck wagon, and there was usually a bed wagon driven by the night-hawk—who slept when he could! Trail herds varied in composition as to the age and sex of the animals, but usually contained two thousand to twenty-five hundred cattle. A greater number was too unwieldly to handle. The hardest herds to drive were those containing cows with suckling calves—for the calves, following an inborn instinct, were continually trying to go back to the bed ground where they sucked last. Fortunately, herds with calves were not common. One old cowboy referred to trailing a herd of this kind as "the hardest cow punching I ever did."

The manner of handling a trail herd did not vary greatly from boss to boss although, of course, there were different ways of doing some things. The following is a description of the task as one old foreman saw it:

An outfit generally consists of eight cowboys, horse wrangler, night hawk, cook and the boss, which is twelve men. As a rule the boys have 9 horses in their string. One is kept for a night horse which is very gentle, *sure-footed*, and well broke to a rope to be on a picket rope at night.

As soon as it is daylight in the morning, the herd is pushed off the bedground and onto the trail. All hands go with the cattle except the cook, boss and wrangler. The boss goes ahead and finds a place to camp for noon and water. There are two on the point—one on each side—two in the swing, two in the flank and the rest at the drags. They are kept on the trail until around 9 oclock then they are thrown off to graze and take it easy on to the water hole, but they are always kept moving and in the direction they are supposed to go. One half of the boys are left with the herd, the others go to camp, and generally get an hour or two rest, some take a nap, and, when the cook has dinner, they eat, catch a fresh horse—for the horse wrangler is supposed to have the horses in the rope corral when the cook hollers "Come and get it"—and they go out and relieve the boys who are with the herd, which by that time should be on the creek or water hole. They are kept on water until about 3 PM then all hands throw them on the trail for a couple of hours. Then they are thrown off agin and grazed in near camp to the bed grounds. If they are full they dont cause much trouble at night. First guard goes on at 8 oclock and stays two hours, then the 2nd the 3rd and 4th. There are always 4 guards [shifts]. There are always two men or guard. [When they are bedded down] the cattle are bunched, but not too close, and the boys ride around them. One rider goes one way and the other the opposite. When the time is up, one goes in and wakes the other [shift]. The cook has breakfast at 4 o'clock [at which time] the night hawk has his horses in the rope corral.[99]

Bedding down was accomplished by allowing the cattle to graze onto the bed ground and, as the cattle started to lie down, riding around the

90. "Trail Herd, Powder River, 1888."

herd to prevent the others from moving farther away. Once they had settled down, the guards began their watch, which involved something more than just riding around the herd. Whether singing helped to keep the cattle quiet, or to keep any stragglers lying at the edge of the herd from being frightened as the night horse felt his way along on a dark night, or whether its principal value was to break the monotony of the work for the guard seems to be a matter of opinion. Certainly a guard had to listen to the sounds the cattle made, or did not make, to tell whether they were resting quietly—or whether the dead silence was the ominous lull that often preceded the sudden, mad rush of a stampede.

Both the presence and absence of water created problems. In watering a herd along a stream, the cattle, as they arrived, were placed on the bank on the upstream side of those that had preceded them. Thus, all were given an opportunity to drink water which had not been roiled. When a dry drive lay ahead, the herd would be pushed off water in the evening and trailed far into the night. The next day was often not too difficult—but the second day was likely to call for all the skill available. As cattle can smell water a long distance, there was no difficulty if a breeze blew in the cattle's faces from water which lay ahead, but if it blew off water at some point in the rear, there was hell to pay. Stuart observed: "I have seen a herd traveling along only a few miles from where they were going to water, when the wind would suddenly blow from a river behind them. The cattle would turn as one cow, start for that water, possibly ten miles distant, and nothing could stop them."[100]

There were various ways of getting a herd started across a stream of swimming water. One foreman wrote: "In swimming a herd across a swollen river, it is best to put them in about sunup of a morning, but not facing the sun. Throw the remuda in first. Get the horses started, have the herd there ready, and put them in right behind the remuda and they will most always follow the horses. Two men are kept on the point to keep them moving, and the men behind the pointers keep them from turning back."[101] Another old trail hand commented that a method he thought worked well was for all the hands to cut out a bunch of fifteen or twenty and push these animals across. This little band was held on the opposite bank where they were allowed to "drip and bawl." The remainder of the herd was then brought down to the bank of the stream, allowed to see the others on the opposite bank, and then fed into the stream. Another method was to cut out a few of the leaders after they had finished drinking and push them across, meanwhile feeding the rest of the herd in behind them. Still another method was to use a few work oxen, if there were any in the herd, to start the movement.

Several prerequisites were necessary to a successful crossing. The sunlight could not be reflected from the water into the animals' eyes for neither cattle, nor sheep, would swim into the sun. There should be no high waves. While waves due to wind action would not vary greatly in size, it was impossible to tell when the rippling of the sand in the bed of a swift-flowing stream might cause high waves to suddenly appear, thus

91.   "The N Bar [N̲] Crossing, Powder River, 1886."

92. Trail herd swimming the Yellowstone at the Fallon Crossing.

creating an unpredictable hazard.[102] Nor should there be a particularly swift current, or floating trees or logs that might break the stream of cattle in midstream and cause them to mill or to try to turn back.

Swimming a herd was a task no one particularly liked. It was too easy for the cattle to start to mill in midstream, thus causing both cattle and riders to be drowned. One lady who grew up near Miles City recalled that, when a girl, she watched many herds cross the Yellowstone. She wrote that on one occasion

> One herd arrived when the river was bank-full and dangerous looking. On this side near the old town the boys began to prepare for crossing. They looked like circus riders in all colors of underwear. As each man loosened his saddle cinches, a young chap who had never ridden in swimming water, tightened his—just another case of thinking the little things in life don't count. . . .
>
> The herd was crowded off the bank into the treacherous looking stream. When part way over the leaders tried to come back, forming a mill. . . . The shouting ceased; cattle, men, and horses all realized what might happen as they drifted.
>
> [One man] Bill Case seemed everywhere, he and his horse giving each other confidence as they tried to break the mill. A shout went out, "Hey, the Kid's gone down!" His plucky horse swam until the tightened cinch cut his wind off. Case managed to go where he saw him last [and] as his head appeared he shouted, "Grab a steer's tail." The silent churning animals took action. The old steer . . . made for shore.
>
> Case kept shouting, "Swim high." The boy was bouncing high when that old steer started for the big cottonwood trees, on the other side. He looked like the weight on the tail end of a kite when he landed on shore. He let loose and began climbing a tree as the herd's hoofs cracked over the stones through the trees and up the hillside. Dripping wet but happy, the kid dropped on the horse of the first rider to reach him.
>
> His saddle horse drifted, came out away down opposite . . . his ears hanging down, having filled with water when he sank, until he looked like a German dachhund. Then the tightened cinch was discovered.[103]

The kid was lucky. All too often an unhorsed rider went out of sight, his body to be found later, if at all, on a sand bar somewhere downstream.

Stampedes were both a fearsome and a fascinating phenomenon. Certainly they were dangerous, for riding a horse on a dead run in close proximity to a mass of wild cattle was bad enough in the daytime, but at night when the horse could not see his footing the rider was gambling with the grim reaper. Strangely enough, fatalities were not a common occurrence: "I've been in a lot of stampedes," observed an old foreman, "but was never hurt, or had my horse fall with me during one." Nevertheless, they could be distinctly unpleasant experiences.

Stampedes were interesting in that a herd might be grazing or lying quietly on the bed ground one moment and a split second later *every* animal might be "rolling its tail" on a dead run. The movement did not propagate like waves from the splash of a rock thrown into a pool of quiet water—the whole herd moved as a unit, and with explosive violence. Causes were legion—the sudden coming of a breeze after a dead stillness

93. Going to the Roundup.

before a storm, the crash from a bolt of lightning, the sudden light from a falling star, or some cowboy prank that created a disturbance. Illustrative of such causes are the following:

Another stampede was caused out on Fallon [Creek]. A windy evening the outfit had made a big drive, [and] cattle, men and horses were all tired. As the cook poured the pound of Arbuckle coffee into the coffee mill a breeze whipped the paper sack into the air. Away went the herd pell mell.[104]

Just as unexpected was the following incident:

We were crossing the Little Missouri once a few miles above Alzada [Montana]. . . . The steers were on water, some drinking, some laying down resting and pretty well scattered along the river. One of the steers was rubbing himself on an old post oak of which there were quite a lot along there. The top was dead and it fell off on top of him. What a stampede! They all went out of there like a flash, and got 10 miles before we could get them checked. Some of the boys on herd said they didn't know what happened, but thought the world was coming to an end. Those steers were pretty spookey after that and gave us a lot of trouble before we got them shipped from Belle Fourche.[105]

The immediate objective in handling a stampede was to keep the cattle from scattering over the countryside. Where possible, the cowboys tried to turn the leaders so that the animals would run in a circle and, eventually, "mill." And whenever it happened, day or night, all hands except the cook and the horse wrangler headed for the scene of trouble and stayed with the cattle until they were under control.

A considerable part of a cowboy's working time from snow to snow was spent with the wagon on the roundup, branding calves, gathering beef, and, in the case of the rep with distant roundups, gathering cattle that had strayed far from their owner's range. These roundups were not run in a haphazard fashion in spite of the fact that the roundup areas were bounded by rivers and divides. Areas of responsibility, the naming of roundup foremen, and other necessary details were worked out each year in the annual meeting of the Stockgrowers Association, which was held a few weeks before the spring roundup started.

In 1885 the two Montana stockgrowers associations united to form one organization. The minutes of this meeting, held in Miles City early in April, give the details worked out for the spring work of that year. After discussing three suggestions, a plan was adopted which provided for twelve districts in eastern Montana. (A year later western Dakota was included and the area reorganized into seventeen districts.) The following is the description of a district as entered in the minutes of this meeting:

ROUNDUP NO. 2. Commence at the mouth of Logging Creek on Tongue river May 13th, 1885, work up Tongue river and its tributaries to mouth of Canyon, up Hanging Woman to Grinnell's Ranch, then join the Wyoming roundup No. 17 at the [state] boundary line, at mouth of Squirrel Creek, working with them on west side of Tongue river to the mouth of Canyon; then commencing at Grinnell's Ranch work Hanging Woman Creek and up east side

94. "The SL Boys at Dinner [1897]."

95. The Pumpkin Creek Pool in the spring of 1907.

of Tongue River to boundary line, then to big bend of Rosebud, and down the same to mouth of Muddy. Foreman, James Davis.

After the arrangements had been decided upon, notices were published in the local papers. The following is an early notice which appeared in Medora's paper, *The Cow Boy*, on May 15, 1884:

> The cattlemen are all supposed to know that the roundup for this section of the Bad Lands begins May 25, at the Beaver Creek crossing of the N.P.R.R. Every stock owner will send enough cowboys to look after his interests, who will be under orders of and subject to dismissal by the foreman, John Goodall. Each cattle owner will provide a mess-wagon or make arrangements with some-one else. At least six good horses will be needed by every man. There will be day and night herding, in which each man must take a part. Branding will be done every day. Every man who wishes his cattle taken care of, must be represented on the roundup. The time taken by the roundup will be six weeks to two months and the extent of territory is about one hundred by fifty miles. In this district there are about 40,000 cattle.

The size of roundup outfits varied, and Huffman's photographs are deceptive in that only the herds being worked give an approximate picture of the true size of the operation. One rancher, included in the photograph "SL Boys at Dinner, 1897," noted that when this roundup started from Powderville there were eleven *wagons* and about one hundred forty men. "Eleven wagons" refers, of course, to chuck wagons—a bed wagon to carry all the bedrolls except the cook's, extra coats and slickers, corral ropes, stake ropes for night horses, etc., being part of the unit represented by the chuck wagon. As this group began to work their district, the wagons began to drop off until at one time all that remained of the group which started were three wagons. As the wagons camped at intervals of three quarters of a mile or more apart, the photograph of a single wagon may show but a fraction of the picture of that immediate area. Although the photograph noted shows only fifteen men, exclusive of the cook, it was not uncommon to have thirty to fifty men eating at one wagon.

The manner in which a roundup outfit did its work was quite simple. One rancher, writing of the heyday of the open range, stated that

> In the old days on the roundups each outfit had its own mess wagon with from 30 to 50 men[106] each man rode from 7 to 11 horses, part circle horses, part cutting horses and a night horse. we had breakfast at 3:30 A M our horses saddled and on the circle at 4 A M. some [circles] were 15 M[iles] some 40 M. you would roundup from 3,000 to 10,000 on each ride. you had dinner when the last man was in, sometimes 9 A M sometimes 4 P M, then changed horses and worked the herd, cut out the beef and cattle that had drifted from their home range and kept them under herd until you reached their home range where they were turned loose. you also branded all calves in the same brand their mother carried. it made no difference whether the owner had a repre-sentative there or not.
> supper was at 6 P M. Then you saddled your night horse, went to the herd you were holding, and relieved the herders. They were through for the day. you got the herd bedded down at 8 P M., left two men to guard them, and

96. "After the Rain in the Rope Corral [*circa* 1897]."

went to bed. the guard was changed every two hours so sometime during the night your sleep was broken and you smoked cigarettes and sung to the cattle for a couple of hours. this was the procedure followed every day and Sunday too. it was never too hot or too cold, rain or snow, to interfere with the work.[107]

While this old-timer's description gives an accurate outline of the work, there are many small details that need to be added to sketch a picture comparable to Huffman's photographs. For the cook the day began in the chill air before the gray light of dawn, when he started breakfast for the crew rolled up nearby in their sougans and blankets inside a heavy bed tarp. Usually, his call to breakfast was an unwelcome intrusion on their dreams— for a cowboy's hours of sleep were few at the best—but occasionally, as after spending a night shivering in bedding soaked by cold rain water that had seeped in from puddles on the ground, the "sleepers" welcomed an excuse to get up. In the fall there would be frost on the tarps and often it was desirable to warm the tin plates before dishing out one's breakfast.

While breakfast was being eaten—and the cowboy never dallied over his food when there was work to do, for it was a disgrace to always be the last one ready to go—the night-hawk brought in the *remuda* and put it in the rope corral adjacent to the nearby bed wagon. As soon as the cowboy

97. "Roundup Outfit Breaking Camp."

98. "Roundup Outfit on the Move, 4:30 A.M."

dropped his tin plate, cup, and utensils into the big kettle of hot water that served for a dishpan, he went immediately to the rope corral and roped and saddled one of his circle horses. When all were ready, the circle leader, who might or might not be the roundup foreman, would ride out with the hands and drop them off at designated spots to comb the next part of the range and to drive their findings to the next designated roundup spot.

In the event the camp moved—and it usually did—all hands took part in breaking camp. The work horses were harnessed, the mess tent—if one had been put up—was taken down, the chuck wagon was packed, the bed wagon was loaded, and everything readied for the cook to hitch his four-horse team to the chuck wagon, the night-hawk to hook a team to the bed wagon and move out when the circle riders left. As this part of the outfit rolled, the pilot—a rider who knew the country round about—led out, followed by the chuck wagon and the wagon with the bedrolls, with the *remuda*, now under the care of the horse wrangler, bringing up the rear. As soon as the new roundup ground was reached, the cook immediately began his preparations for the midday meal; the night-hawk—relieved of his duties at last—rolled out his bed and prepared to get his daily quota of sleep; and the horse wrangler stretched his ropes for the corral.

There was quite a knack in setting up the ropes for this corral. The rear side of the corral was anchored to a wheel of the bed wagon by slipping a loop between the spokes from the inside out and then down around the hub, the sides were supported by forked sticks so that the rope was held about three feet off the ground, and the ends of the rope were anchored by short stakes. The gate was an opening about thirty feet wide which the horse wrangler opened and closed by means of a loose end of rope. Strange as it may seem, it was very seldom that a horse made a break over this low,

WITH COATS OF ARMS ON RAWHIDE 177

100. "Telling Off Men for the Circle."

flimsy barrier, though care was taken not to make the corral large enough to permit much movement of the *remuda.*

Scattering the riders, as the circle for gathering the herd for the afternoon's work was often called, followed a fairly definite pattern. The circle leader would usually lead out at a trot until the riders got the "kinks" out of the backs of any snaky horses, and then he would change to a lope. In working the area the most practical subdivisions to use were those represented by the various parts of the drainage system. Thus the drive would usually encompass the watershed of a particular creek, with riders being dropped off around its outer edge to comb each of the smaller laterals down toward the main channel. Sometimes the party would stay more or less intact until the head of the divide was reached. At this point it was common practice for the circle leader to stop and allow the men time for a smoke, to straighten up their saddle blankets, and get set for the drive.

Often the roundup boss allowed each rancher to lead the circle on that part of the range with which he was most familiar. There was one tall, lean Texan, the foreman for an English outfit in the valley of the Tongue, who was obnoxious because of the fact that he rode a string of fine horses numbering double the usual number. As usually happened when cowboys were imposed upon and mistreated, the riders on one roundup laid plans to humble this particular individual. The story of this ususual incident is best told in the words of "the Kid" who, on a horse named Gray Eagle, turned the trick.

Sam B——— was foreman for the ——— Creek roundup. he rode twenty one highly bred horses. besides his own men there were about thirty reps from other outfits working with him and it was his delight to see how many men he could set afoot. on leading circle he would leave camp on the run and it would only take five or six miles until he had winded the cold blooded horses the Reps were riding. (I might say here that the difference in a hot blooded horse and a cold blooded horse Is that the hot blooded horse will never quit. if urged he will give to his last breath. The cold blooded horse when winded will quit and when he gets his wind will go again) if you rode up along side of him and he thot you were riding a good horse he took no chances he would turn you off down the first creek. There was a Kid who was repping for another outfit that rode eleven horses in his string, and believe me they were all you could ask for in a cold blooded horse that is if you could keep right side up when you forked one of them.

One night some of the boys said Kid you are a light rider and you ride good horses. tomorrow we have a long circle to make. you ride your best horse and see if you can go all the way around with Sam. when Sam saw the Kid was going to keep up with him he turned him off down the creek. the Kid said Sam I want to go all the way around with you I want to take it out of this horse. Sam waved his hat for a man to go down that creek hit his horse and said come on and we will see if you can go the route. he never slackened his pace down hill and up. the Kid would lay off the pace down and up hill so his horse could catch his wind. Sam would think he had him but when they would hit the level the Kid would lead him and make him set a faster pace. the other men were left entirely and it was a race unto death. when they had gone thirty some miles Sams horse suddenly dropped dead. Sam broke down and cried as

101.   "Throwing Rangers to the Roundup."

102. "Branding Calves in a Corral."

this was his top horse and his pet. he said to go to camp and bring me a fresh horse. the Kid said it serves you right. pick up your saddle and walk. you will be here until hell freezes over before I will bring you a horse. when the Kid got to camp they all said where is Sam? he said he is about ten miles out sitting on a dead horse bawling like a calf. they said are you going to take him a horse? he said I should say not. but one of his men did.

Sometime in the late forenoon or early afternoon the cowboys began drifting in to the new roundup ground with the bunches of cattle gathered on their part of the circle ride. A new herd of cattle began to grow for the cutting and branding activities, one of the most colorful of all range operations. In later years, where timber was available, corrals were sometimes built at convenient intervals along the streams and, after each outfit had cut its cattle, the branding was done in these enclosures. At other times and places all the work was done in the open, and it was this sort of operation that provided Huffman with subject material for some of his most interesting photographs. Likewise it provided certain horses and their riders an opportunity to take the spotlight in the center of the stage, for the star actor of the entire ranch cast was the cutting horse.

After a substantial—but quickly eaten—dinner, each rider caught a fresh horse, the cutting horse of their string if their duties so demanded, from the *remuda* the horse wrangler had driven into the rope corral. Then the labor began. Representatives of the various outfits rode into the herd and cut from it, usually one at a time, those animals bearing the brand or

103.   Noon at a roundup camp.

brands with which they were concerned. Calves were roped and dragged
to the branding fire, their identity usually being established by the markings
of the anxious mother following close behind. However, she was not
allowed to approach the branding fire too closely lest she make trouble—
all that was necessary was that she be identified. If there were only a few
stray cows and calves in the roundup herd, these calves were branded first
before there was an opportunity for them to become separated from their
mothers. A little care on such details often prevented mistakes in branding
occasioned by the milling resulting from working the herd.

Several of the fine points in the technique of handling calves are
illustrated in these photographs but, like many other things, may easily be
missed by those not familiar with the work. In those pictures taken in a
corral it will be noted that the calf was heeled, or caught by the hind legs.
Although another photograph taken in the open shows the same procedure,
the accepted manner of roping in the open was around the neck for this
provided the smallest chance of injury to the animal.[108] When the calf was
brought to the fire, the *calf wrastlers*, working in pairs, took over.

A calf roped by the neck might be thrown in one of three ways. If the
wrastler reached over the animal's back, grabbed the opposite front leg and
the flank, and flopped the animal on its side, the procedure was called
flanking. Another method was to trip the calf by reaching under, grasping
the opposite front leg, and pulling this member toward the wrastler. In the
third method the animal was tripped by "running it over the rope." When

104. "At Rest."

105. "Branding Fire. Waiting for the irons to heat."

106. "Waiting for the Next Calf: Big Dry, 1904."

107.   "Bringing a Calf to the Branding 'Fiah.'"

108. A heeled calf about to be thrown.

working with calves that had been heeled, one wrastler would grab the rope about three or four feet from the calf, and a second man, working on the opposite side of the rope, would grab the calf's tail. Then—without a word being spoken—both would give the calf a jerk, flopping it on its side. The man with the tail hold would drop quickly on the animal's neck and it would be stretched out as described in the following paragraph.

Once the calf was flat and the lariat thrown off, one wrastler seated himself on the animal's neck while the other, sitting on the ground behind the calf, hooked the heel of one boot over the hock of the lower leg and pushed it forward and, using both hands, pulled the top leg as far to the rear as possible. This stretched the skin smooth for the application of the hot iron, and eliminated the possibility of trouble from flying feet when a bull calf was being castrated. The hot iron was applied just *so*—it had to leave a clean-cut imprint, burned neither too shallow nor too deep.

In addition to the brand, the calf usually lost part of one or both ears in cuts of certain shapes and location. Earmarking provided a quick, easily recognizable means of identification for riders on the range; and sometimes

109. Branding a calf.

characteristic cuts were also made in the dewlap. Standing by while all this was happening, was the tally man who, with a pencil and little book, recorded the number of calves of the various brands that were marked. And if, perchance, the calf was branded with the wrong brand, this man would direct that the next calf of the owner who profited by the mistake be "traded" for the one wrongly branded. Total counts were generally kept by tossing the end of the scrotum of castrated bull calves into a pile, and putting a part of the ear of heifer calves in another. A count of these piles at the end of the day gave an accurate total of the day's work.

Branding and earmarking gave rise to a vernacular perculiar to the range. If the end of the ear was cut off, it was said to be cropped. If a piece was cut out on top, it was an overbit; and if cut from the bottom side it was underbit; or the end might be split, sloped, or shaped in some other recognized variation, all of which had their descriptive names. Any animal with untrimmed ears was known as a slick ear, a term synonymous with maverick.

All brands, except those that represented a design of some kind, were made up of combinations of letters, figures, short dashes or *bars*, circles, and fractions of circles. Such brands are quite easy to read as the universal procedure is to read from the top down, left to right, left to right and down, and from the outside in. Figures or letters lying on their side are said to be lazy, if cocked at an angle are said to be tumbling, if joined to one another are sometimes said to be connected, and if anything that resembled wings stuck out on either side the symbol is said to be flying. Thus Pierre Wibaux's W̲ was called the W Bar; Davis, Hauser and Stuart's D-S was the DHS; 7⌣ was the Seventy-one Quarter Circle; Huffman and Lamphere's Hh was the H Lazy L, sometimes called the H Half H or H 7 connected. Ҏ of the Judith Mercantile & Cattle Company was the P Lazy N; ꟻF was read FUF; the Ǝ2 of Concord Cattle Company was the reverse E Two or sometimes just E Two; ⌣ was read JA, as "A's" were often made without a crossbar; and of course Ⓐ was Circle A. Some brands spelled names as D♡ which identified cattle of the De Hart Land & Cattle Company, and Sack Brothers SₓS . Others were not so easy to identify. The Northern Pacific Refrigerator Company—Marquis de Mores' firm— used the Y Cross Ψ ; ⊥ was the famous Hashknife of Arizona, Montana, and Dakota fame; ⅄ was read Bug; ⊂⊃ was Milliron, and Roosevelt ran the Maltese Cross ✠ and the Elkhorn, ⅄ .

To return to the branding fire, the cow and her calf, if far off their home range, would be thrown into a small herd held separately and called a *cut*. If a rep found only a few cattle of his brand, he threw his animals in the *stray herd* or, sometimes, with the cut of some other outfit until he had collected enough to make a trip back to his home range. Often when the herd rounded up was very large or when several wagons were working close together, the cattle would be held in several herds scattered along the valley in close proximity to each other. When this occurred, riders worked each herd in turn, cutting out their stock. When the cuts were completed,

110. "The Mill Iron Rawhide."

111. "Working a Herd Among the Buffalo Wallows."

112. "Herd Moving from Cash Creek on Powder River."

each would be "thrown back" on the owner's range at the proper time and place as the roundup crew moved across the range.

When the rep who was a long way from his home range had collected enough cattle to warrant his return, he would announce to the outfit with which he was holding his cattle, "I want to pull away from you this morning." Then he would cut out his cattle and head for home. "It was remarkable," remarked an old rancher, "how one man could handle a bunch of fifty or sixty cattle and his string of horses with his bed roll packed on one of them, though he usually tried to stay overnight at some ranch where there was a fenced pasture or a corral to hold his bunch."

Sometimes in working the herd there would be trouble with ill-tempered animals, usually called snuffers from their habit of blowing through their nostrils to express their displeasure. In the description for one of his pictures Huffman noted:

> It frequently happens on the roundup that a "snuffer" has to be tied down until the cutting out of cattle is finished. A "snuffer" may be any old Texas or native that's on the fight and will dive at to gore and overthrow any rider who tries to cut them from the herd. One charge at a rider generally gets them into trouble, and in less time that I have been telling you the circling lariat has them in its toils, one at the head, one at the heels, and they are thrown and stretched; one forefoot and one hindfoot lashed together. Their mad antics as they struggle to rise the boys call "beating their selves out flat."

On one roundup Huffman saw experienced cowboys "job" a beginner with one of these mean animals.

> It was a certain hot day in July some years ago that I chanced to be with the big Powder River Roundup. We had moved camp at 3 oclock in the morning. There were three immense herds to work and word had gone out that there would be no circle that day. Each rider was on one of his "cut horses." Great clouds of dust rose in columns that one could see ten miles away like the smoke of battle. After the first hour horses and men all looked the same color so thickly were they covered with the stifling smother of dust. As the work waxed fast and furious there were great feats of horsemanship. Sulkers had to be roped and dragged from the herd. Snuffers caught and hogtied. Brands there were to be picked[109] to determine ownership. The "Montgomery Ward" puncher was there with his new "center fire" saddle and rawhide rope. A M W puncher is a new recruit who tries to "cut her" like the real article. They come to grief mostly and seldom fool anybody but theirselves.
>
> Orl. Sayers was holding forth to a bunch of the fellows who were letting their horses blow for a spell. "There's an old Arizona Texas Rawhide that I've seen in every roundup the past eight years between Grand River and the Crow Reservation," and he pointed out a big tawney-white ox with a pair of horns that loomed up conspicuously. "If any of you children want practice [roping] fly at him. He savvys the rope all right. Old Top Segrist met him last year up on Bay Horse [Creek]. Top got insulted when old Whitey bowed to him. Top never would take anything from snuffys. He just took down his rope and sailed into him and it took two good men to help Top out of his trouble. If you cattleboys want some fun just go over to Montgomery W there and tell him to rope old Whitey that we want to examine the brand."

113. "Picking a brand to determine ownership."

Montgomery tightened up his rigging, pulled his hat string under his chin and sailed in. It was a scratch but he caught old "Mexico" off his guard landing the noose in such a way that old Whitey had it round his neck with one fore leg through it. Then for ten minutes there *was* a circus and M W's horse only escaped disembowling by lively dodging, indifferently guided by his badly rattled rider. The spectators yelled, "St-a-y with him Monte." "Good hoss." "Tear him in two." "You've got him faded." Then something happened. The latigo of Montgomery's new "center fire" saddle gave way. Its rider went one way, and the horse another. And only after the cinch rigging had burst did they lend a hand to stretch the old white "snuffer" out [and retrieve] Monte's new saddle he'd "captured" and round up the riderless horse.

After supper the night horses were staked out near the bedrolls where they would be easy to find in the dark, and the crew relaxed. In the short interval between supper and bedtime they smoked, did minor repair jobs on their clothing and equipment, and perhaps were entertained by some cowboy who, after slapping the dirt out of his mouth organ, essayed some range ballads. If the day's work had not been too strenuous, there might be a singing or storytelling session. The stories might be funny or tall yarns, or they might be reminiscences of unusual incidents that had been observed. Often the latter kind of storytelling session was touched off by some event of the day's work.

Huffman wrote in one of his diaries that while with a roundup on

114. "Evening at the Roundup: Big Pumpkin [Creek]."

July 28, 1904, there was a stampede and two cowboys ran a steer over a high cut-bank. Later he wrote of the storytelling that resulted from this incident in a short sketch which he entitled "Old Sixteen's Jump." Although his diary indicates Huffman took a bit of liberty in setting the scene, his photographs show that the story he set down was not a tall yarn.

Its when we are in camp near Hungry Creek Springs last July at the edge of the breaks of the big Missouri that I first hear of old 16 and his big jump. Also its the sixty-fourth day since the roundup starts work at Buffalo Creek over a hundred and 50 miles to the southwest as a crow flies. With the reps there must have been a hundred and 25 riders in all and say eighteen hundred saddle horses. Then theres the herd of maybee 5000 cattle and four more herds half as big being held flanking the camp for miles on all sides, a gigantic wild west show worth talking about, the likes of which you will travel far and not see a year or two hence. The country's so broken and rough that the day's gather the circle brought in had to be worked ("sorted") on a narrow bench breaking off at the back of our camp—the Hat X—in a sheer decent of thirty odd feet.

Its about supper time, the horses are behind the ropes, the men changing, roping fresh mounts for the night. There's an omninous lull in the roar of the gale thats been increasing in fury for hours. Up from the crest of the near hills to the west rises a cloud, inky black with a white wooley roller atop, spitting lightning flashes like fierce tongues of flame so near and so low they fair lick the ground as it bears down on us. No one needs orders now. No man Jack seeks shelter but pulls his latigo a hole or two tighter, mounts, and cuts for the herds as fast as good horseflesh can pack him. "There's sure hail a plenty comin in *that* and there'll be hell and a bawlin and rollin of tails when she strikes."

Its just when the dust clouds and the spume of the squall is almost upon us that someone shouts, "Look! Look!," and, from the crest of the bank at the place of its sheerest decent, crowded hard by two rope swinging riders leaps headlong to death a big four-year-old steer. We have only time for a glance at the miracle of the two riders emerging, still mounted, unscathed. Then its ten minutes of pandemonium, booming of great guns, blackness, bellowing trampling herds, blinding buffeting pelting drenching [storm], popping of guy ropes, ripping and thrashing of canvass, oaths and neighing of horses. When it's past the little valley as far as you can see up and down is a mass of moving, lowing cattle. All hands fall to straightening the camp and skinning and hanging the beef old "Loose Twist" and "Never Slip" brings us.

Its this job that gets us started on "Jumps We Have Known." Starbuck of the Js starts the game. "Im coming up the trail last summer from the end of the track with a Cross Anchor herd. We camped back here in the Porcupines. One evening when Im off guard and down under the bank beside camp washing myself and a bunch of socks, parin my hoofs and getting into some clean underwear, whilst I am down there Old Cronkey, the trail boss, comes in and unbeknownst to me stakes his horse, a half-broke, big black snuffer, between me and camp. When I comes up that bank packin' my rags—it being hot I'm wearin only my drawers and boots—Cronkey's old horse just tears up the ground, pulls his pin, and breaks out for the hills.

Cronkey's hot as a wolf and jumps me all spraddled out for paradin round naked thataway. I dont wait to be sent but hustles on my shirt, mounts my stake horse and cuts out to the herd to head off that runaway. He gives me a long chase but I works him into the breaks where finally I crowds him close enough for a cast with any rope, and it's just my damned luck to get the loop over the horn of that saddle 'stead of his neck. My nags a good roper and he setts back sudden pulling the saddle high up on the black's rump the first turn where it sticks. Say children! there's some doins now. Old Shiner—thats the horse I'm riding—he's the real thing as I says, he's close to ten hundred [pounds] and, with a fair catch he'd snub evry livin thing up to ellerfunts, throws down his head just grubbin up the greasewood [and] rocks a slidin all fours trying to hold that black, and the black bawling and pitchin to beat four aces. It's no use. Shiner's gettin rattled and its here I has a wise hunch to turn him loose like I orto have done. No! thats not the only wise hunch I turns down that day. I'm ambitious to make good bringing in old Cronkey's hoss, so I takes chances, throws off the turn, gives him slack, [and] jumps old Shiner in to throw him.

This brings us down to the edge of a cut about 5 times higher than this one these boneheads puts their beef over, but I am mad clear through now. Old Shiner's blood's up, I gives him slack again when this 60 foot stake rope and heavy green club of a [picket] pin the black's still draggin gets into my game —gets fouled in a half hitch round one of Shiner's hind legs and starts *him* to buckin. In no time he changes ends and twists us up in both them ropes in such a shape I'm plum helpless to get off which I sure fears to do. I'm using a one eard bridle and no throat latch. Say! Cattleboys! she sure gets complicated when one of them ropes saws down old Shiner's neck when he makes a duck and skins off that bridle and both hosses sifts straight down the hill for that cut. Shiner gets there a length ahead of the black and goes over. The black rears back to save himself, there's a yank that cuts me nearly in two but breaks my fall. My cinch rig gives way. The black gets both saddles and ropes. Shiner and me loses some skin and patches of hair. The worst that happens to me is I has to walk that four long miles back to camp—afoot."

"The biggest jump," chips in Manager Wells of the Hat X, "any horse ever makes and lives is when Old 16 of the Bow-Gun bolts with the sheep herder down South Sunday [Creek] way when we are starting on the roundup last spring. This herder that gets a string plays himself off on Bob (Bob Martin foreman of the Bow-Gun) the evening before for a puncher. Bob's short a man or two when this rooster rides into camp looking for work. Next morning somebody ropes Old 16 for him to ride for a try out. This old stampeder breaks away and jumps off a bank sixty feet high, neither horse or man hurt."

Mr. Martin said, in response to an inquiry when I visited him at the ranch a few weeks later, "There's the horse—sound as a nut. We will take him down to the place for his picture, and you can measure the leap for yourself. Its just back here on the bench where we are camped. This locoed sheepherder rides in on a 79 hoss, thats what throws me off. I takes him for a puncher and gives him a job. I gets suspicious the next morning when I sees him saddling 16 that some obliging cuss ropes for him but I dont want to let him out before he begins. It's plain enough when he gets hold of the cantle instead of the horn and swings up with a slack rein that something's going to happen. Old 16 is the worst stampeder in the bunch. No matter what kind of a bit, he swallers it. You cant sort of bend him but once he's had his dash he settles down to his work, and goes to the rimrock with the best.

"This maverick aint hardly in the saddle till he's off straight for the creek, and at the brink of this bank he never stops. He rises like a hurdler and disappears. For a spell nobody wants to take a look over reckoning—of course —that they are both drove into the earth and killed. Somebody finally takes a squint, and when we get's down to the creek bed there's this sport holding Old 16 by the head, talking to him like a crazy man. Barring being hatless, wet and muddy he's as good as ever. When he sees us coming he turns the

115. Old Sixteen at the foot of the jump-off.

bridle loose and, still talking to himself, pulls out across country afoot and that's the last we ever sees or hears of him."

Then we measured the leap. My lariat is 46 feet long. Mr. Martin stood at the top and threw one end down. The bank measured 43½ feet.

Storytelling sessions were not common occurrences. Usually the cowboy "went to bed with the chickens" and by the time it was dark most of them were in their bedrolls. However, in some notes made in 1897, Huffman recorded that—even at night—they were

Always ready to swap yarns. Last night was dark as a root cellar. I am a light sleeper and, being unused to sleeping on the hard ground, lay awake listening to the guards chaffing each other as the reliefs came and went through the night. Alex was on second and when Billy called him he said, "Old man, this is sure dark. An owl'd sure get bogged."[110] Alex made answer whilst putting on his boots. "A owl kant discount me none. Onct me and old Brig—fore he got kicked to death with a bronck two years back—was herdin beef near ———— creek. One [dark] night a big white owl ole Brig jumped goin out flew agin a tree 'n hooked one of his dukes. An there he was hangin next morning. Old Brig tuk him and had him stuffed with hay 'n he's hanging in old Brig's shack yet." [Then Huffman heard] "Whoa, Mokey." A rustle of the slicker and a patter of Mokey's hoofs and he was off without asking which way the herd lay. Mokey took him there.

On their weary round in the darkness the guards often fought to keep

116. Branding in a chute.

from going to sleep in the saddle. Singing to the cattle helped. Many of the tunes used were simple religious airs—though the composers would probably have turned over in their graves had they heard the words improvised for them. But in due time the shift would be over, and one would ride in and awaken the next shift while the other awaited their coming. Then the two who had been relieved could crawl into bed again and sleep until the cook's "R-o-l-l o-u-t an' take it away" heralded the starting of another day—another circle, another roundup herd to be worked, and another guard to stand.

Occasionally there were rainy days. To men living in the open these with their—usually—wet beds could be brutal. And the cook, though *he* might have a dry bed in the chuck wagon, had to cook in the rain and struggle to keep a fire going with wet wood. Although a canvas fly to cover the "kitchen" was adopted early, it was not until about 1897 that the cowboys began to use little tepees shown in some of these pictures. These provided protection from falling rain but not from water that might run under the edges.

When these slack days occurred, the roundup work stopped and the men turned to other activities. It was on such a day that "the Kid" completed the humbling of Sam B——— whom he had previously set afoot. This incident, and the circumstances which led up to it, are told best in the vivid language of this old cowpuncher.

There was a silver mounted Rep from an outfit in Wyoming with the outfit. he had a silver mounted saddle, bridle, spurs, and chaps. he looked like one of the latest inventions Sears Roebuck had turned out. Sam took him under his wing and made a pet of him whenever he had to ride a long circle or go on herd or wrestle calves. he did all the roping.

Sam had one horse he was afraid to ride so one bright sunny morning Sam asked Fancy Pants to ride him. Sam snubbed the horse to his saddle horn

117. End of the roundup.

for him to mount and then hazed him—that is rode along side of him to keep him bucking straight so he could not sunfish. the Kid remarked he bucked straight but he made him pull leather just the same. If a man pretends to be a rider and has to reach down for the apple it is very humiliating. Sam said maybe you think you could ride him. the Kid said if he was in my string I would ride him. Sam said I will bet you twenty five dollars you can't. the Kid said I only have ten but if some of the boys will take the other fifteen I will take a whirl at him. the money was covered and Sam turned the horse loose. they said arn't you going to let the Kid ride him? [Sam replied] not until I get ready. that horse is going to have a good rest.

Several weeks later [when] we were camped on a hill side there was such a downpour of rain that morning we could not work. Sam said we will have that ride this morning. the boys said Sam this is not fair. you know that horse cannot hold his feet on this hill side in this mud. he will fall and hurt that Kid. Sam said he will ride him now or forfeit the money and there won't be any hazing. he has got to ride him slick. the Kid said on the quiet boys if you can get Sam to bet any more money take him on. I promise you I will not let you down. I think they got up something like sixty dollars more. unknown to Sam the Kid twisted some hairs from a horse's tail into the rowels of his spurs so they would not spin, and what you can do to a horse with your spurs locked is a shame. well the horse stayed on his feet. the Kid stayed in the middle of him and scratched him from the cinch to his hips. the horse finally gave up and just squatted and squealed.

John A——— another cowman who was with the outfit said Sam you have given the Kid the worst of it all the way. now if you are game I will bet you five hundred dollars he can ride any horse you own. Sam said I would not let him get on one of my horses for five hundred.[111]

The fall roundup, as has been indicated, was held to gather the cattle that were ready for market and to brand any stray calves that had been dropped late. The manner in which it was conducted was similar to the spring roundup, except that the beef were gathered into what was called the *beef herd,* and at the close of the roundup were taken to market. In this movement to market an old-timer recalled:

A beef herd is never thrown on the trail, or shouldent be anyway but some people dont know any better and do anyway. They should feed from the start off the bedground, let scatter out but not too much, and just kept moving slowly along feeding as they go. 4 men are all that is necessary to be with the herd at a time.[112]

Such trailing was not without its troubles as the following incident indicates. On this occasion a wagon boss failed to follow the old frontier rule of thumb which decreed that—if at all possible—all streams should be crossed before camping for the night. In 1903 the LO and the TA[113] spent three weeks rounding up their fall shipment of beef. They ended up beside the Little Missouri near the southeastern corner of Montana en route to Belle Fourche, the shipping station. At this point the LO had about a thousand head of four- and five-year-old steers.

It began to rain early in the morning of Sept. 10th, and kept it up all day. The TA wagon crossed the river late in the afternoon and made their camp on the east side having previously cut out their herd. Rodman of the LO decided to camp on the west side thinking he could easily cross the next morning. The rain turned to snow and the cattle drifted with the storm, the guards being unable to hold them. The horses also drifted away as the night hawk was powerless to keep them together. Two of the horses on night picket for guard change chilled to death. This storm lasted for three days. . . . The TA went right on and got their herd to market. . . . and the LO outfit started out to re-gather the drifted steers. . . . The wagon went back the way it came gathering what they could by covering each creek and divide and shipped from Miles City three weeks later.[114]

When the beef herd was delivered, the major part of the work for the season was over. Then, as one old cowboy put it,

> when the last critter was in the car the boys would jump on their horses run them into town stop at the first saloon rush in and yell give me the biggest beer you have. then draw their pay dress themselves up, call on the girls, have a few more drinks get into a poker game go broke and in three days [be] ready to go back to the ranch and start life anew.[115]

The next year the same cycle would be repeated, and the next . . .

As few cowboys kept diaries, most of the recollections of range life are subject to the shortcomings of the human memory. However, in 1904 Huffman kept a diary while he was with a roundup outfit which, together with the pictures he took, provides a vivid and precise picture of this two-week period. Unfortunately some of the charm of these notes scrawled by a tired and sweaty hand in the evening twilight has been lost when they were translated into neat type on a clean page.

> Crow Rock Mont (Dawson Co.) July 17th (04)   Arrived at noon camp 1 mile below Cooks ranch at 11-30 AM leaving McRaes 21 mile ranch (old "stone shack") at 6-50 AM. the distance is fully 26 miles but a fine road. Guy Truscott and I are looking for the roundup. We passed the remains of beeves they used on this creek 3 days ago. leaving Miles City at 3-30 PM yesterday— (16th) we have passed but two ranches, stone shack and Cooks 47 miles with 35 to travel to the nearest one — We surprised an antelope doe — early this morning on Grimes Creek — she had kids hid in the tall grass nearby.[116] Saw 50 old sage hens in one bunch and 30 young — they have weaned the chicks already. Made view of Crow Rock

> No remains of the Crows are visible in the trees after 28 years.[117]

> July 18th 04   Sun rises 4-20   Yesterday we left Crow Rock at 3 PM and drove to Mr. Hedstroms on the head of "Timber Creek" which has not changed much in 26 years. We missed the roundup by one day and pulled back to the mouth of Crow Rock where we camped for the night with my old friend Wm Stiller who like myself had not been here since the buffalo days. We had young sage chickens for our supper. During the drive to Timber Creek we came close to a wreck — rattler in the trail made the little gray bolt. Here is a rider from the roundup they work ten miles down Little Dry today. barring accidents we

118. "Camp of Hat X Outfit, General Roundup, Big Dry, 1904."

dine with them at noon today. All well. Guy is writing a boys journal of the trip. Dine with LU—.

10-35 A.M. 19th   We are at the Hat X wagon. The drive is large today and the roundup ground near camp. The   herd is large and watering just below camp on the Big Dry 15 miles below mouth of Little Dry. Mr. Wells and wife and 2 children came out to visit the wagon and brot the boys new peas — string beans   lettuce which is being prepared for dinner. Mr. W. is manager for the hat. He told me a snake story today that skunks my best one in a walk. He was at the Le Vally ranch 12 miles above here on Timber Creek about the ——— of ——— with two hat men. Mr. Le Vally told him of a rattlesnake den in their pasture a half mile from the ranch — they got a pole, fastened a rake to the end of it and armed with quirts and clubs went out to make war on the snakes. The dens are in volcanic rocks on a little butte. Thousands of snakes were in sight in a little depression suning themselves. They raked and mauled until they were all nauseated with the stench arising.   counted up 146 and all agree enough escaped to fill the bed of this mess wagon. I am going to investigate on our return if I can rustle some boots and sheet iron leggins.

July 20th 04   Camped with the XIT boys near the hat ranch which is on Timber Creek near the Dry. Got bogged in the deep crossing near mouth of Timber this morning. Charley Morris, Bob Fudge and Johnnie Woodruff happened along and found me in the water getting the team out after unhooking them. The boys hooked on the hind ex [axle] with 3 lariats to their saddle horns and made 3 or 4 hard pulls breaking some good grass ropes before we got it out. On return to camp I found a bed wagon—hat X—4 mules bogged at this same hole   the pictures will tell the story.

21st   We breakfasted by the firelight 3-30 and broke camp at 4 moving down to Nelson Creek.   the drive is in early — about 6000 cattle on the ground and in the herds. The winter must have been tough — branded only about 130 calves yesterday and today. The CK boys turned over their mess wagon but no body killed — steep rocky hill.

21st camped with LU bar. This morning Homer Lewis saddled his private "Sorrel Top" — sorrel pitched with the saddle went off a bank into the Dry 25 ft below turning completely over.   crossed the bar and a CK boy roped him he pitched on the rope and the boy took a fall out of him breaking his near fore leg. Poor Sorrel he was beautiful. Homer looked pretty sad when he drew the gun to put him out. Heres a little ranch and a garden.   lettus is good without mayonnace. Last night Butch held forth on his travels in India — the Nigger question and the crabs. Butch has been cooking and trying to wean the boys from their vices for 25 years and the old man is as sunny and good tempered as one could wish. And he *can* cook. Our supper last night was stewed corn, steak, sour dough biscuits, hot apple sauce and coffee. Here we are 5 miles down and in camp with the hat again at 7-20. My team are gaining on grass alone and I can almost hook them up without help.

July 22nd 3-30 am   We breakfasted by firelight.   too hot for eat   the horses are in and we will be off before the sun rises

23rd
Camped with the CK boys. Roundup on sand opposite Maguire Creek 110 in shade and hot wind   too hot for write.   Water getting worse — rain needed very much though grass is fine.

119. "Hot Noon Beside the Roundup, July 19, 1904."

120. "XIT Roundup Outfit Pitching Camp, Hungry Creek, North Montana, 1904."

121. "Rest and Water [Hungry Creek, August, 1904]."

24th Hotter today than yesterday. Roundup large over 100 calves to brand   XIT threw back an immense herd this morning at daylight.   made 18 pictures today.

Monday 25th July We are 10 miles from the big Mo [Missouri] and making the last camp on the sand flats of the Big Dry. Here are the big sand ridges in which cottonwood trees are buried so that only the tops are to be seen — trunks 30 ft high and 18″ or 20″ in diameter having formed roots the entire length so slowly have they been embedded. some in like manner have been uncovered showing natures efforts to clothe roots with bark again.

Tuesday 26th
7 to 10 m [thousand] cattle in three great herds. We moved to Bear Creek making a dry camp at sundown. It was beautiful looking from our camp 4 miles from the Big Dry, horses and cattle moving as far as the eye could reach.

Wednesday 27th
Rounded up Bear Creek, fine grass, clear sky, no mosquitoes or flies up here. Bathed and washed our clothes in the rain water holes and as I write we are pitching a dry camp where we can look over into the breaks of Hungry Creek.

Thursday 28th
In camp on Hungry Creek CK   Hat X & XIT all near together   CK immense herd. 10 miles from Mo 15 miles west of CK ranch. It has been a hard day but the pictures paid for the extra effort saw 4 men thrown today one remoota [remuda] stampeeded. Neverslip and Loose Twist ran a big CK steer off a 25 ft cut — killed the steer but men and horses unharmed — picture I am writing in the dark too tired to do anything more —— heres for the sleeps ——
or would have been had not the wind rose and made us hustle to tighten pegs and guys. The thunder and lightening grew more intense all night long and at 4 oclock this morning the height of the storm broke upon us from the north. it turned inky black. every tent but our little tepee went flat. the roaring, bellowing and trampling with shouting and cursing went on for an hour when it cleared. The herds must have mixed which would mean lots of hard work for the tired boys. Cyclone Ed had a bucket of stewed raisins in his bed. The ⌐ ̄⌐ cook's table went down in the ruck. 6² 8² [6½ x 8½] camera is badly smashed. Its glue and nails for the forenoon.

Friday 29th   The circle took in the Mo bottoms and Hungry Creek which furnishes the great "general" for the year. the calf branding has been very light, 30 to 70 a day. the largest about 130. The CK ought to have branded from 50 to 250 — this tells the story of last winter losses.

Saturday 30th
We drove from Hungry back to Bear Creek where the final working of the big herd is going on. There are about 60 riders and every man is helping at cutting or holding — anxious to start home with his cattle.

A few years more and the homesteader—or *honyocker*—put most of the big cattle outfits out of business. Scenes such as these Huffman photographed were passing—like the buffalo he had hunted years before. The frontier was almost a thing of the past.

122. "Roping the Maverick."

While the life of the cowboy has not passed as completely as has that of the hide hunter, bull-whacker, steamboat captain, Indian scout, and others, what remains is but a shadow of the life that once was. "The Kid," who retired to a warmer climate to spend his remaining years, wrote

I was back in Montana three years ago   it was a sad sight for an old cow hand, the flats all ploud up, the grass ruined, the open range fenced up, and all big outfits out of business. In our section of the country the big Companies . . . counted their cattle by the thousands   now those that are left "and they are very few" count them by the hundreds.

I found that the most of the old cowpunchers had saddled a cloud and ridden into the great beyond. the few that were left are retired, spend their time talking of the good old days and cussing the Hon Yocker.

Epilogue

Huffman made his last big buffalo hunt just south of the Missouri in the valleys of the Big and Little Dry and their short tributaries. In the days immediately following, he realized that it was doubtful if he would ever have such a hunt again. The last big cattle roundup he photographed was held in the same locality. Perhaps the reason he made so many photographs of this one was because he realized that the last bit of prairie frontier—like the buffalo herds of those years long past—was almost gone. Four short years later the big outfits in this country began to ship their cattle and close out their holdings, and in another four years all that remained of the days of the big roundup and the chuck wagon were memories.

Just as the Sharps of the hide hunter rang the knell of the great buffalo herds, so did the plow of the honyocker bury the days of the open range. For there was a man named Jim Hill who saw in these open prairies room for many farmers—who, in turn, would provide business for his railroad. Hill was not unique. He merely promoted a movement that others also supported and fostered. A flood of settlers surged over the prairies and swept the old life before it.

With reluctant pride Huffman watched the development of the prairies the buffalo and cattle had ranged, and he added to his meager income by interviewing new settlers and writing copy for the publicity department of the Chicago, Milwaukee, and St. Paul Railroad. On one occasion, to the

123. "One of the Earliest nesters and family in Powder River."

west of the Missouri in Dakota where part of the lands of the Standing Rock Reservation had been opened for settlement, Huffman visited with an old man who had come to this country to start anew. The settler told him:

"I sold the old place, staked my boys, put something by for a 'rainy day' and here we are bound for the Grand River country, south of Lemmon [South Dakota]. Counting Cousin Mary, four of us will enter land. We will then have a holding of a section of this fine, black loam, all that we need, all we can use. My motto is, 'Not to use is to lose.'

"My oldest boy is an engineer and already has a chance to run one of those big steam plows. . . . The younger is a carpenter, and I am going to be of use again. Say, friend, grub has not tasted so good in ten years. I have my old-time, prairie appetite back again, like when Mother and I led a cow behind the wagon and camped on the Illinois prairies almost fifty years ago. I can ride a horse and drive as well as ever. I am not going to rust out, never fear. . . ."

Then we had Sunday dinner. I was the guest of honor. The table was improvised on boards, boxes and bundles, and overhead was the wonderful high sky with its fleecy clouds racing above us. And from sundry boxes and barrels, mysteriously came savory eatables, prepared in advance for just such emergencies as this. Withal there was much interesting talk, of the wonderful sod houses they would build, how warm they were in winter and how cool in summer, with their dead air space in the walls two feet thick; and what sort of collar beams beneath the roof and of the modern fireplaces adapted to the use of lignite coal which underlies this whole prairie country, and outcrops in nearly every rough brake.

Next day I drove South toward the much talked about Grand River and Big Meadow country where there still may be found some excellent claims. Going out that 25 miles we passed 30 teams returning a longer road further West toward Lemmon; the next afternoon we met 63 teams, not including 3 motors and every known sort of light vehicle, outbound. Not since the old Red River days have I witnessed such an out pouring of people literally possessing and being possessed by a new country.

But this was not a hospitable, well-watered country like the Middle West. Even as some viewed the prospects through rose-colored glasses, others recalled the years when the searing summer heat had parched the ranges and dried up the streams. To allay feelings of doubt Huffman wrote:

> And this country which I have just been describing, is not going to have all its eggs in one basket, be confined to a dead level of wheat, wheat, wheat, but its people are going to grow a great range of crops, and they are going to empound storm water in a thousand natural reservoirs by inexpensive means for stock watering, and for irrigation of specialized crops, and as an insurance against drouth years, which soon or late come to every country under the Sun.
>
> And then it rained some more. . . . It rained 15 out of the 22 days of my trip. The record is about 4½ inches of precipitation for May at Hettinger, to nearly 6 inches in the same time at Terry and Miles City. And that is the story all along the line for 400 miles.
>
> From Mobridge to the Musselshell, flax, speltz, gardens and the waving grain and grasses of the prairie are a sight to gladden the settler's heart.

Part of the things Huffman foresaw came to be—years later—and the disaster the cautious ones predicted came also. The pioneer-farmer, more often than not, has been a plunderer of the soil, and homesteaders who came to the Dakota and Montana prairies believed that land that could be plowed was suitable for cultivation. That was not true—and many a settler paid for his lack of knowledge and judgment with heartbreak, privation, and futile toil. A quarter of a section was usually not enough for a farmer to eke out a living. There were dry years—sometimes two or three in succession. In the end Mother Nature revenged herself on those who turned the buffalo and grama grasses—as an Indian is alleged to have aptly put it— "wrong side up."

One by one many of those who had come with high hopes abandoned their fields and their sod shanties and their little tar-papered shacks. To stay was to starve. Even though most of the honyockers were able to hold on for but a short time, they stayed long enough to push out all those cattlemen who depended upon an abundance of free grass. When faced with this flood of people, the big outfits gathered their cattle and drove them to market. Then they sold their chuck wagons. The honyocker's plow killed the buffalo and grama grasses, and, when the fields were abandoned, the tumbleweeds took over. It is no wonder the cattlemen were bitter about the farmers ruining that which they could not profitably use.

Even though Huffman appeared to write enthusiastically of the agricultural development of the prairie lands, deep in his heart he had no love for the change. Closer to the real truth was the statement he penned for Sam Gordon that

> Everywhere I go in the Yellowstone country, twice on long drives to the south and east, within the past few weeks, tells me this, that soon if I am to gallop the little gray mare it must be in a lane, and you do not care, but I do; that makes me sad: I would that there were yet a few waste places left untouched by the settler and his cursed wire fence, good in its way, but not for me.[1]

Of these days Huffman wrote but little—he preferred to recall more pleasant things. He never recorded his feelings when, in the sunset of life, he looked back to the days at the close of the Indian wars, to the days of the hide hunter, and to the days of the cowboy riding free across the range. However, there can be no doubt that he wholeheartedly agreed with the thought one of his friends put into verse:

> There wasn't a fence in the world that we knew,
> For the West an' its people was honest an' new,
> And the range stretched away with the sky for a lid—
> I'm old, but I'm glad I lived when I did.[2]

124. "The Honyocker."

Notes on Photographs

1. "So well trained do cow-horses become that the wrangler, unaided, can in an incredibly short time bunch them anywhere, so that the riders can change without loss of time. To look at this rope corral, stretched to portable tripods and wheels of the bed wagon, one uninformed would not believe that two or three hundred 'snorty' horses could be penned there with only a taut rope three feet from the ground to hold them." L.A.H.

6. "This shows a buffalo hunter's log camp in the wild inaccessible butte and bad-land country in the Hell and Snow Creek region of North Mont. The cabin has back of it what we once termed a lookout butte, from the top of which we looked over to the south and west in the morning time at the open spaces where the last great herds of American bison ranged and were slaughtered for their tongues and robes. Young pines and creeping cypress has grown up in the trails which were once used to the springs which lay below in the gulch, now dried up...." L.A.H.

   There are good reasons for believing that Huffman hunted from this camp.

8. "This subject is [from] . . . an old wet plate. It shows the skinner-hunter beginning the work of taking the robes and tongues." L.A.H.

14. The old log courthouse, which was the scene of the "corking" incident related in note 4, Chapter One, is the second building from the right edge. (The log walls are plainly visible.)

16. The rifle is a .44 caliber Kennedy. Because of its small caliber, Shields some-times referred to it as "Huffman's pea slinger."

17. One purpose of this trip was to hunt timber suitable for the government sawmill. No doubt it also provided a desirable change from tedious duties at the post.

18. Tall Bull is in the lead on the dark horse, Woman Leggins rides beside him on the paint horse. The rider in the rear is Zac. Rowland, half-breed son of the scout Bill Rowland. For other identities see the note for Plate 110 of Brown and Felton, *The Frontier Years*.

19. "Young Plenty, as we used to called him, is rather an aristocratic young Cheyenne warrior. He obliged me one day in June by sitting down in his sweat lodge so that I might show in some detail how the thing was constructed and used. The Indian 'Turkish bath' is well known and still used as a method of cleansing among all the remnants of our Plains Indians." L.A.H.

20. "[Sits Down Spotted] was a sporty lad at this time. He had many horses. Was much married in his Indian way, a fashion not so bad for Indians. He was a gambler [first], last and any old time, and played them pretty high. He was living less than two years ago but the gay glamour of his life and the finery of his dusky wives, and the multiplicity of his horses all passed away." L.A.H.

   Huffman confused this Indian with Carries His Food, a Crow who was noted for being a good provider for his household. The old-timer who made this correction added this note: "The notes are perfect for Sits Down Spotted, and was as I heard about him except it could be added that he was a trickster and very much of a practical joker."

21. The overhead cable and the pulley to which the two ropes were attached are not shown. By lengthening or shortening a cable the "forward" end of the ferry could be pointed upstream and the pressure of the current flowing along the hull would then propel the ferry to the other side. There the adjustment would be reversed for the return trip.

23. "This scene is typical in all respects. Here is the perfect grass country, where in the years just prior to this scene, the slaughtered cousins of the grass eaters in this picture grazed only to be annihilated by the buffalo hunters. Here is the typical roping pony and roper. A ranahan straight, pigeon-breasted, long-backed cow puncher, always riding the horse between his legs from the bottom of his stirrups to the top of his hat. He is tied hard and fast with a bellowing calf on the end of his manilla, reluctantly being dragged to his baptism of fire, with the proverbial 'anxious mother' always following." L.A.H.

25. "The big red broncho bolted and threw 'Dutchy' at the third pitch. The photograph is not over sharp, but shows 'Dutchy' high in the air, however it does not show the three deep purple blats that the horse uttered as he bucked to 'get his man.' There is nothing more terrifying at first, than the bawl of a maddened broncho, but you soon get used to it, for it goes on every day at the roundup. You soon grow to like it—if some other fellow is doing the riding." L.A.H.

26. "Bitter Creek flows into Powder River not far from the Montana-Wyoming line. The ranch stands a couple of miles from the river and is still intact with its scoria roof and its memories of the 'Days that Were' when it was the S.A. Cow Camp. In addition to a bunch of Spear children, it sheltered many a trail driver and not a few outlaws." L.A.H.

28. Some hint of the location of this line camp is contained in the words "Crow A[gency?]" stenciled on one of the boxes in the background. It may belong to some outfit with a lease to run cattle on the Crow Reservation.

29. "This ranch, made famous by the Phillips Brothers of Chicago who have long since passed away, is now only a hole in the ground." L.A.H. (Note the post office sign over the door.)

31. The banjo case is marked with a Diamond D. Bread dough is undoubtedly rising in the dishpan beside the stove.

33. Shown are Manager Hugh Wells and family and an unidentified cowboy. The object in the "front yard" is a merry-go-round for the children.

40. "This picture was taken at high noon on the Powder River, and, like many others, cost some days of patient waiting. It shows a beautiful stretch of water. The camera was located in the midst of the band." L.A.H.

41. "These were the first sheep to graze in the lower Powder River region so far as I know. Billie Guthrie and John Ming, old time cowmen of Helena, owned them and Guthrie said to John in my hearing, 'Now you've got to learn to blat and smell like a D—— blankety sheep or we'll never make a dollar off'n them in a thousand years.' " L.A.H.

43. "This picture was made in the Powder River badlands near the old crossing of the Deadwood Stage Line which led from Fort Keogh on the Yellowstone to Powder River crossing, thence to Deadwood. There was an old saying in those days which still persists,—when natives wanted to compliment a faithful man in any endeavor they would say of him or to him, 'There is a man who can get along with hot sheep.' Hot sheep won't move but each ducked his head under his neighbor and the wise herder would not dog them under those conditions. The picture shows greasewood and red scoria outcrop, and the Powder River in the dusty and dim distance." L.A.H.

44. The features and dress of this man indicate that he was a Basque. These people occupy the border provinces of Spain and France and have been described as being simple, brave, and independent. Note the 1873 model Winchester, the favorite repeating rifle of the times, and the bundle of coyote skins.

46. "This picture was made overlooking one of the bitterly alkaline pools in the channel of Big Dry Creek, not far from Smoky Butte. The herder and his dogs are very typical of the time." L.A.H.

47. "This picture shows the little white wagon, the sheepherder's home and the band lying in a protected cup in the hills back of the wagon, also the herder's high water mark [stone pile] on the butte at the right. This was taken at a time when, in Montana, the reference to the little white wagon meant trouble for the range cattle man. The herder with his little home on wheels, when the grass got short, could at once move his band and his home wherever there was good grass and water. Whereupon the new grass and water became very distasteful to the cattle herds and so the old saying of the cowboy was, when he would see the little wagon in the distance, 'That's putting the boys out of business.' " L.A.H.

48. "Go where you will between the first of May and the first of December on the range country of Montana, Wyoming or elsewhere, you will meet sheep, stock bands, mutton sheep bands being ranged to market or to their new owner's range. There are heroes in the sheep business as well as in all other occupations known to man, for the dust and heat, the smell of the sheep, bad water, long hours and the dreariness and weariness of it all must be endured. Here is the herder on his pony beside Cap Butte in the Bad Lands, and the sheep are [being] herded through the pass making for water." L.A.H.

49. Williamson started ranching in 1897 and became one of the largest operators in eastern Montana. When he started, he hired a herder to teach him the business "from the ground up."

50. "Quite the prettiest sight may be seen on the range of any of the wool growers of the Northwest. This picture was taken at four o'clock in the afternoon. Lambing camps are situated, when possible, upon some flat, smooth bench land or bottom ground. As the lambs become strong enough, they gambol on the short, green buffalo grass by the thousand. The picture shows them grouped thickly on the grass and their mamas engaged in the intricate task of sorting out their babies preparatory to moving to the bed ground for the night." L.A.H.

51. "Every well regulated sheep ranch is now equipped with a wagon fitted with from twelve to eighteen compartments arranged on the sides, with sliding panels, so that in bad weather, and there is usually a good deal of bad weather during

lambing time, a lamb may be picked up in its very infancy, placed in a small, dry box in the back of the bin or compartment, the mother then caught [with a sheep hook], as shown in the picture, and placed head outward in such a position that she cannot lie upon or injure the lamb during her ride to the sheds." L.A.H.

52. "Each year between the 15th of May and the 15th of June the sheep are brought to the shearing pens, a bower is erected, and the professional shearers begin the annual harvest of the wool crop. These are professionals; some of them are able, when the sheep are not too dirty or too large, to shear and tie up the fleece of from 150 to 200 sheep in a single day [other estimates indicate that 80 to 120 was a good day's work]. They are hardy men and well trained. They travel from southern Colorado, beginning in March, to the British possessions, ending in June, and do little else. The tramper is working on his lofty perch; the owner with his scales is weighing a fleece." L.A.H.

53. The wagon and trailer in the left foreground probably has a load of about three and a half tons. As the distance from the ranch to market might require several days' travel, the two-wheeled "field kitchen" (known as a *coaster*) shown at the extreme left was a necessity. The building in the background is the wool warehouse in Miles City, Montana.

56. The brand records show that this brand, the C Dot, was recorded by Gerald T. Archambeault, Fort Peck, Montana. (It was a horse brand—not a cattle brand.)

57. "It frequently happened on the roundup to be more convenient to work, or sort, small bunches of cattle where they were first found; so instead of driving those they didn't want on the long trip to the roundup grounds they would work the bunch and leave the others behind, undisturbed. Through eastern Montana and northern Wyoming during mid-summer the Bad Land creeks are dry from ten to twenty miles; then among the rough scoria-topped hills at their heads will be found good water in abundance. This picture is good of this operation and shows a calf breaking away with a cowboy after him." L.A.H.

59. Left to right: Bill Crowder (foreman), unidentified, Conrad Kohrs.

64. "T. H. Irvine . . . was one of the old time sheriffs of Montana. The man at his right got his early education man-hunting with the Texas Rangers. . . . At this writing only one of the five has passed in his checks. These men could write interesting stories, but are not built that way, they were men of action." L.A.H.

Left to Right: Billy Smith, Jack Hawkins, Tom Irvine, Louis King, and "Eph" Davis. (Louis King and Billy Smith were in the posse which arrested the Indians who burned the Alderson-Zook ranchhouse as related in Chapter Two.)

67. "The real cowboy with his 'six-pistol,' his leather leggings, sombrero and all the rest is fast disappearing from the plains; few new ones are being brought up to the business. One may now travel with many roundups and find only now and again the thoroughbred, who had his early education in the chapparal and on the trails leading from those cattle nurseries to the plains of the Northwest. Here are shown in this picture three men just as they came off herd; neither they nor the mounts they ride have ever known anything else but the cow camp and the trail." L.A.H.

The style of the chaps and the saddles brand this picture as having been taken in the 1880's. Left: Lou Iron; center and right are unidentified.

70. "With each mess wagon that leaves the home ranch to spend the summer on the range goes the cook, two horse wranglers, one hundred to one hundred and fifty saddle horses, and a quota of cowboys. The night wrangler drives the bed wagon, the [day] wrangler [drives] the saddle stock, and the cook drives the mess wagon when the roundup is on the move." L.A.H.

71. "Here is a good race between a cutting horse and a cow, with the cut and roundup in the middle of the picture, and the cook tent and cavvy in the far distance." L.A.H.

73. "The cook and his outfit are shown. The horse wrangler is 'pie-biting' on the side. The mess box is open, exposing to view the modern arrangements for quick work in the field. The roundup cook must be an expert and have his necessities handy; and he must possess the ability and the deftness to put up three 'squares' of substantial 'chuck' for from twenty to forty riders every day. This close shot of the kitchen on an old dutch oven outfit is typical in showing the familiar scene of a hungry horse wrangler having pie and coffee." L.A.H.

76. Left to right: "Older, unidentified, J. Woods, Geo. Mc Donald, Jap Reu, unidentified, John Burgess (standing), Pinto, unidentified (sitting), unidentified (mounted), unidentified (sitting), 'Appetite Bill'—night-hawk, 'Crow Dog'—unsaddled horse." L.A.H.

77. "This picture was taken on Crow creek, a tributary of Big Powder. . . . The picture was taken on a lowery, cloudy morning; . . . The choice of the situation cost more than a week of riding, watching and waiting." L.A.H.

78. "The famous roundup cook of the early days at work at his kitchen table, which is the rear end of the chuck wagon." L.A.H.

79. "This picture was taken on Big Pumpkin. The wagons are camped along the stream as usual, and each day at sundown the word goes out that the Box T or the WL, the SH or the YT are 'going to kill,' and someone is told off [from the outfit to butcher?] the two-year-old which has been cut out of a nearby herd, and this beef must always bear the mark of the owner upon whose range the roundup is then at work. The riders dash after it, rope it by the head, or if it is not too heavy, sometimes by the heels, and drag it at a gallop to a point near the wagon, and the cook sallies forth with his axe. The picture shows him in the act of dispatching the beef." L.A.H.

81. "A hackamore is the bitless bridle, so to speak, which is put on a wild horse as his first introduction to the bridle. It's the broncho busters most useful piece of equipment and a young horse during the hackamore stage of his training generally learns a lot which he never forgets. 'But who cares about hackamores,' says the curious little colt in the background, who really steals this scene." L.A.H.

82. "There are many ways of accomplishing this feat. The cowboy in this picture, a professional broncho-buster, proceeded to rope, blindfold and bridle the gray horse, then took him outside the corral at my request, and flung on the saddle, holding the horse by the bridle and hackamore. The picture was made just at the instant when he gave the first pull at the latigo, cinching the saddle." L.A.H.

89. ". . . about the slicker in the horses face. I kept a slicker on the Corral fence, as I all ways rode a bronck in the corral three times before riding outside. so on the second saddle I picked the slicker off the fence and [did] what was called slicker brokeing to get the young horse used to the slicker when some cowboy had to wear a slicker in the rain." Lee Warren.

91. "The old N Bar at the mouth of Cash Creek was owned by Zeke [E. S.] Newman of El Paso, Texas. Jessie Haston was General Manager and paid off in cash in 1882—thus Cash Creek got its name. This picture shows the famous old N Bar Crossing of Powder River. It was on the trail leading from the south into Montana and was made famous later by Andy Adams' story, *The Outlet*. This Niobrara Ranch was the first cow camp and was bought from two old trappers. It was the first to have a log and rail fence and the first in Powder River valley to enclose a saddle horse pasture. The red scoria roofs beckoned to many a tired puncher when road ranches were 'pretty darned far apart.' Welcome in those days was well expressed by one old friend who said, 'You are just

as welcome as you would be to drink out of the old river when she's abooming.'

"This picture was taken in the early morning, when light was not at its best, but it is a remarkable picture in many respects. It shows the old ranch on the river bank [and] the fine sweep of river on one side of which the herd is pouring into the water, swimming in the center, and the point coming out on the opposite shore." L.A.H.

94. "This is the old Dutch oven outfit of the SL owned by Judge Loud and Fred Hitzfeldt on Tongue River. . . . In the background is the 'cavvy' in the rope corral and the Biddle tepees. Biddle of the 70L was the first to introduce tepees for the cowboys." L.A.H.

Reading from left to right (individuals will be designated *upper* if in background, *center* if in center of group, and *lower* if near to the camera): Fred Hitzfeldt, Charlie Decker, Ad Rickards, George Snyder, Chippy Coloraw, Colville Terrett, "Fatty" Hamilton, Frank Woods (lower), Charlie Mosgar (center), Luther Dunning (upper), Ed Cross (upper—with black hat), Bob Harper (center), Ed Whitbeck (upper), Mac Rickards (lower), Black Henry—the cook, and Jim Glenn—the horse wrangler.

Huffman's notes need some amplification. The SL was owned by the Hereford Cattle Company and was located on Pumpkin Creek (a tributary of the Tongue River). Judge C. H. Loud was manager and Fred Hitzfeldt was foreman. When the company closed out, the manager and foreman took over and moved the outfit to the location of the M Diamond on Foster Creek, although they continued to operate the ranch on Pumpkin Creek. Thus all but the old-timers associated the SL with the Foster Creek location. Also, it is believed this picture was taken a year or two before the new owners took over.

The ⌐O⅃ (reversed 7 and L) was owned by Ferdon and Biddle, and the ranch was located six miles above Powderville. S. F. J. Biddle was a member of a famous family in Philadelphia. The ⌐O⅃ went out of business and Biddle established the ☧ (Cross) ranch on Little Powder about 30 miles above its mouth. There is still a Biddle post office.

95. Reading from left to right, with the name of the outfit represented enclosed in parentheses: Charlie Taylor—"Dirty Charlie," the cook; Eldon Runkel (SL); Jack Whitbeck (Ed Whitbeck); Jimmie Gibson (LO); Billy Glenn ("Lord" Horkan); Billy Crawford (himself); Price Terrett (JO); Sid Smith (himself); Hugh Daily (Arthur Kelsey); Fred Hitzfeldt (SL); Millard Shy (Scott & Decker); Dan Gaskill (himself); Harry Daily (Al Berry); Charley Wesley (Cross S); Walton Baker ("Lord" Horkan); Billy Coleman (W. C. McDowell); Nels Neilson (Horton Bros.); Tom Scott (himself); Tepee Dick (Johnny Ramer); Jimmy Drake (TA); Eva Carey—the night-hawk; Art Algar (George Harkan); Johnny Moore (SY); Ray Mitchell (George Mitchell); Beaver Slide (George Liscomb); John Kraft (OU); Jud McKelvey (the Bug); Flayto—the horse wrangler; Sam Shy ("Dinner Rep"); Charlie Decker (himself); and Lee Wilson (Link Wilson).

96. "This close scene of the cavvy in the corral shows the activity of catching horses for the move. Many of the horses have been rolling in the mud, the ropes are stiff, and it isn't so pleasant sometimes." L.A.H.

97. "This shows a little alkali spring, mess wagon, bed wagon and the old Ⅎ2 saddle bunch against one of the old scoria buttes at the head of Squaw Creek between Tongue River and Powder River. The Ⅎ2 was the Concord Cattle Co., wagon boss, Nate Spangler. This picture is especially interesting in showing the general activity suggested by the title. In the center right on a white Bar V (∇) horse is Frank Murphy and directly beyond him notice the man with a hobbled bronc. This side of him on the blaze-face bay is Ed Phillips. Coming down to the dust in the rope corral we see a man's head and shoulders and he is evidently

roping. Directly in front of the team at the bed wagon is a cowboy tightening his cinch and keeping his distance. All around the corral are men saddled and ready to go on the circle. To the left is the real excitement. A cowboy is trying to hold a horse which is rearing. He cannot hold him because he has one foot through the loop and the loop is way back on his withers. Directly down the hill from this horse we see a buggy belonging to L. A. Huffman, who drove out to take the pictures. This rearing horse fell over the buggy tongue, breaking it. Frank Murphy and Ed Phillips fixed it with a rawhide from the beef killed the night before." L.A.H.

98. "This subject shows the Pilot on the right, the cook, mess wagon and four horses in the slanting light of morn and the bed wagon trailing along followed closely by several hundred saddle horses belonging to the old Capital Syndicate [XIT] then ranging cattle between the Missouri and Yellowstone, owned for the most part by the Farwells of Chicago. The gray horse shown on the bed wagon is 'Old Eagle,' pensioned by O. C. Cato who for many years was range foreman and manager for this company. Eagle outlived the man who planned his emancipation. Peace to their ashes, they were God's best creatures—both." L.A.H.

99. "At evening time when the roundup is in camp and after each rider has caught his night horse—and no cowboy turns in till he has done that—the balance of the saddle stock is again turned out to graze for the night, the wagon boss tells him which way to throw them, then the 'night hawk' (night wrangler) begins, in moonlight or pitch darkness, rain or snow, heat or cold, his nightly vigil. At about 2 a.m. he slips away to camp, calls the cook, lights the fire for him, and by the time its 'raining tin dishes' as each man drops his empty plate and cup into the kettle that sizzles by the flickering firelight, he brings in the horses, and in less time than it takes to tell it the roundup moves. At what time the new camp is made he unrolls his bed, and while the boys are on the circle the 'night hawk is in his nest.' " L.A.H.

100. "The foreman of the roundup must know his country. In the gray of the morning his rough riders gather near to be told which creek or draw each is to ride to the head of, driving before him on his return to the new roundup ground, six to ten miles ahead, every horned creature he finds, and the place that knew him yesterday is 'tromped flat,' still and lifeless, tenanted only by the wild creatures and here and there a worn out cow-horse left behind or a distracted mother crying for her baby (calf) that 'wandered away with the show.' This scene is most familiar to all old cowboys. Its 4:30 AM and the ꓱ2 wagons are rolling in the background amid the cavvy. In the center is the foreman, Nate Spangler, with his cowboys; his hand is raised in giving instructions to one of them. His words are something like this: 'Ed, you take five men and start your drive on Bay Horse. Drive down the creek. We will roundup at Buttermilk flats.' Ed Phillips is on the W horse directly in front of Spangler and Frank Murphy is directly behind Spangler wearing a white muffler." L.A.H.

101. "This scene is laid on the old Con Kohr's range in the Prairie Elk country near the Missouri. The picture is unique in that the cattle had been held on a dry camp the night before just beyond the distant hills. They needed no driving as they were headed toward the nearest water they could smell so the photographer was not bothered by any ambitious cowboys getting between him and the herd to get their 'pitcher tooken.' They were at the wagon enjoying a rest and putting on 'taller.' The cattle could be trusted to go to the nearest water and remain there for some hours for it was in the hot mid-summer." L.A.H.

Note: An old cowman once estimated that there were 3000 cattle shown in this photograph.

102. "At what time they finish cutting out cattle, whether it be nine o'clock in the morning or four in the afternoon, they hie themselves to the branding pens or corral, and these pens are situated from five to ten miles apart on all streams, and near the pens are gathered all the unbranded cattle. These are sorted into bunches according to the mark they will bear; a fire is built, the irons are brought from the wagon and heated, one or two men go into the pen on horseback, rope the calves or yearlings, one at a time, by the heels and drag them to the fire, where they are seized by the men, and with knife and the branding iron are 'dealt all sorts of misery' in a short space of time. The iron must be very hot, and it must be burned deep into the animal's side or hip, in addition to which the ears are split or forked, and the dewlap cut so that it may be easily identified at a distance. If an animal is found with a horn that needs to be amputated it is included at the branding pens, and it is sometimes a sight worth seeing when a two or four year old steer must be roped and thrown in one of these pens." L.A.H.

104. "This picture was taken on the head of Little Pumpkin. The night wrangler's tepee is in the foreground. The roundup moved early this day, and the cattle are now being held in the background while the men are eating their dinner. The horses are held behind the ropes. In a few minutes everything will be in a turmoil, and fifty men will be charging up and down the flat sorting these herds, and the wrangler in his tepee, surrounded by the dust and all obvious of noise and hurrying feet, will sleep until the cook notifies him in terse language that it is time for him to 'get a move on himself.' " L.A.H.

106. "In this we have the tired, sweaty cow ponies in the foreground glad to huddle together and rest while their riders work. This is work of the hardest sort as it is plain to see these rastling sets are mopping sweat from their brows." L.A.H.

107. "This picture tells how the cow punchers knew which brand to put on each calf when they came crying and struggling at the end of the rope in the hands of the calf wrestlers to have their dewlap cut, the brand burned on their tender hide and, in the dust and hurry of the branding hour, to have a lot of other things done to them. The brand on the mother is visible to the lookout lad in the left of the picture, and it will be so ordered that the calf bear the same mark. Observe the wise and powerful rope horse who made no more ado about dragging, if the center fire did not slip, a twelve hundred pound bull, than the calf which is giving him no sense of effort. The writer has had a leg over that horse and the feeling was that he could pull the bend out of a crick [creek], if need be." L.A.H.

110. "In the right foreground is shown the famous old Mill-Iron brand, trailed here by Roosevelt's friend, Colonel Simpson, who also owned the Hash-knife brands. This one, lone rawhide was found on the edge of the roundup in the big Missouri country, one hundred miles from the old range and ten or more years after the Colonel had passed away. Strange as it may seem, eight other famous old brands show in this picture. Among them are the fish, the mitten, bug, shaving mug, the letter D, flying eight, and Piere Wibaux's W Bar, also HOW." L.A.H.

111. "This picture shows plenty of action in the working of the roundup, with four cuts from the main herd. In the distance flows the Little Missouri amid the cottonwoods. In the foreground is a buffalo wallow half full of water from a recent rain. It seems but yesterday, so swiftly time runs on, that I saw buffalo wallowing here enjoying the June grass by the thousands." L.A.H.

112. "Each outfit from day to day as it finds cattle bearing its brand and the brands of other owners it represents begins at once the formation of a herd. When this herd begins to grow unwieldly the foreman orders it worked. Working the herd means that every owner or 'rep' sorts out his cattle and men are told off to throw them back to the range on which they belong." L.A.H.

114. "In the distance leisurely grazing is the day herd. All is quiet. The day's work is done and the night-hawk will soon start his vigil with the cavvy while the night guards sing to the cattle." L.A.H.

   This picture was taken in the spring of 1907; and the location was 20 or 25 miles from the head of "Big *Punkun*." The rider in the foreground is probably Eva Carey, the night-hawk, or perhaps Flayto, who was the horse wrangler with this Pumpkin Creek Pool.

118. "It's July 19, 1904 and the Hat X day herd is lying down resting on the sand bar across the creek while the horse wrangler is for the first time corralling the cavvy at this location. The boys will soon be in from the morning circle, and will want dinner and a fresh horse." L.A.H.

119. "This is a much closer shot from the same direction as in [Plate 118] showing the horses drinking and enjoying the water after a long hard ride, with the day herd just beginning to string out in the distance for their afternoon graze." L.A.H.

120. The horse wrangler is throwing the ropes from the rope corral from the bed wagon, while in the background the cook's tent is going up.

121. "This shows the Hat X foreman on a crazy gray horse not rope wise working in the lead, throwing a two year old maverick cow to make sure before branding her to the owner on whose range she was found." L.A.H.

123. The nester was the forerunner of the homesteader or honyocker who came in droves later.

124. "Then came the Honyocker, with his cow in lead, his plow and his spotted sow, and it looks as though he has come to stay." L.A.H.

Notes on Text

PROLOGUE

1. Badger Clark, "The Passing of the Trail," *Sun and Saddle Leather*, pp. 171–172.
2. "The Old Cow Man," *ibid.*, pp. 92–93.
3. See Clarence S. Jackson, *Picture Maker of the Old West, William Henry Jackson*.
4. Erwin E. Smith and J. Evetts Haley, *Life on the Texas Range*.
5. The first half of this two-volume study on the work of L. A. Huffman.
6. J. Evetts Haley, "Focus on the Frontier," *The Shamrock*, (September-October, 1955), p. 6.

CHAPTER ONE

1. Colonel E. G. Ovenshine (U.S. Army, Retired) came to Fort Keogh just before Huffman arrived. His interesting letter to the authors about the early days at this frontier post is reproduced below. The error noted in regard to Mrs. Miles is undoubtedly due to the fact that Huffman wrote the reminiscences in question thirty-three years later. The most logical explanation for what appears to be an inaccuracy in regard to the barricade is that its location was probably at the Tongue River Cantonment where they may well have been a need for it in the winter of 1876–77.

Colonel Mark H. Brown
Trails End Farm, Iowa
Dear Sir:

I have just finished reading your very interesting and well written book, "The Frontier Years," and thought you might be interested in hearing that there is at least one person alive who knew many of the places, soldiers, Indians, and incidents that you write about. I lived at Fort Keogh from the fall of 1878 until about August 1885. . . .

My father was a captain in the 5th Infantry and went with General Miles when he went up to Montana just after the Custer fight. He left there late in the fall of that year and was sent east for duty.

In the fall of 1878 he returned to Montana with his wife, two girls and two boys. We took the "Josephine" at Bismarck and went up the Missouri to Fort Buford, crossed the Missouri and went into camp with the escort and transportation that had brought Mrs. Miles and her baby from Keogh to Buford. That night there was a prairie fire and my mother and children fled to the river bank while the soldiers started a backfire. Fortunately the wind shifted and blew the fire away.

In this connection, isn't Mr. Huffman in error when he says that he handed a note to Mrs. Miles after his arrival at Keogh December 11, 1878?, as when we met her at Buford the middle of October she was on her way east and did not return to Keogh until about June 1879.

I used to see Two Moons, Rain-in-the-Face, Spotted Tail, Little Wolf, and others of the well known Chiefs often. Little Wolf at one time had his tepee pitched near the post guard house for protection, and I went there several times and he strung a couple of bows for me with sinews. His tepee was later removed to a small knoll along the road leading to the Yellowstone and several of us boys would take him sugar and other things in my small toy wagon. He made moccasins for my brother and myself.

. . .   .

The night before the Sioux were evacuated from Keogh to the Standing Rock Agency in 1881, they were camped along the Yellowstone and I and several boys spent the evening in and out of their tepees. We thought they were cooking their dogs. I would have liked to have seen a picture of their camp. There were five boat loads. The "Eclipse" with 418 Ogallalas, the "Josephine", 323 Sans Arcs, Spotted Eagle the Chief, the "Helena", 528 Minneconjous, the "General Terry", 181 Hunkpapas and the "Sherman", 191 Brules.

In connection with the picture . . . of the bridge over the Tongue River [between Fort Keogh and Miles City], unless my memory is wrong, Captain Logan had built a previous bridge which was also destroyed. A number of us children from Keogh used to go to a school in Miles City run by a Rev. Mr. Horsefall and his wife, driving there and back behind a four mule team. When the river was high we would cross on the ferry, or the bridge if it was there; in the fall when it was low we would ford and in the winter when the river was frozen we would cross on the ice.

My first two or three years at Keogh we would look out of our kitchen windows and see the hills across the Yellowstone covered with buffaloes. In the fall of 1881 enroute to a camp at the mouth of the Powder River, to guard supplies being landed from steamboats unable to pass the rapids on the Yellowstone, and to protect Northern Pacific graders, I saw the remains of hundreds of buffaloes with just the hides removed.

I remember the hunting party [from Fort Keogh, which returned with ten six-mule wagons heavily loaded] . . . and seeing all the game hung up in the stable in rear of General Miles' quarters and watched its distribution.

. . . Although as a boy I was all around Keogh and from about 1881 to the day I left there I used to ride all over the vicinity with a shot gun hunting, I have no knowledge of any barricade built around the post. At first, cord wood was stacked around the post hay stacks to prevent animals grazing on them but after the stacks were burned by incendiary fires, and the government had baled hay shipped in, the wood was stacked in various places, but not as barricades. It was open all around.

. . .   .

One more incident: I remember seeing a man who apparently had been scalped calling on my father. He had no hair on top of his head, which was very red, showing the veins. He kept a bandanna handkerchief on his head under his hat, and had the ends of all his fingers cut off. Who he was and how it happened I never knew.

Sincerely yours,
E. G. Ovenshine/s

2. Hunting was a favorite pastime of Huffman's. From time to time he wrote of his experiences to his father as, apparently, this sport was enjoyed by both. Several letters are reproduced in part in chapter 3 of *The Frontier Years*, and part of another has been copied here, together with a story from a manuscript which Huffman titled "Pop Shots." In the letter the word "pheasants" refers to ruffed grouse. The killing of the elk took place while a party from Fort Keogh was hunting timber suitable for sawing, and the picture of a camp (Plate 17) may have been taken on the same trip.

Miles City, M.T.   August 30, 1885

Dear Father,
Yours of recent date at hand yesterday—Lizzie [his wife] Bessie [oldest daughter] and I have Just been out at the foot of the mountains with a Mr. Towers and wife   made our headquarters at Hunters Hot Springs and bathed and lounged to our hearts content for a little more than a week— I killed young chickens [sharp-tailed grouse?] and blue grouse every day which with trout made high living— In fact we dont want any more chicken or fish for some time. . . . Old Pard [George O.] Shields comes tomorrow on his way to Bitter Root Range and finds plenty of fault because I am not going along— I will have to content myself with Ducks geese and maybe a few whitetail deer nearer home. I have a new Colt shot gun that you would dote on for the above shooting 10 guage extra heavy breech 32 inch modified choke and weighs 11 lbs. scant— I have killed sage grouse too dead at 60 to 75 yards. and I think with 5½ to 6 drams Hazard electric [powder] that Red Heads and canvas backs at that distance will be out of luck. Do you hunt *Fezzants* [*sic*] or partridges any more.   there are none in this country that I have ever seen neither have I ever found a hunter who ever saw one — but I had an experience with one or a bird that imitated him exact one evening last spring while passing along the foot of the Crazy range in my little boat — N[ate Barnard] was with me and strange to say we were talking about the groves of Iowa and Minnesota and at the very moment pheazants [*sic*] were mentioned If one did not commence drumming in the woods within a hundred yards—We at once went ashore made camp and hunted for him for an hour with no success though we often heard his drum during evening   I shall never forget how that mellow indescribable sound came to my ears and yanked me back to scenes and recalled experiences dearest of all my boyhood — saturdays and vacation time expeditions. . . .

Yours Truly
Late

Extracted from "Pop Shots":
It was in the late seventies . . . that I accompanied a government timber exploring expedition along the Wolf Mountain divide to the Big Horn Mountains. Capt. [Frank D.] Baldwin . . . was in command. Lieut. O. F. L. [Oscar F. Long] was our adjutant. On our return trip one morning the captain and myself were lounging in the ambulance. Lieut. Long with his orderly were

leading the command as usual and keeping a lookout for game. As we approached what was then known as Deep Creek Springs near the Rosebud Buttes we noticed adjutant Long rein up suddenly and give a sign which we instantly interpreted as "game ahead." The captain and myself hurried forward with our rifles to see moving swiftly up a little creek bottom and so far ahead as to look no larger than antelope, 2 bull elk. We lost no time but at once began "blasting away" at them with our .45–70 guns, turn about. Long sitting his horse nearby watching through his glasses and calling out "that one went behind, too high, too far ahead," etc., as he noted the dust spots kicked up by our bullets. At about the tenth shot the game in crossing the creek disappeared for a moment among the scattering bushes when Long cried out, "Captain, your last shot got one of them. Only one in sight now, and he's so far away he dont look bigger than a "John [jack] rabbit."

Meantime the command had come up and halted. We resumed our mounts and quickly located the dead bull. I got out my camera—no kodaks, films or dry plates in those days—a 5 x 8 wet plate outfit—and photographed the captain and his prize then before the skinning and taking of the head began. Some one asked the captain, "Where did you hit him?" A careful examination was made for "where he was hit." The bull was turned and scrutinized minutely but not a drop of blood or a scratch was to be found anywhere on his fat, smooth body or limbs. Camp was made at the nearby springs, the bull's head was hung up against the hind wheel of an escort wagon. Dinner over and pipes lit again, the captain was chaffed as to how the beast came to his sudden and bloodless death. All sorts of guesses were made in jest and earnest. Late that evening when the subject seemed exhausted and dropped, it occured to me that I could place my finger in that bullet hole which I promptly did, finding it just underneath and neatly hidden by the coarse hair and the projecting ring at the very base of the horn where it had entered and lodged at the vital point where head and body hinge together, causing the beast's instant collapse and death without spilling a drop of blood.

3. The daughter of an early rancher in the valley of the Rosebud recalled: ". . . all I remember hearing my father tell about Huffman was that he was the finest photographer of all times—he compared him to Brady of Civil War fame, but that he was not cut out for a rancher." Bertha M. Randell to authors; November 17, 1955.

4. Huffman wrote to his father of another Fourth of July as follows:

July 4th 1883

This is the day we celebrate and the music commenced at 12 last night and lasted until 6 this morning — exhausting 130 sticks of giant powder — fortunately we had things well planned and no one was killed or maimed but everybody complains of a headache and not a few of broken rest and window glass. our first salute was a daisy — a skyrocket was the signal for the lighting of 20 blasts 1 lb. each in as many different localities of the town — and when they began to go it was as though the last day had come — It was a complete surprise and we had more solid fun than you can imagine

Today we marched in grand array — soldiers — artillery — Calithumps — cowboys & etc   Tonight fireworks and lots of amusements — I have spent the afternoon at Bro Will Skinners with Col Comstock and family — a quiet dinner and cigars Hammocks & etc afterwards. . . .

Yours with regards to all
Late

.   .   .   .

Typical of the pranks in which Huffman was often involved was the "corking" incident he described to Sam Gordon, veteran editor of *The Yellowstone Journal*, Miles City's newspaper at that time. This reminiscent letter was provoked by an incident Huffman witnessed while working at a sportsman's show in New York. The Tom Irvine whom he mentions was one of his good friends and, at one time, deputy sheriff at Custer County.

Sam,

   .   .   .   .

   But Sam, maybee it would be easier on your "brane" to decide what the
dad blame reason is that, when a feller's as busy as I ought to be here talkin
Injin to these gothamites and any of the 6 to 10 thousand ites that I can
catch onto as they stream through here from noon to ten at night is the very
time his imagination will be impressed with something, or sound, or face or
funny fracas that moves at the stroke of the hand back to Judge Conger's
courtroom so one can hear and see the Judge and Old dad Grimes, so late
expired at old Milestown.

   The old log building where Judge Strevell's is now [right foreground,
Plate 14], Hot July morning, No sidewalks then, Here and there a sage bush
growed against the wall, Two yellow dust deep paths, One rounded toward
the jail the other off "up street to old John Smith's" would lead you in
either case. . . .

   The low and dirty windows raised "wide up" The high backd benches
ranged in rows and packed for Walker he was tried that day. Walker was a
bad man youll remember him, he once worked for the diamond R [Freighting
Co.]. The "Court" was late. He'd spent the night with Cox [seeing the bright
lights of the town]. . . .

   The sheriff chowowed at the open door. The "court" was on. The prisoner Walker sat within a yard of Old dad Grimes. When the Judge did
question him (Grimes) on his qualifications as a Juror asking, "Do you
know the def[endant], Mister Grimes—There! There! you need not rise to
answer me." But old dad Grimes was up and would not down till he
announced in accents strong while he shook his fist in Walker's face, "Do I
know him. I do and he's a son of a —— that ought tove been hung long
ago." Sam LeRoy and Tom Irvine were there and they roared Judge
Conger promptly fined them for cause and then "pasted" Dad Grimes a
hundred for contempt and bade Kelly take him "AT ONCE"

   And now we're almost to the point. There was no more court that forenoon. A man—you know him—he's still one of your (ours) first rate (?)
citizens—being about half full and sleepy from gaming all night sneaked into
the cool empty courtroom and laid down to rest behind one of the benches.
Some loafers always happen along and we were "on time." You wouldent
have missed it if you had been in town but being in St. Paul you missed a
good thing. We corked him a plenty with seven or eight big red headed
parlor matches whittled sharp at one end and stuck into the top of the cork.
It took two to work it. his hands and his head were thrown carelessly back
and he was "mowing it down" getting even on shrinkage in sleep all uncon-
cious of us and the fact that the Judge had suddenly entered to resume State
vs Walker quite sober and over his tiff of the morning. Then Abe he jabbed
with a stick the hand of the sleeper while I put my cigar to the matches.
. . . Judge Conger served notice right then while the "sleeper woke" over-
turning his bench, that, "if there is any more of this damd confusion in
court, some fellows will get a plaster that will stick." . . . What's corking?
. . . You split a cork, trim her up with matches, set the split gently, Oh so
gently, stride the sleeping victim's nose. have lighter and jabber work
together, "Then take to the hills."

   .   .   .   .

Late

5. A comprehensive biography of L. A. Huffman is contained in Brown and
Felton, *The Frontier Years*, chapters 2 and 5.

6. See Brown and Felton, *The Frontier Years*, chapters 2 and 5, for other material not included in this volume.

7. "One must make tintypes. that is we small fry must so one must keep a bath

and when at leisure we can snatch the face of a cowpunch at a cost of ½ Cent saving 12 cents each time   it does not prevent resorting to the dry [plate] when crowded for time." L. A. Huffman to Perrin Cuppy Huffman, April 5, 1885.

CHAPTER TWO

1. Frank Bird Linderman, "Cabins," *Bunch-Grass and Blue-Joint*, p. 26.
2. Nannie T. Alderson and Helena H. Smith, *A Bride Goes West*, pp. 26–30.
3. Granville Stuart, *Forty Years on the Frontier*, II, 145.
4. *Ibid.*, p. 239.
5. *Miles City Daily Star*, May 24, 1934, Section III, 15.
6. Fictitious name.
7. Name withheld, letter to authors, December 19, 1951.
8. *Ibid.*
9. *Miles City Daily Star* (May 24, 1934), Sec. III, p. 10.
10. Lincoln Lang, *Ranching with Roosevelt*, pp. 94–99.
11. *Miles City Daily Star* (May 24, 1934), Sec. III, p. 12.
12. Alderson and Smith, *A Bride Goes West*, pp. 32–33.
13. Theodore Roosevelt, *Ranch Life and the Hunting Trail*, pp. 97–98.
14. *Miles City Daily Star* (May 24, 1934), Sec. III, p. 15.
15. One ranch wife remembered one of their hired men irritated her greatly by always licking the spout of the syrup jug after helping himself.
16. Alderson and Smith, *A Bride Goes West*, pp. 229–230.
17. *Ibid.*, p. 231.
18. *Ibid.*, pp. 131–132.
19. Meaning, in a way, silly or foolish.
20. Alderson and Smith, *A Bride Goes West*, pp. 188–190.
21. *Ibid.*, pp. 190–191.
22. Lang, *Ranching with Roosevelt*, pp. 163–164.
23. *Miles City Daily Star* (May 24, 1934), Sec. III, p. 12.
24. One of the Eaton brothers—later dude ranchers at Wolf, Wyoming, after the honyockers forced them to move their "ranching" activities from the Little Missouri country.
25. George O. Shields, *Rustlings in the Rockies*, p. 139.
26. Several outfits sent chuck wagons when a large roundup crew worked together.
27. *Miles City Daily Star* (May 24, 1934), Sec. III, p. 21.
28. A rep was a cowboy sent to represent his employer at a roundup. Occasionally he might be authorized to act for other neighboring outfits if the roundup was at a considerable distance from the home ranch. His chief duties were to see that the stock of his employer was branded properly and, when operating a long way from home, to bring back to the home range any cattle that might be found.
29. *Miles City Daily Star* (May 24, 1934), Sec. III, p. 12.
30. Alderson and Smith, *A Bride Goes West*, pp. 123–124.
31. Dr. L. F. Townsend, interview with authors, October 8, 1950.
32. *Miles City Daily Star* (May 24, 1934), Sec. IV, p. 9.
33. *Ibid.*, pp. 9–16.
34. Alderson and Smith, *A Bride Goes West*, pp. 101–102.
35. Abbott and Smith, *We Pointed Them North*, pp. 186–196.
36. *Ibid.*, p. 198.
37. *Ibid.*
38. Alderson and Smith, *A Bride Goes West*, pp. 111–112.
39. *Ibid.*, p. 148.

40. *Ibid.*, p. 146.

41. A. C. Huidekoper, *My Experience and Investment in the Bad Lands of Dakota and Some of the Men I Met There*, pp. 51–52.

42. Frank Bird Linderman, "Cabins," *Bunch-Grass and Blue-Joint*, p. 27.

CHAPTER THREE

1. Badger Clark, "The Sheep-Herder," *Sun and Saddle Leather*, p. 163.

2. *Miles City Daily Star* (May 24, 1934), Sec. II, p. 3.

3. Howard L. Conrad, *"Uncle Dick" Wootton*, pp. 249–279.

4. Edwin L. Sabin, *Kit Carson Days*, p. 356.

5. John F. Bishop, "Beginnings of the Montana Sheep Industry," *The Montana Magazine of History*, Vol. I (April, 1951), No. 2, p. 5.

6. *Ibid.*, pp. 5–8.

7. Edward N. Wentworth, *America's Sheep Trails*, pp. 294–295.

8. Eleanor Banks, *Wandersong*, pp. 166–171.

9. William B. Gaw, *Map of Southeastern Montana, Showing the Great Stock Ranges Embraced in Custer County*, etc., 1884.

10. Wentworth, *America's Sheep Trails*, pp. 298–299.

11. Particularly instructive on this and similar subjects are Archer Gilfillan, *Sheep*; Hughie Call, *The Golden Fleece*; and Winifred Kupper, *The Golden Hoof*.

12. In the case of a small flock the leader or a tame sheep might be carried across and tied down on the opposite bank. In crossing trail herds, one method was to take a long strip of canvas, cut out a bunch, and, using the canvas like fishermen would a seine, "pull" a bunch out into swimming water. Being able to see only the shore in front and the wall of canvas behind, the bunch would strike out for the distant shore. The others would then follow. Charlie Coyle, interview with authors, November 11, 1951.

13. Charlie Coyle, interview with authors, November 11, 1951.

14. N. H. Thorp and Neil M. Clark, *Partner of the Wind*, pp 42–43.

15. John Clay, *My Life on the Range*, pp. 59–61.

16. William MacLeod Raine and Will C. Barnes, *Cattle*, p. 255.

17. Levitt, a rabid Southerner, was also a roundup cook and something of a character. His saloon was unique in that he later dug a well directly in front of it so that his customers would have a ready source of water to counteract the fiery liquids he sold across the bar.

18. George R. Milburn, a prominent judge living in Miles City.

19. 1870–1900. Wentworth, *America's Sheep Trails*, p. 285.

20. Bishop, "Beginnings of the Montana Sheep Industry," *The Montana Magazine of History*, Vol. I (April, 1951), No. 2, p. 8.

21. Raine and Barnes, *Cattle*, pp. 251–266.

22. Lee M. Ford, letter to authors, February 17, 1951.

23. Name withheld, interview with authors, December, 1951.

24. Fictitious name.

25. Name withheld, letter to authors.

CHAPTER FOUR

1. John A. Lomax (ed.), "The Texas Cowboy," *Cowboy Songs and Other Frontier Ballads*, p. 231.

2. Granville Stuart, *Forty Years on the Frontier*, II, 97.

3. *Ibid.*, p. 98.

4. Lee M. Ford to authors, February 17, 1951.

.. Ray H. Mattison, *Ranching in the Dakota Bad Lands.* Reprint from *North Dakota History*, Vol. XIX, Nos. 2 and 3, pp. 3–8. Wallis Huidekoper, *The Land of the Dacotahs*, pp. 8–9.

6. Nephew of General Nelson A. Miles who was employed at Fort Keogh.

7. *Miles City Daily Star* (May 24, 1934), Sec. III, p. 3.

8. Huidekoper, *The Land of the Dacotahs*, p. 9.

9. Ray H. Mattison, *Roosevelt and the Stockmen's Association.* Reprint from *North Dakota History*, Vol. XVII, Nos. 2 and 3, p. 4.

   Mattison's articles (quoted in footnotes 5 and 9, and his "The Hard Winter and the Range Cattle Business," in *The Montana Magazine of History*, Vol. 1 [October, 1951], No. 4, pp. 5–21) are particularly useful as they contain sizable quotations from contemporary newspapers and rare source material, as well as interview material secured from knowledgeable old-timers. Olaf T. Hagen and Ray H. Mattison, *Pyramid Park Where Roosevelt Came to Hunt.* Reprint from *North Dakota History*, Vol. XIX, No. 4, is of value for an account of the very early development of the Little Missouri country.

10. Huidekoper, *The Land of the Dacotahs*, p. 9.

11. The term is of Spanish derivation, apparently from *de' brocha gorda* which means "painting poorly done." Such animals had spotted or mottled faces.

12. Mattison, *Ranching in the Dakota Bad Lands*, p. 40.

13. Huidekoper, *The Land of the Dacotahs*, pp. 9–10.

14. Stuart, *Forty Years on the Frontier*, II, 178, 185–186.

15. John Clay, "The Passing of Conrad Kohrs," *The Breeders Gazette* (December 2, 1920), pp. 1162–1163.

16. William MacLeod Raine and Will C. Barnes, *Cattle*, pp. 216-217.

17. Mattison, *Ranching in the Dakota Bad Lands*, p. 75. The *Wibeaux Pioneer Gazette* (August, 1939) put the figure at 60,000 head.

18. Illustrated and Historical Edition of *The Yellowstone Journal* (September 27, 1900), pp. 39–41; Bertha M. Kuhn, "The W Bar Ranch on the Missouri Slope," *Collections of the North Dakota State Historical Society*, V, 161.

19. Lewis F. Crawford, *Ranching Days in Dakota*, p. 43.

20. Arnold O. Gosplen, *The Career of Marquis De Mores in the Badlands of North Dakota.* Reprint from *North Dakota History*, Vol. XIII, Nos. 1 and 2, pp. 5–56. Lincoln Lang, *Ranching with Roosevelt*, pp. 68–76; Herman Hagedorn, *Roosevelt in the Bad Lands*, p. 348.

21. Stuart, *Forty Years on the Frontier*, I, 39–272.

22. E. C. Abbott and Helena Huntington Smith, *We Pointed Them North*, p. 159. Abbot was known far and wide by his nickname "Teddy Blue."

23. Men who cut wood for sale to the steamboats.

24. Stuart, *Forty Years on the Frontier*, II, 195.

25. "Between the months of November 1880, and April 1881, three thousand head of cattle were wantonly butchered by Indians in Choteau and Meagher counties; there was therefore in six months a destruction of $60,000.00 worth of property by the malice of Indians." *Ibid.*, p. 154.

26. *Ibid.*, pp. 214–223.

27. Ford to authors, February 17, 1951.

28. Stock detectives are still employed by the cattlemen's organizations. Their efforts are now supplemented by brand inspectors stationed at the major cattle markets. Perhaps the most colorful of the range detectives—certainly the most controversial figure—was Tom Horn who was employed by interests in Wyoming. Horn, a government scout in Arizona and a packer during the Spanish-American War, was an outstanding frontiersman. He was noted for coming and going unexpectedly. One Wyoming night-hawk long remembered visiting with Horn on a "dense black" rainy night when the detective, wearing a black slicker and

riding a dark-colored horse, suddenly appeared beside him, and then vanished as suddenly. John K. Rollinson, *Pony Trails in Wyoming*, pp. 147–150. Horn was convicted of shooting a fourteen-year-old boy on the basis of evidence obtained by an officer who plied Horn with liquor. He was hung in November, 1903; and the case is still argued pro and con.

29. Cowboy slang for being in an exceptional hurry. Cattle and horses, when running from some object that has frightened them, invariably raise their tails high above their backs.

30. A cousin of the writer.

31. As the Eatons had many visitors from the East, they drifted naturally into the business of "dude ranching." They probably were the first dude ranchers and their ranch, now located at Wolf, Wyoming, is still in operation.

32. Huidekoper, *The Land of the Dacotahs*, p. 14.

33. Stuart, *Forty Years on the Frontier*, II, 195–197.

34. *Ibid.*, p. 197.

35. Huidekoper, *The Land of the Dacotahs*, p. 15.

36. Stuart, *Forty Years on the Frontier*, II, 197–198.

37. Said to have been a cousin of Jesse James.

38. Said to have been the son of F. H. Burr, the well-known engineer who was with Lieutenant Mullan (who laid out the road between the heads of navigation on the Columbia and the Missouri), and also a nephew of Granville Stuart.

39. Mueller thinks this party contained fourteen, perhaps sixteen, men. He doubts that Stuart wrote this description although the details, with the exception of two names and the date, appear to be correct; and he claims that the account is in error in naming Frank Hanson as one of the killed, and in including Bill Williams, "a reputable man," as one of the gang. Another account states that the alarm was given by two guards who discovered the vigilantes, and that the date was July 20. Oscar O. Mueller, "The Central Montana Vigilante Raids of 1884," *The Montana Magazine of History*, Vol. I (January, 1951), No. 1, pp. 29–33.

40. Stuart, *Forty Years on the Frontier*, II, 207–209.

41. Deck hands who carried wood on board and did other heavy manual labor.

42. William Burnett, a DHS cowboy who was a member of this group of vigilantes, recalled this incident fifty-seven years later. Unless there were two steamboats in the vicinity at the time, either Zogbaum glossed over some aspects of this meeting or Burdett's memory is faulty. Burdett recalled the meeting this way: "The next morning after the smoke had cleared away we caught our pack horses to get some breakfast. We found our grub soaked with muddy Missouri water from swimming the river. We was 100 miles from the ranch without grub and there wasn't a chance to get anything from the rustlers camp since both of their cabins was burned down. . . . Right then a steamboat came up the river. Granville hailed the boat but it passed us up—he did not like that— so he says 'Get on your horses we will head them off.' When the captain saw a lot of Winchesters and a bunch of hungry riders, he landed. Granville told him that we was stockmen who had had some bad luck with our mess outfit and that we wanted to buy some bacon and flour. The captain shows us the commissary and says, 'Help yourselves, no charge.'" Statement by W. C. Burnett of Gilt Edge edited by Michael Kennedy. "Judith Basin Top Hand," *The Montana Magazine of History*, Vol. III (Spring, 1953), No. 2, p. 22.

43. Rufus F. Zogbaum, *Horse, Foot, and Dragoons*, pp. 150–156.

44. Stuart, *Forty Years on the Frontier*, II, 208.

45. Huidekoper, *The Land of the Dacotahs*, p. 15; Huidekoper to authors, December 21, 1950.

46. Usher L. Burdick, *Life and Exploits of John Goodall*, p. 16.

47. Huidekoper, *The Land of the Dacotahs*, p. 15.

48. Theodore Roosevelt, *Ranch Life and the Hunting Trail*, p. 14.

49. *Ibid.*, p. 14.

50. Quoted in Mattison, *Roosevelt and the Stockmen's Association*, p. 15.

51. Roosevelt had a camera with him, and one of his men photographed him guarding the prisoners. This is probably the nearest thing to a picture of rustlers in the hands of a "vigilante" party that exists. William B. Edwards, "The Guns of Teddy Roosevelt," *Guns Magazine*, Vol. II, Nos. 1–12, p. 32.

52. Roosevelt, *Ranch Life and the Hunting Trail*, pp. 112–128.

53. Quoted in Mueller, "The Central Montana Vigilante Raids of 1804," *The Montana Magazine of History*, Vol. I (January, 1951), No. 1, pp. 23–35.

54. This account of these activities is of necessity, like all others, rather fragmentary. Two over-all accounts that are quite informative are Mueller, "The Central Montana Vigilante Raids of 1884," and part of Mattison, *Roosevelt and the Stockmen's Association*, pp. 6–15.

55. Term applied to the practice of earmarking an unbranded calf running with its mother so that anyone observing the animal would assume that it was branded. Later the calf would be branded by the rustler and the earmarking altered to conform with the brand. It is a range practice to *both* brand and earmark an animal.

56. Patrick T. Tucker, *Riding the High Country*, p. 118.

57. A. C. Huidekoper, *My Experience and Investment in the Bad Lands of Dakota and Some of the Men I Met There*, p. 48.

58. C. B. Powers to authors, November 17, 1950.

59. Animals of inferior size and quality. Obviously the beef supplied the Sioux was of low quality.

60. William Rowland served here and, later, at the Northern Cheyenne reservation at Lame Deer, Montana, as an interpreter. He was a Cheyenne squaw man and a respected scout. See Brown and Felton, *The Frontier Years*, p. 105.

61. The officer to whom they surrendered was Captain Johnson of the Third Cavalry. George Bird Grinnell, *The Fighting Cheyennes*, p. 399.

62. John K. Rollinson, *Wyoming Cattle Trails*, pp. 220–228—who quotes *The Yellowstone* (November 20 and 27, 1941).

63. Cattle with marked coins hidden under the skin were hard to "explain" even though the rustler had done a first-class job of altering the original brand.

64. Snowboy, a full-blooded Mission (Canadian) Indian who worked in the Little Missouri country in the 1880's, carried and used expertly a riata of the "unprecedented length of eighty feet." Lang, *Ranching with Roosevelt*, p. 199.

65. Philip Ashton Rollins, *The Cowboy*, p. 23.

66. On the circle, riders are scattered at widely separated points. These then ride toward the designated roundup location driving before them all the cattle they can find.

67. Name withheld, letter to authors.

68. Lang, *Ranching with Roosevelt*, pp. 191–196.

69. A rough estimate of what the rancher *thought* he had—not an actual count.

70. Charles M. Russell, *Trails Plowed Under*, p. 3.

71. Abbott and Smith, *We Pointed Them North*, pp. 84–88.

72. Lang, *Ranching with Roosevelt*, p. 174.

73. See note 28 in Chapter Two, for a definition of this term.

74. So called to distinguish from another man of the same name known as "Hot Water" Howard.

75. Irvin S. Cobb, Will Rogers, and John Wilson Townsend, *Piano Jim and the Impotent Pumpkin Vine*, pp. 21–23. Also in Charles M. Russell's *Rawhide Rawlins Rides Again*, pp. 16–19.

76. Russell, *Trails Plowed Under*, pp. 1–2.

77. "Biddle of the 70L was the first to introduce tepees for cowboys." L.A.H.

78. *The Cattleman* (May, 1934), p. 5.

79. Huffman's notes indicate this may have been Jack Taylor of the Hash Knife.

80. John D. Childress to authors, December 10, 1950.

81. Stuart, *Forty Years on the Frontier*, II, 234–235.

82. *The Miles City Daily Star* (May 24, 1934), Sec. III, p. 19.

83. Stuart estimated their losses at 50 per cent in this storm alone.

84. Stuart, *Forty Years on the Frontier*, II, 236.

85. Illustrated and Historical Edition of *The Yellowstone Journal* (September 27, 1900), p. 4.

86. Lang, *Ranching with Roosevelt*, pp. 250–251.

87. For a comprehensive account see Mattison, "The Hard Winter and the Range Cattle Business." *The Montana Magazine of History*, Vol. I, No. 4, pp. 5–21.

88. Long Lance, *Long Lance*, pp. 202–206.

89. L. A. Huffman, "The Last Busting at the Bow-Gun," *Scribner's Magazine* (July, 1907), pp. 80–85.

90. *Ibid.*, p. 77.

91. Lee Warren to authors, April 11, 1951.

92. Rounding up in rough country where the cook had to move his equipment and supplies on pack animals.

93. "Spectacled."

94. Huffman, "The Last Busting at the Bow-Gun," *Scribner's Magazine*, pp. 75–87.

95. The cause of this loss is not evident as Tingle was following a well-defined road used by freighters.

96. Neil M. Clark, manuscript for "He Captured the Vanishing West Before It Vanished."

97. Rollinson, *Wyoming Cattle Trails*, pp. 28, 99, 125–152.

98. Stuart, *Forty Years on the Frontier*, II, 188–189; Abbott and Smith, *They Pointed Them North*, frontispiece; Crawford, *Ranching Days in Dakota*, p. 38; Raine and Barnes, *Cattle*, p. 230.

99. John Childress to authors, June 4, 1950.

100. Stuart, *Forty Years on the Frontier*, II, 192.

101. Childress to authors, June 4, 1950.

102. So-called "sand waves."

103. *Miles City Daily Star* (May 24, 1934), Sec. III, pp. 20–21.

104. *Ibid.*, p. 20.

105. John Childress to authors, January 1, 1951.

106. This applies to an outfit in its home country. Reps from distant ranches ate with the others of course, thus thirty to fifty men represented more than one outfit.

107. "The Kid" to the authors.

108. Charles M. Russell's picture, "The Roundup," shows a calf being heeled in the open. Another cowboy artist told the author he once exhibited such a picture at a Texas stockmen's convention—and was roundly criticized for not knowing his subject matter better!

109. "Picked"—to cut away the hair and expose an obscure brand for closer examination.

110. Meaning it was so dark that an owl could not see to fly.

111. "The Kid" to the authors.

112. John Childress to authors, December 10, 1950.

113. This outfit headquartered about twenty miles south of Powderville, Montana, and should not be confused with the outfit of the same name that was involved in the Johnson County War in 1892.

114. John Childress to authors, December 10, 1950.

115. Name withheld, letter to authors.

116. Although Huffman loved to hunt, antelope was one kind of game he would not shoot. This attitude stemmed from an experience he had in the early days when out for camp meat. He detailed the incident, and his reactions in part of a manuscript titled, "Pop Shots."

> But never do I speculate about pop shots but that one in particular comes back, always with it's pang of keen regret. I was crossing the once famous hunting ground lying between the Powder River and the Dakotas in the early eighties when one evening, casting about for a likely camping ground for my self and [my] jaded horses, I fell most unexpectedly plump upon the new-made ranch house of an old timer friend, [Oscar] Brackett, among the Cabin Creek hills. We had a good many dropped threads to pick up and my horses needed rest so it took little pressing to induce me to lay over for a spell. Brackett was out of meat [so] taking a fresh mount from B's little bunch and my Winchester I set out the next day in quest of antelope. I had sighted small bands within a mile of the ranch on my way in the previous day, but now that I wanted one none were in sight. Riding a wide circle to the south without success I finally climbed a butte, dismounted and began carefully to scan the immense basin commanded by my elevation. Something was moving along a narrow strip of buckbrush that fringed one of the distant depressions. A thousand, yes fifteen hundred yards, it must have been so far that I speculated as to whether the moving thing was an antelope, deer or prowling wolf. Twice the creature disappeared among the buckbrush for a brief space then twice made a complete circuit of the spot, then by a series of peculiar zig zags came well out into the plain where it settled to graze in a perfectly unstalkable position, still so far away as to make it difficult to decide whether it was a deer or an antelope. Then I did what a sportsman never ought to do—elevated my sights to the top notch and took a chance shot at that object which, had it been fixed and the distance known, I could not have expected to hit in a hundred trials. To my surprise the animal suddenly disappeared. I mounted and galloped to the spot to find that my bullet falling short had glanced on the hard, dry earth and neatly cut the throat of an antelope. One glance sufficed to show that it was a young doe suckling young. I knew then what I could find in that patch of buckbrush [but] had no heart for the search. I felt like a . . . murderer and there and then made a vow which though often tempted I have faithfully kept and shall keep to the end of my hunting days. I have not killed a pronghorn since.

117. "In 1869, the Sioux, as described in Chapter 16 of my *Sitting Bull*, attacked a party of thirty Crows who had 'forted' on a flat hill with a natural rock rampart around the top. This affair is mentioned and somewhat inaccurately described on Page 320 of the Montana State Guide.

"This was one of the bloodiest battles in all tribal warfare on the Plains. Though the Sioux wiped out the thirty Crows, they lost fourteen warriors in the fight and eighteen Sioux were wounded. Of course the remains of the Crows were not buried in the trees in that region. The Sioux burials were made the summer following the winter fight, but the bones of the Crows were left where they fell and found there many years later." Stanley Vestal to authors, October 22 and 28, 1955.

EPILOGUE

1. L. A. Huffman, from the manuscript for a story in *The Yellowstone Journal* (July 8, 1907).
2. Frank Bird Linderman, "Cabins," *Bunch-Grass and Blue-Joint*, p. 27.

Bibliography

A. MANUSCRIPTS, etc.

Huffman, L. A.
    Miscellaneous manuscripts, letters and notes.

B. NEWSPAPERS and MAGAZINES

Arizona Highways
The American Magazine
The Billings Gazette
The Breeders Gazette
The Cattleman
Country Life
Evening Montanan
The Fergus County Argus
The Frazier Journal
Guns Magazine
Helena Independent
The Judith Gap Journal
Miles City American
Miles City Daily Star
The Mississippi Valley Historical Review
The Montana Magazine of History (now *Montana, the Magazine of Western History*)
The Montana Stockgrower

The National Geographic Magazine
North Dakota History
The Outing Magazine
The Panhandle-Plains Historical Review
The Saturday Evening Post
Scribner's Magazine
The Shamrock
The Square Butte Tribune
The Wibaux Pioneer Gazette
The Yellowstone Journal

C. PAMPHLETS

Burdick, Usher. *Life and Exploits of John Goodall.* The McKenzie County Farmer, Watford City, 1931.
Cobb, Irvin S. *Piano Jim and the Impotent Pumpkin Vine or "Charley Russell's Best Story—To My Way of Thinking."* Blue Grass Book Shop, Lexington, 1947.
Golpen, Arnold O. *The Career of Marquis De Mores in the Badlands of North Dakota.* Reprint from *North Dakota History*, Vol. XIII, Nos. 1 and 2. State Historical Society of North Dakota, Bismarck, 1946.

Hagen, Olaf T., and Mattison, Ray H. *Pyramid Park Where Roosevelt Came to Hunt.* Reprint from *North Dakota History*, Vol. XIX, No. 4. State Historical Society of North Dakota, Bismarck, 1952.

Huidekoper, A. C. *My Experience and Investment in the Bad Lands of Dakota and Some of the Men I Met There.* Wirth Brothers, Baltimore. 1947.

Huidekoper, Wallis. *The Land of the Dacotahs.* Montana Stockgrowers Association, Helena, n.d.

Mattison, Ray H. *The Indian Reservation System on the Upper Missouri, 1865–1890.* Reprint from *Nebraska History*. State Historical Society of Nebraska, Lincoln, September, 1955.

———. *Ranching in the Dakota Bad Lands.* Reprint from *North Dakota History*, Vol. XIX, Nos. 2 and 3. State Historical Society of North Dakota, Bismarck, 1952.

———. *Roosevelt and the Stockmen's Association.* Reprint from *North Dakota History*, Vol. XVII, Nos. 2 and 3. State Historical Society of North Dakota, Bismarck, 1950.

D. BOOKS

Abbott, E. C., and Smith, Helena Huntington. *We Pointed Them North.* Farrar & Rinehart, New York, 1939.

Adams, Andy. *Cattle Brands.* Houghton Mifflin Co., Boston, 1906.

———. *The Log of a Cowboy.* Houghton Mifflin Co., Boston, 1903.

———. *The Outlet.* Houghton Mifflin Co., Boston, 1905.

———. *Reed Anthony, Cowman.* Houghton Mifflin Co., Boston, 1907.

Adams, James Truslow, ed. *Atlas of American History.* Charles Scribner's Sons, New York, 1943.

Adams, Ramon F. *Come An' Get It.* University of Oklahoma Press, Norman, 1952.

———. *Cowboy Lingo.* Houghton Mifflin Co., Boston, 1936.

———. *Western Words.* University of Oklahoma Press, Norman, 1945.

Adams, Ramon F., and Britzman, Homer E. *Charles M. Russell.* Trails End Publishing Co., Pasadena, 1948.

Alderson, Nannie T., and Smith, Helena Huntington. *A Bride Goes West.* Farrar & Rinehart, New York, 1942.

Baber, D. F. *The Longest Rope.* The Caxton Printers, Caldwell, 1947.

Baldwin, Alice Blackwood. *Memoirs of the Late Frank D. Baldwin, Major General, U.S.A.* The Wetzel Publishing Co., Los Angeles, 1929.

Barnes, Will C. *Apaches and Longhorns.* Ward Richie Press, Los Angeles, 1941.

Birney, Hoffman. *Vigilante.* Grosset & Dunlap, New York, n.d.

Borein, Edward. *Borein's West.* Schauer Printing Studio, Santa Barbara, 1952.

———. *Etchings of the West.* Edward Borein Memorial, Santa Barbara, 1950.

Branch, Douglas. *The Cowboy and His Interpreters.* D. Appleton, New York, 1926.

Bronson, Edgar Beecher. *Cowboy Life on the Western Plains.* Grosset & Dunlap, New York, n.d.

Brown, Mark H., and Felton, W. R. *The Frontier Years.* Henry Holt and Company, New York, 1955.

Brown, Jessie, and Willard, A. M. *The Black Hills Trails.* Rapid City Journal Company, Rapid City, 1924.

Burt, Struthers. *Powder River, Let'er Buck.* Farrar & Rinehart, New York, 1938.

Call, Hughie. *Golden Fleece.* Houghton Mifflin Co., Boston, 1942.

Clark, Badger. *Sun and Saddle Leather.* Richard G. Badger, Boston, 1922.

Clark, William Philo. *Indian Sign Language.* R. L. Hamersly & Co., Philadelphia, 1885.

Clay, John. *My Life on the Range.* Lakeside Press (privately printed), Chicago, 1924.

Cleaveland, Agnes Morley. *No Life for a Lady.* Houghton Mifflin Co., Boston, 1941.

Crawford, Lewis F. *Ranching Days in Dakota and Custer's Black Hills Expedition of 1874.* Wirth Brothers, Baltimore, 1950.

Dale, Edward Everett. *The Range Cattle Industry.* University of Oklahoma Press, Norman, 1930.

———. *Cow Country.* University of Oklahoma Press, Norman, 1942.

Dick, Everett. *Vanguards of the Frontier.* D. Appleton-Century Co., New York, 1941.

Dobie, J. Frank. *The Longhorns.* Little, Brown & Co., Boston, 1941.

———. *The Mustangs.* Little, Brown and Co., Boston, 1952.

Dobie, J. Frank, Boatright, Mody C., and Ransom, Harry H. *Mustangs and Cow Horses.* Texas Folklore Society, Austin, 1940.

Dodge, Theodore Ayrault. *Riders of Many Lands.* Harper & Brothers, New York, 1894.

Forrest, Earle R. *Arizona's Dark and Bloody Ground.* The Caxton Printers, Caldwell, 1936.

Freeman, Lewis R. *Down the Yellowstone*. Dodd, Mead & Co., New York, 1922.

Gilfillan, Archer B. *Sheep*. Houghton Mifflin Co., Boston, 1929.

Grinnell, George Bird. *The Fighting Cheyennes*. Charles Scribner's Sons, New York, 1915.

Guernsey, Charles A. *Wyoming Cowboy Days*. G. P. Putnam's Sons, New York, 1936.

Hagedorn, Herman. *Roosevelt in the Bad Lands*. Houghton Mifflin Co., Boston, 1921.

Haley, J. Evetts. *Charles Goodnight*. Houghton Mifflin Co., Boston, 1936.

————. *The Heraldry of the Range*. Panhandle Plains Historical Society, Canyon, 1949.

Hamner, Laura V. *Short Grass and Long Horns*. University of Oklahoma Press, Norman, 1943.

Horn, Tom. *Life of Tom Horn, Government Scout and Interpreter*. Louthan Book Co., Denver, 1904.

Hough, Emerson. *The Story of the Cowboy*. D. Appleton & Co., New York, 1897.

Hunt, Frazier. *Cap Mossman, Last of the Great Cowmen*. Hastings House, New York, 1951.

Jackson, Clarence S. *Picture Maker of the Old West William H. Jackson*. Charles Scribner's Sons, New York, 1947.

James, Will. *All in the Day's Riding*. Charles Scribner's Sons, New York, 1946.

————. *Cowboys North and South*. Charles Scribner's Sons, New York, 1926.

————. *Lone Cowboy*. Charles Scribner's Sons, New York, 1932.

Kelly, Charles. *Outlaw Trail*. Charles Kelly, Salt Lake City, 1938.

Kelly, Luther S. *"Yellowstone" Kelly*. Yale University Press, New Haven, 1926.

Kupper, Winifred. *The Golden Hoof*. Alfred A. Knopf, New York, 1945.

Lang, Lincoln. *Ranching with Roosevelt*. J. B. Lippincott, Philadelphia, 1926.

Langford, Nathaniel Pitt. *Vigilante Days and Ways*. A. C. McClurg & Co., Chicago, 1923.

Linderman, Frank Bird. *Bunch-Grass and Blue-Joint*. Charles Scribner's Sons, New York, 1921.

————. *On a Passing Frontier*. Charles Scribner's Sons, New York, 1920.

Lomax, John A. *Cowboy Songs and Other Frontier Ballads*. The Macmillan Co., New York, 1925.

Long Lance. *Long Lance*. Cosmopolitan Book Corporation, New York, 1928.

McLaughlin, James. *My Friend the Indian*. Houghton Mifflin Co., Boston, 1910.

Mercer, A. S. *The Banditti of the Plains*. University of Oklahoma Press, Norman, 1954.

Miles, Nelson A. *Personal Recollections and Observations of General Nelson A. Miles*. Werner & Co., Chicago, 1897.

(Montana). *Contributions to the Historical Society of Montana*. Vols. I-X. Historical Society of Montana, Helena, 1876-1941.

(Montana Stockgrowers Association). *Brand Book of the Montana Stock Growers' Association for 1890*. Montana Stock Growers' Association, Chicago, 1890.

————. *Brand Book of the Montana Stock Growers Association for 1899*. Montana Stock Growers' Association, Helena, 1899.

————. *Brand Book of the Montana Stock Growers' Association for 1910*. Montana Stock Growers' Association, Helena, 1910.

(North Dakota). *Collections of the State Historical Society*. State Historical Society of North Dakota, Vol. V, Grand Forks, 1923; Vol. VII, 1925.

Noyes, Al. J. *In the Land of Chinook or the History of Blaine County*. State Publishing Co., Helena, 1917.

Osgood, Ernest Staples. *The Day of the Cattleman*. University of Minnesota Press, Minneapolis, 1929.

Pelzer, Louis. *The Cattleman's Frontier*. The Arthur H. Clark Co., Glendale, 1936.

Perkins, Charles Elliott. *The Pinto Horse*. Fisher & Skofield, Santa Barbara, 1937.

Price, Con. *Memories of Old Montana*. Trails End Publishing Co., Pasadena, 1945.

————. *Trails I Rode*. Trails End Publishing Co., Pasadena, 1947.

Raine, William MacLeod, and Barnes, Will C. *Cattle*. Doubleday, Doran & Co., Garden City, 1930.

Remington, Frederic. *Drawings*. R. H. Russell, New York, 1897.

Ritch, Johnny. *Horse Feathers*. Naegle Printing Co., Helena, 1940.

Rollins, Philip Ashton. *The Cowboy*. Charles Scribner's Sons, New York, 1924.

————. *Jinglebob*. Charles Scribner's Sons, New York, 1927.

Rollinson, John K. *Pony Trails in Wyoming*. The Caxton Printers, Caldwell, 1946.

————. *Wyoming Cattle Trails*. The Caxton Printers, Caldwell, 1948.

Roosevelt, Theodore. *Hunting Trips of a Ranchman*. G. P. Putnam's Sons, New York, n.d.

———. *Ranch Life and the Hunting Trail.* The Century Co., New York, 1920.

———. *The Wilderness Hunter.* 2 vols. G. P. Putnam's Sons, New York, 1907.

Rush, Oscar. *The Open Range.* The Caxton Printers, Caldwell, 1936.

Russell, Charles M. *Forty Pen and Ink Drawings.* Trails End Publishing Co., Pasadena, 1947.

———. *Good Medicine.* Doubleday, Doran & Co., Garden City, 1930.

———. *More Rawhides.* Montana Newspaper Association, Great Falls, 1925.

———. *Rawhide Rawlins Stories.* Montana Newspaper Association, Great Falls, 1921.

———. *Rawhide Rawlins Rides Again.* Trails End Publishing Co., Pasadena, 1948.

———. *Trails Plowed Under.* Doubleday, Page & Co., Garden City, 1927.

Russell, Charles M., and Stuart, Granville. *Studies of Western Life.* J. L. Robbins Co., Spokane, n.d.

Santee, Ross. *Cowboy.* Grossett & Dunlap, New York, 1928.

———. *Lost Pony Tracks.* Charles Scribner's Sons, New York, 1953.

Shields, George O. *Rustlings in the Rockies.* Bedford, Clarke & Co., Chicago, 1883.

Smith, Erwin E., and Haley, J. Evetts. *Life on the Texas Range.* University of Texas Press, Austin, 1952.

Strayhorn, Carrie Adell. *Fifteen Thousand Miles by Stage.* G. P. Putnam's Sons, New York, 1915.

Stuart, Granville. *Forty Years on the Frontier.* The Arthur H. Clark Co., Cleveland, 1925.

Sweetman, Luke D. *Back Trailing on the Open Range.* The Caxton Printers, Caldwell, 1951.

Taft, Robert. *Photography and the American Scene.* The Macmillan Co., New York, 1938.

Taylor, Joseph Henry. *Kaleidoscopic Lives.* Joseph Henry Taylor, Washburn, 1902.

Thorp, N. H., and Clark, Neil M. *Pardner of the Wind.* The Caxton Printers, Caldwell, 1945.

Towne, Charles Wayland, and Wentworth, Edward Norris. *Shepherd's Empire.* University of Oklahoma Press, Norman, 1945.

Tucker, Patrick. *Riding the High Country.* The Caxton Printers, Caldwell, 1933.

Vestal, Stanley. *Short Grass Country.* Duell, Sloan & Pierce, New York, n.d.

Wellman, Paul I. *The Trampling Herd.* Carrick & Evans, Inc., New York, 1939.

Wentworth, Edward Norris. *America's Sheep Trails.* Iowa State College Press, Ames, 1948.

Wheeler, Homer W. *Buffalo Days.* Bobbs-Merrill Co., Indianapolis, 1925.

———. *The Frontier Trail.* Times-Mirror Press, Los Angeles, 1923.

Wheeler, Olin D. *The Trail of Lewis and Clark, 1804–1904.* 2 vols. G. P. Putnam's Sons, New York, 1926.

Wister, Owen. *The Virginian* ("Russell" Edition). The Macmillan Co., New York, 1911.

Wyman, Walker D. *Nothing but Prairie and Sky.* University of Oklahoma Press, Norman, 1954.

Yates, Haydie. *70 Miles From a Lemon.* Houghton Mifflin Co., Boston, 1947.

Zogbaum, Rufus Fairchild. *Horse, Foot, and Dragoons.* Harper & Brothers, New York, 1888.

ACKNOWLEDGMENTS

INTO THE melting pot, from which this book came, went various bits and pieces. Foremost among these, of course, were the Huffman pictures. Also, there were reminiscences of old-timers, suggestions and criticisms, and other assistance. The authors are grateful for this opportunity to express their thanks.

It would have been impossible to compile the material for this book without the kind cooperation of Ruth Huffman Scott of Miles City, Montana, who owns the Huffman negatives.* Bessie Huffman Felton provided the file of her father's letters and also supplied much other information. Thanks are likewise due to Vernon L. Scott who, in addition to supplying helpful data, handled details pertaining to the reproduction of prints from the negatives. Assistance provided by others varied widely in nature.

While it is not the intent of the writers to single out anyone for particular mention, the reader may be interested to know that John D. Childress of Tucson, Arizona, and William "Montana Bill" Roberts of Miles City, Montana, rode with herds bound for the Montana ranges. Colville Terrett of Billings, Montana, was a horse wrangler when Huffman visited the roundups at which he worked. The memory of Wallis Huidekoper, veteran rancher of Big Timber, Montana, spans almost the entire period of the days before barbed wire. Lee R. Warren of Long Beach, California, provided some of the fine details about the bronc snapping at

* Prints from these negatives are still available to collectors.

which Huffman photographed him at the "Bow Gun." Charlie Coyle of Omaha, Nebraska, trailed flocks of sheep from Oregon to the Midwest; and Dr. L. F. Townsend of Belle Fourche, South Dakota, drove half-broken broncs over the trails of southwestern North Dakota and southeastern Montana to visit the sick and injured, among them Calamity Jane in her last illness. Thanks are due to "The Kid"—nameless at his request—who put his reminiscences of the days of the open range into the terse, vivid diction of the cowpuncher: the authors "apologize" for refusing to spoil this material by rewriting as they were requested.

Others who were particularly helpful were William C. Almquist of Miles City, Montana; Casey E. Barthelmess of Miles City, Montana; Badger Clark of Custer, South Dakota; Lee M. Ford of Great Falls, Montana; Louis F. Grill of Miles City, Montana; Sam Hotchkiss of Stacey, Montana; Historical Society of Montana—with special mention of Anne McDonnell, assistant librarian; Ed Holt of Miles City, Montana; E. A. Phillips of Helena, Montana; C. B. Power of Helena, Montana; Julian Terrett of Brandenburg, Montana; R. Price Terrett of Paso Robles, California; John Wilson of Lewistown, Montana; and Ben Woodcock of Miles City, Montana.

In addition to those who supplied data, others helped in various ways. Professor Walter Campbell (Stanley Vestal) of the University of Oklahoma advised on the plans for the manuscript and gave many helpful suggestions. J. Evetts Haley of Canyon, Texas, gave the photographs a critical evaluation. Paul I. Wellman of Los Angeles, California; Ross Santee of Arden, Delaware; Harold Bugbee of Clarendon, Texas; and Carl Norcross of Dobbs Ferry, New York; were helpful in various ways. Dr. Raymond Estep of Montgomery, Alabama, read the manuscript with meticulous care and offered many valuable comments both large and small. Charles B. Dull of Bellevue, Nebraska, also read the manuscript and offered helpful criticism; and Jack Coffrin of Miles City, Montana, toiled patiently over the old negatives to make the best possible prints.

Others who lent a helping hand are Clara A. Barley of Rosebud, Montana; S. B. Bean of Savage, Montana; A. Bond of Brockway, Montana; M. P. Browne of Lambert, Montana; Harry R. Chamberlain of Ekalaka, Montana; Elizabeth B. Cox of Birney, Montana; Charles R. Cutts of Billings, Montana; M. H. Duffy of Paxton, Montana; Patty Alderson Eaton of Wolf, Wyoming; W. R. Felton, Jr., of Sioux City, Iowa; V. G. Hooker of Glendive, Montana; Claude Ivers of Omaha, Nebraska; J. H. Lemmon of Lemmon, South Dakota; Whitman Longley of Forsyth, Montana; Dr. John D. Lutton of Sioux City, Iowa; Montana Stockgrowers Association, Inc., of Helena, Montana; Jack Milburn of Grass Range, Montana; Colonel E. G. Ovenshine of Washington, D.C.; Anna Polk of Miles City, Montana; J. K. Ralston of Billings, Montana; Bertha M. Randell of Bentley, Alberta; L. F. Sheffy of Canyon, Texas; Ethel Cato Tarbutton of Kyle, Texas; I. E. Thomas of Terry, Montana; Lillian Wheat of Baker, Montana; and Natalie Brown Woodward of Birney, Montana.

The following authors, author's agents, and publishers have kindly given their permission to use material from:

Forty Years on the Frontier, by Granville Stuart. Copyright, 1925, by The Arthur H. Clark Company. Reprinted by the permission of the publishers.

The Land of the Dacotahs, by Wallis Huidekoper. Reprinted by permission of Wallis Huidekoper.

"Beginnings of the Montana Sheep Industry," by John F. Bishop. Copyright, 1951, by The Montana Magazine of History. Reprinted by permission of the publishers.

Life and Exploits of John Goodall, by Usher Burdick. Copyright, 1931, by Usher Burdick. Reprinted by permission of the author.

Sun and Saddle Leather, by Badger Clark. Copyright, 1917, by Richard G. Badger. Copyright, 1942, by Chapman and Grimes, Inc. Reprinted by permission of the publishers.

Cattle by William Mac Leod Raine and Will C. Barnes. Copyright, 1930, by the authors. Reprinted by permission of William Mac Leod Raine.

Piano Jim and the Impotent Pumpkin Vine, by Irvin S. Cobb. Reprinted by permission of John Wilson Townsend.

A Bride Goes West, by Nannie Alderson and Helena Huntington Smith. Copyright, 1942, by Farrar and Rinehart. Reprinted by permission of the authors.

Cowboy Songs and Other Frontier Ballads, by John Lomax. Copyright, 1938, by The Macmillan Company.

"The Last Busting at the Bow-Gun," by L. A. Huffman. Copyright, 1907, by *Scribner's Magazine.*

Bunch-Grass and Blue-Joint, by Frank Bird Linderman. Copyright, 1921, by Charles Scribner's Sons.

Trails Plowed Under, by Charles M. Russell. Copyright, 1927, by Doubleday, Page and Co.

We Pointed Them North, by E. C. Abbott and Helena Huntington Smith. Copyright, 1939, by Farrar and Rinehart.

Ranching with Roosevelt, by Lincoln Lang. Copyright, 1926, by J. B. Lippincott & Co.

Last, but by no means least, thanks are due to the writer's wife, who lived patiently for months with the clutter of books and papers essential to a work of this kind, and often lent a helping hand.

Mark H. Brown

Trails End Farm
Alta, Iowa
July 2, 1956

Key to Symbols Used on Map

▲ DRY HOUSE, WHERE HIDE-HUNTERS CURED BUFFALO MEAT.

✂ DILTS FIGHT, WAGON TRAIN FORCED TO BUILD EARTHWORKS FOR PROTECTION.

✕ HOLE IN ROCK, A NOTED WATERHOLE.

The following brands mark ranch headquarters:

CK CK—PIONEER CATTLE COMPANY

D⌐S DHS—PIONEER CATTLE COMPANY

Ǝ2 REVERSED E2—CONCORD CATTLE COMPANY

ⴚF FUF—GREEN MOUNTAIN STOCK RANCHING COMPANY

Ⱨ H LAZY L—HUFFMAN AND LAMPHERE

Ⱨ HT—LITTLE MISSOURI HORSE COMPANY

⋉ CROSSED JL—GREGOR LANG

JO JO—CHARITON MONTANA CATTLE COMPANY

LO LO—MIZPAH LIVE STOCK COMPANY

L̲U̲ LU BAR—PHILLIPS CATTLE & LAND COMPANY

M◇ M DIAMOND—MANKATO CATTLE COMPANY

MC MC—M. C. CONNORS

N̲ N BAR—NIOBRARA CATTLE COMPANY

N-N N BAR N—HOME LAND & CATTLE COMPANY

O⊂ O LAZY U—THOMAS J. BRYAN

O✕ OX—TOWERS & GUDGELL

P̬ P LAZY N—JUDITH MERCANTILE & CATTLE
COMPANY

◠S̲ QUARTER CIRCLE S—JIM SHARP

SⱧ SH—NORTHERN CATTLE COMPANY

SL SL—HEREFORD LIVE STOCK COMPANY

VVV THREE V'S—CLAY & FORREST

W̲ W BAR—PIERRE WIBAUX

WL WL—HOLT & MURPHY

XIT XIT—CAPITOL FREEHOLD LAND & INVESTMENT
COMPANY

⅄ Y CROSS—NORTHERN PACIFIC REFRIGERATOR CAR
COMPANY (MARQUIS DE MORES)

δ 7OL—MONTANA SHEEP & CATTLE COMPANY

ⲄOⳑ REVERSED 7 & L—FERDON & BIDDLE

777 THREE 7's—BERRY-BOICE CATTLE COMPANY

79 SEVENTY-NINE—MONTANA CATTLE COMPANY

⌁ BOW AND ARROW (BOW GUN)—REA CATTLE
COMPANY

✡ BUG—GEORGE M. MOOREHEAD

⊖ MILL IRON—CONTINENTAL LAND & CATTLE
COMPANY

⚒ HASHKNIFE—CONTINENTAL LAND & CATTLE
COMPANY

✠ MALTESE CROSS—THEODORE ROOSEVELT

𝜦 ELK HORN—THEODORE ROOSEVELT

♉ SUGAR BOWL WITH SPOON—
ZOOK AND ALDERSON

⊖ CIRCLE BAR—HOWES, STREVELL & MILES

⌐✕ HAT X—WELLS & MALONE